SECRETS & MYSTERIES

ABOUT THE AUTHOR

Denise Linn is an international healer, writer, and lecturer. She has taught seminars in 19 countries and has written 17 books, including the bestselling book *Sacred Space* and the award-winning book *Sacred Legacies*. She has also appeared on *The Oprah Winfrey Show* and in numerous documentaries, as well as on TV programs on the Discovery and Lifetime Networks and BBC television.

Denise lives in the central California wine region, where she and her husband, David, are planning a small vineyard and winery ("Sacred Oak") dedicated to producing sacred wine. Using organic farming, sustainable agriculture, landscape feng shui, and by connecting with the spirit of the land, the wine they will produce is intended for sacred purposes. Denise is also creating a woman's Mystery School.

BY DENISE LINN

SECRETS & MYSTERIES

The Glory and Pleasure of Being a Woman

Denise Linn

HAY HOUSE, INC.
Carlsbad, California • New York City
London • Sydney • Johannesburg
Vancouver • Hong Kong • New Delhi

Published and distributed in the United States by: Hay House, Inc.: www.hayhouse.com •
Published and distributed in Australia by: Hay House Australia Pty. Ltd.: www.hayhouse.com.au •
Published and distributed in the Republic of South Africa by: Hay House SA (Pty), Ltd.:
www.hayhouse.co.za • **Distributed in Canada by:** Raincoast: www.raincoast.com • **Published in
India by:** Hay House Publishers India: www.hayhouse.co.in

Editorial supervision: Jill Kramer • *Illustrations by:* Mai Soon Lee

First published in 2002 by Rider, an imprint of Ebury Press, Random House, London, England:
ISBN: 0-7126-0518-5

Library of Congress Cataloging-in-Publication Data

Linn, Denise.
 Secrets & mysteries : the glory and pleasure of being a woman / Denise
Linn.
   p. cm.
Includes bibliographical references and index.
 ISBN 1-40190-103-4 (pbk.)
 1. Women-Psychology. 2. Women-Conduct of life. 3. Women-health
and hygiene. 4. Self-realization. I. Title: Secrets and mysteries. II.
Title.
 HQ1206.L513 2002
 305.4-dc21

                                          2002010508

ISBN 10: 1-4019-0103-4
ISBN 13: 978-1-4019-0103-5

11 10 09 08   6 5 4 3
1st Hay House printing, September 2002
3rd printing, February 2008

Printed in the United States of America

CONTENTS

I dedicate this book to you, Meadow,
my daughter and my joy. I love being your mother.
I am a richer and fuller woman for having you in my life.
Thank you so much.

ACKNOWLEDGMENTS

First, I'd like to thank everyone at Hay House for letting me be a part of their team. Additionally, my husband, David, has been a remarkable source of understanding during my late-night and early-morning writing sessions. Also, the following individuals have deepened my realization of the glory and pleasure of being a woman, especially Lynne Franks, Amber Dotts, Cynthia and Shumway Poole, and Pattie Hanmer; as well as Collette Baron-Reid, Terah Kathryn and Brian Collins, Shari Carr, Louise Hay, Steve Heliczer, Debbie Kaminski, Monica King, Matthew Manning, Dr. Kim Muczynski, Leon Nacson, Jamal Rahman, Caroline Reynolds, Nancy SantoPietro, Stratton Semmes, Maree Thomas, Ruth Toledo, and Reid Tracy. And my eternal gratitude to Marika Burton.

PREFACE

"You're just a girl!" they taunted. Hot tears streamed down my face.

We had been playing baseball in an empty lot—the neighborhood boys and me. I was seven years old. It was my turn up to the plate. The first ball came flying toward me. I clenched the bat, held my breath, and swung as hard as I could. Wow! I knocked a ball completely out of the lot and over a far fence.

I could never remember anyone ever doing that as long as we had been playing. I grinned ear to ear with exuberance as I raced around the bases.

I thought everyone would be cheering and hollering at my success as I crossed the home plate. Instead, there was a grim stillness. What had happened? I had just made a great play. "Hey, guys, did you see what I did? Wasn't it great!"

No one said a word. Then the pitcher said, "You're just a stupid girl."

"Yeah," said another. "You're just a girl."

What did they mean, *I was just a girl*? These guys, who had all been my friends, now seemed to be a part of an exclusive club in which I wasn't allowed. (In the fifties, girls weren't supposed to beat a boy at sports, but I didn't know that at the time.) What did they mean when they called me a "girl"? I thought we were all the same. As the boys heckled me, I suddenly realized that people were divided into two groups: boys and girls, men and women, and one group was considered better than the other. Slowly an awareness flooded through me, *I was in the inferior group*. I felt like I'd been slugged.

I ran home sobbing in great heaves. Stumbling up the stairs of our home, I slammed the front door, found my mother, and accosted her. "Why?" I cried. "Why did you make me a girl?!"

She didn't have any answer for me other than, "That's just the way you were born." In an ancient time, my mother might have drawn me close to her and whispered the secrets and mysteries of being a woman. She could have said that being a woman is a sacred thing and life on earth is sustained by divine feminine energy. Yet my mother was a product of her generation, as I was a product of mine. So she said nothing that could soothe my anguish.

It was the worst day of my young life. I was doomed to be the "inferior" sex my entire life, and there was nothing I could do about it. In the male-dominated atmosphere of the fifties, I really believed I was the lesser sex. It was years later that I discovered the absolute glory of being a woman . . . in fact, now I wouldn't want it any other way. However, the road to this realization wasn't an easy one.

Shortly after the discovery that I was the "inferior" sex, I decided to prove that I wasn't, by beating boys at whatever they did. I got in fistfights with boys, and I always tried to run faster and be tougher than they were. As a pre-teen, when my girlfriends didn't want to participate in sports because they might develop unsightly muscles (they honestly said that!), I was highly competitive. I used to work out with the boys' track team, which the boys hated because they didn't like a girl who could run faster than them.

As a teenager, my body and attitude changed and I became interested in dating. In the American Midwest farming community where I lived, boys wanted to date a girl who was soft and feminine, not someone who was wild and assertive. So I suppressed my spirit and became sweet and compliant and had lots of dates.

Then I went to college! The feminist movement was growing, and I attended protests where we marched down the street yelling, "Male Chauvinist Pigs!" at the top of our lungs. I took karate and wore military-style clothes. It was liberating and exciting.

After college I had a guru who said that to be spiritual, a woman needed to be gentle, domestic, and supportive of males. I wanted to be spiritual, so I tried being servile to the men in my life. I bought flowery dresses, baked cookies, and was very domestic. At first I loved feeling feminine and soft, but after a while I began to feel confined and constricted, so this period didn't last very long. My life then became a series of fluctuations back and forth between what I perceived as masculine and feminine qualities. I couldn't seem to grasp the essence of my gender.

For decades I was perplexed by what it meant to be a woman, but I continued to peel back layers of my being, challenged by the questions: "Who am I?" "What does it mean to be a woman?" In my quest to discover the secrets and mysteries of being a woman, I uncovered ancestral wisdom from many cultures. I spent time in native cultures to understand the mysteries of the divine feminine spirit. I also explored modern-day truths.

I have gained so much on my journey, and I'm continuing to grow. I'm learning to be a woman who lives without fear. I'm recognizing how to find my truth, speak it, stand for it, and be it. I'm on a mission to love both myself and others deeply and fully . . . and to be loved deeply and fully. I am on a journey to discover the glory, pleasure, and true measure of being a woman.

INTRODUCTION

E VERY life has turning points. Sometimes, when we look back over our personal history, we can locate these pivotal moments that have changed our direction. The episode that led to this book was such a juncture in my life. It occurred in the early morning about a year ago. Although it was not a dramatic incident, it initiated the sequence of events that have transpired over the past twelve months . . . and maybe it even saved my life.

I woke up tired, exhausted, and depressed. Stumbling out of bed into the bathroom, I splashed water on my face and looked at myself in the mirror. My eyes were red and my face was puffy. Bracing myself, I stepped on the scale. Arrgggh! Up another pound. What happened? When did I get so out of shape and start to feel so old and depleted? When did I forget how to embrace each day with joy? Increasingly, every morning had been permeated with these small despairs.

Looking closer into the mirror, I tried to find some glimmer of myself beyond the limp hair and dull skin. Suddenly, superimposed over my face in the mirror, an image of a snake appeared. It wavered before me, like heat above a road on a hot summer day, and then disappeared. A snake! I was shocked. It happened too fast for me to be scared. Where did it come from? And why?

Bewildered and confused by what I had seen, wisps of a dream from the previous night began to filter into my memory. In broken fragments, I remembered a dream about a snake. It was fat and yellow, its back was criss-crossed with black lines, and it moved slowly and sensuously. I was terrified, but fascinated by it at the same time. Although the snake in my dream looked healthy, I had the feeling it was dying. Something about this dream struck a chord buried deep inside me. Standing before the mirror, I was overwhelmed with emotion and began to sob. I didn't really know why I was crying, but I knew that something was wrong with my life.

For a few years prior to this incident, I had been feeling sluggish and uninspired. Something inside me seemed to be slowly dying. Occasional depression had nearly turned into an everyday occurrence. I was gaining weight and feeling stagnant. The only exercise I ever got was walking down the stairs from my bedroom in the morning to the desk and computer in my home office and going back up the stairs to the bedroom at night. Several times I'd joined a gym, but I would go twice and never go back again.

Whenever I wanted to be athletic and get fit, I'd go shopping for athletic equipment and then *never use it.* I even bought a kayak from an outdoor store, but used it only once. Every time I became anxious about my weight and my lack of exercise, I would buy an exercise video, which would then sit on the shelf unopened. (My anxiety about not exercising seemed to cease after each purchase.) I decided that maybe I needed a less aggressive approach to exercise, so I began buying yoga videos, which again I never used.

When I was home after a seminar or book tour, I'd watch repeats on television for hours. I even started ordering exercise equipment from the television shopping channel, which I never used.

My professional and family life were good, but when I was alone, I was often filled with a quiet desperation. Friends said it was menopause and aging, but when I looked at myself in the mirror and saw the snake, I knew it was deeper than that. I had the feeling that unless something changed in my life, my health would suffer and I could die.

Although I've been blessed with a strong body, I've also had the potential for poor health as a result of injuries I sustained as a teenager. When I was seventeen years old, I was shot by a gunman in a random violent act and had substantial damage to my body including the loss of my spleen, one of my kidneys, and an adrenal gland. I also had a bullet hole through a part of my spine (though I can still walk) and a plastic tube inserted to replace my aorta.

While in the emergency ward of the hospital, I had a near-death experience. I had been in tremendous pain, but abruptly the pain subsided and everything became very quiet and still. I felt myself lifting out of my body and entering a soft, dark sphere that cocooned and protected me. I don't know how long I was there, but suddenly a piercing light penetrated the darkness and I found myself in a realm of exquisite golden light. It was so peaceful and beautiful. I didn't want to leave, but a calm, resonant voice told me I couldn't remain there because my time on earth wasn't complete. I tried so hard to stay, but I was pulled back into my physical form.

After coming back into my body, something remarkable began to happen. The radiant energy flowing out of people, plants, and objects became visible to me, and everything on the earth seemed to be enveloped in an ocean of energy, light, and sound. The world was so alive. I marveled at the grass on the hospital lawn because every blade shimmered in its own light and seemed to hum its own song. My body healed very quickly. It was as if somehow during those few moments when I was thought to be dead, I had tapped into a life force that was very healing. I eventually became a healer, using the insights that I had gained for my own health to assist others in their healing process. But over the last few years, I had felt my vitality and energy waning. The ailing snake in the bathroom mirror and in my dream seemed to be a sign that my body wouldn't hold out if I continued living in the same way.

I have always watched for signs, omens, and coincidences. Possibly this is a quality passed down from my Cherokee ancestors, who depended on portents to give them daily guidance. By observing the movements of the clouds and actions of animals, my predecessors gained valuable information about organizing the activities of their lives. Perhaps, however, I developed this ability as a child to help me endure a painful childhood. I grew up in a home filled with violence and abuse. To make survival easier, I taught myself to watch for signs. For example, a red-winged blackbird in the morning was a good sign for me. It wasn't necessarily a Cherokee omen, but it had significance for me because I noticed that after I saw one, something positive would usually happen; it was a recurring pattern. Every time one appeared, I knew I didn't have to be so vigilant and

on guard for that day. Although watching for omens may seem supersti-
tious, it helped me survive my childhood.

No matter where the ability to interpret signs came from, I knew the
appearance of the snake in the mirror and in my dream had an important
significance in my life. The image was still floating through my mind as I
sat down for breakfast and randomly picked up a nearby book to read.
When I opened it, the word *snake* jumped out at me. I scrolled down the
page to read a paragraph about the serpent being a powerful symbol of
the divine feminine spirit and of the Goddess. The Goddess? The divine
feminine? Was the snake in my dream there to nudge me in this direction?

As I stared at the book, I felt a rumble arise within me, like a mountain
being born from fire. In that moment, I dedicated the next year of my life
to awakening my divine feminine spirit. I gave myself a full cycle of the
seasons—spring, summer, autumn, and winter—to nurture and rejuvenate
myself. This decision not only changed the course of my life, but I believe
that it also saved it.

With the book open in front of me, I remembered a previous experience
that involved a snake and the power of womanhood. It had occurred many
years before when I had spent time with Aboriginal women in a remote part
of the Australian outback. My friend Lynora, who worked for the
Pitjantjatjara Aboriginal Women's Council, had invited me to this remote
part of Australia. As I flew into Alice Springs, unseasonable rains poured
down on the outback, turning the red sand into what looked like a huge
pink lake below. The rain pounded down on Uluru (also called Ayers Rock),
a sacred monolith for the Aboriginal people, creating powerful waterfalls
surging down the red rock and making deep pools around its base.

After a day's drive from Uluru in Lynora's Land Cruiser, over bumpy dirt
roads, we arrived at the Aboriginal gathering. The women elders were
performing ceremonies and dancing. For each dance, they decorated their
breasts with colorful paint. Every design they used had been passed down
for generations and had meanings appropriate to the dance. The women
urged us to come with them to learn some of their dances. We followed
them into a special lean-to made of tall sticks that served as a makeshift
dressing room on the desert sand.

I watched as the women carefully decorated each other's breasts in
preparation for the next dance. A large woman with a round face and
gleaming white teeth instructed me to take off my shirt to expose my
breasts. She looked at my breasts and then looked at the nonchalant
expression I was struggling to make. She gave me a huge smile.

An old woman ambled next to me, reached gnarled fingers into a pot of
paint and, examining my breasts, carefully made dabs and strokes above

and around the nipples. There was something primitive and primal about my breasts being so carefully adorned. I liked the way her fingers felt against my skin. They were rough and yet soothing at the same time. My breasts were treated as sacred and yet ordinary. In my life, my breasts had been ogled, squeezed, caressed, and pinched . . . but never treated so reverently.

From behind a screen we could hear the male elders beginning their drone-like song, using click sticks to set a rhythm. The sound was undulating and hypnotic. This song was sung to call the women out to dance. All the women were leaving the stick shelter to go and dance. I didn't know what to do. I was hesitant to dance in front of men with my breasts exposed. One younger woman laughed at me and gave me a playful shove, so that I found myself stumbling out from behind the lean-to. My shyness disappeared into the rhythm of the music, and I began to dance. At first, I felt awkward and clumsy, yet as I danced, I could feel an energy surge upwards from the earth and through my body, as I disappeared into the sound. It was exhilarating.

After several days with the women, I returned in the late evening with Lynora to set up camp for the night in an area not far from Uluru. The moon was full and the air was warm. As we approached our campsite, an enormous snake, thick and undulant, majestically wove its way across our path. Illuminated by the moonlight, she carried herself like a queen, with splendor and grace. We felt like ladies-in-waiting, pausing for her to pass. Lynora explained that seeing the serpent was auspicious because the women had been honoring the snake in their dances. I fell asleep under the full moon thinking of the snake, barefoot dancing and the Pitjantjatjara woman elders. The next morning I woke up feeling alive and vital. A crimson sun was rising on one horizon while the plump orange moon was setting on the other. In the distance, Uluru rose like a great fertile mound. I stood naked on the red sand and stretched my arms into the sky. I felt glorious, sumptuous, and free. I loved both myself and my body. I was a passionate woman, celebrating myself and ready to take on any challenge life brought me. It was a splendid moment.

Over time, however, my vitality and joy waned. I got stuck in routines, responsibilities, and cultural beliefs about getting old. I went into menopause and often felt tired. Self-contempt grew as I drudged through my life until the morning the snake surfaced in my reflection. I knew that the snake was a harbinger: a sign that I should delve into the divine feminine. I instinctively knew that I had been given a key to a powerful gateway and it was time to open that sacred portal.

Thus began my year-long journey through the sacred passage of feminine secrets and mysteries to reclaim my spirit, and the glory and pleasure of being a woman. For a year I have gone on retreats—inner and outer—to understand more about the mysteries of being a woman. I also interviewed remarkable women to find out their secrets of womanhood, and I researched our ancestral roots as women. The journey that began with a dream and a vision in a mirror has culminated in this book . . . and I feel stronger, clearer, and wiser for having taken the journey. Both my body and my spirit are more vital. Self-doubt and self-loathing are being replaced with self-love and self-celebration, and every day I'm growing in love, compassion, and wisdom. It is my sincere desire that my journey and the information in this book will serve to heal, balance, and strengthen you as well.

BECOMING A GLORIOUS WOMAN

THERE is a magical and mysterious place inside every woman. It is a place where the past embraces the future, where an ancient womanly wisdom dwells, old Goddess legends can be found, and new legacies can be created. It is a sacred realm that can nurture your soul with compassion to make you whole. When you discover this secret place, you truly know the glory and pleasure of being a woman.

My journey to becoming a glorious woman has taken me into many crevices in my soul. On the way, I have honestly explored my darkness and learned to celebrate my light. Even though I have been committed to a spiritual path for most of my adult life, over time I had begun to feel listless and uninspired. For a number of years, my inner landscape had been dry and parched. After the appearance of the snake in my bathroom mirror, however, I became fertile soil for spiritual growth.

Five months passed. It was an amazing time: I meditated in the early mornings, wrote in my journals, prayed, and spent hours of solitude in nature. I also visited spas (which I believed were the closest thing that we have in present time to ancient female mystery schools). With every passing day, I reached deeper into the inner wellspring of the feminine spirit. Every day brought some new self-discovery. It was an exciting and exhilarating time as old negative patterns began to drop away. When the student is ready, the teaching appears, and I believe that those five months were a preparation for what was to come, because abruptly—it was November 16th—my inner journey plunged me even deeper into that secret place.

It's 4.30 P.M. I'm sitting in a stark, sterile-looking room at the hospital waiting for the results of a routine mammogram. A brusque, no-nonsense doctor ushers me into a room with x-rays of my breasts clipped to the side of a wall-mounted light box. She points to one picture of my right breast and says, "In this area there is a 50 percent chance that this is cancer." And then points to another area of the breast, "There is a 95 percent chance that this is cancer." Everything is so matter-of-fact. I ask her matter-of-fact questions. She answers in a matter-of-fact way, suggesting that I have surgery. I thank her. It's all so pleasant and even mundane.

I get in my car to drive home. I can't start the car. My hands are shaking. My legs shake. My body shakes. My soul shakes. My foundation is crumbling.

"Cancer? I don't have cancer. I can't have cancer."

The car starts with a jerk, and I drive out of the hospital parking lot. The light turns green. The guy behind me honks his horn. My car lunges forward and I drive through the light. I feel numb. I'm scared. And even more than my fear of physical suffering, almost irrationally, I'm afraid of being judged by well-meaning people. I imagine them saying, "Oh, she has cancer: what did she do to bring that on?" I feel alone and, somehow, even ashamed of myself for having cancer. At home, I can't talk about it. I fall asleep in shock and in denial.

The next morning, I begin to take stock of my life. The first thing I think about is death. I ask myself if I am ready to die. Surprisingly, I am willing to die. Meadow, my daughter, has graduated from college. I have already attained most of my dreams. My husband, David, will miss me, but I know he'll be okay. I've lived a good life and, if I have to, I *am* willing to die.

The next question is much harder, "Am I ready to really live?" I start to wonder if having the potential of cancer is a symptom of a much deeper problem. I feel that to "really live" I'm going to need to make some big shifts in my life. I have always been a people pleaser and have made major decisions in my life based on what other people wanted from me, rather than listening to my own needs. This negative pattern hounded me for decades, even though I had done an immense amount of personal growth work. I felt that if I was going to heal myself, I would have to change this troublesome recurring pattern. I believe that the vision of the snake five months before was a foreshadowing of this insight.

There is an expression, "If you listen to the whispers, you don't have to hear the screams." The Universe had whispered to me five months ago and I made some changes . . . but now it was screaming at me! I knew I was *really* going to have to make some changes. I knew I needed to start by honestly asking myself, "Am I really ready to live?"

The questions pour out of me. "Am I willing to stop putting other people's needs ahead of mine?" "Am I ready let go of the need to please everyone?" "Can I stop taking care of everyone else, and start caring for myself?"

I don't know the answers to these questions. I'm scared. I'm also mad at all the people that I feel that I can't tell because I'm afraid they will judge me. I'm don't want to hear, "Denise, you created this, what's eating away at you?" or "I knew you had to slow down, you were working too hard."

I long for compassion, understanding, and support. But I'm so judgmental of myself that I don't think that I can bear others judging me, too, so I don't reach out for help. The belief that we create our own life circumstances can be valuable in helping someone to stop feeling victimized by life, but it can be damaging when it is used to condemn or judge yourself and others. I want to yell, "Cancer! Cancer! Cancer!" as loud as I can to drown out my anguish. I don't want to be the kind of person who cares what others think. But I do care. I care very much. So I only tell my husband and daughter, and a couple of close friends.

The doctors want me to come back for more tests, but I want to wait for a month. I need time to ponder my options. I immediately begin to learn everything I can about cancer: traditional, alternative, and psychological approaches. I also do some deep soul-searching to see if there were any submerged issues in my life that might have contributed to the cancer. It was an uncomfortable process but very revealing. Then one day it hit me: I'd been waiting for my real life to begin, but I suddenly realized that I'd been living my real life all along. When I was in high school, I thought that when I finally moved away from the violence and upheaval at home, that my life would begin. But when I moved out, nothing changed. When I finally got into college, I was sure it would happen then, but it didn't. I thought, *When I get a job and am in the "real world" then my life will start.* When that didn't work, I knew that I had to get married to be complete. But that didn't do it either.

It seemed that there was always some future goal that I had to fulfill before my real life began, such as owning our own home, having a baby, writing a book, or traveling to other countries. All the time, I kept waiting for my life to begin—my real life. But there was always some obstacle in the way. There was always something I had to do or accomplish first. I thought that when I was done with my "to-do list," then I could relax and do what *I* wanted to do, but I never got it all done. Consequently, I never really relaxed and I always postponed my heart's desires.

Confronted with the possibility of death, I suddenly realized that this *is* my life. It *has* begun. It dawned on me that the obstacles to my "real" life actually *were* my life. I understood there was no better time to be happy than right now, because if not now, when? I realized that there wasn't a pathway, filled with requirements that you have to meet, to get to fulfillment. Happiness is how you experience each moment. This realization was a defining moment for me.

I know that life will always be filled with challenges. But I don't need to wait for everything to be perfect. I need only believe that I am on the right path. And I *am* on the right path . . . and so are you; we all are. In fact we always have been, *even when we didn't know it.*

I believe that every experience that we each have had—whether we judge it as good or bad, whether we liked it or didn't like it—has been a vital part of our path. Every aspect of life is important and valuable. Every experience is essential for our growth as a spiritual being. The more that I recognize this, the more I understand that there is no "way" to happiness. Happiness is the way. Happiness is a journey, not a destination.

When a woman stops waiting until she loses ten pounds, gets a degree, gets a job, has kids, her kids leave home, she retires, gets married or divorced, or until she's sober or wins the lottery, or even until she has confidence and self-esteem, she is then able to enjoy every moment. I know that this is one of the secrets of being a joyous and Glorious Woman. I also know that this is the time, right now, to step forward and uncover who we are as women, who we are as human beings.

In December, a month after the first series of tests, I went back in for more. They couldn't find any cancer. They said they must have got it wrong the first time. So either the first test was wrong, or all the inner work I did helped heal my body. I was relieved, but most of all I was so immensely grateful for the entire experience because I had come to know myself so much more fully because of it. If it weren't for the downside, I would suggest that every woman get a deadly diagnosis. When confronted with your mortality, you are forced to assess your life with honesty, and to realize what is truly important and what isn't.

I had gained so much insight from the soul-searching I had just done that I decided to continue. So I spent seven weeks of solitude in an empty house in the country. I had a pad on the floor to sleep on and a rocking chair on which to sit. There were no newspapers, magazines, or television. I didn't answer e-mails, telephone calls, or mail. I am often contacted by people who have read my books or attended a seminar, and I have always felt that I needed to respond to everyone personally. This has meant three hours of e-mail a day, three hours of letters, and two hours on the phone, while trying to write books, teach seminars, and have a family life in the remaining time.

It felt so good just to stop. For the first time in my life I was alone with myself. (Even during the two years I lived in a Zen Buddhist monastery, there were other people around.) For the first time I could remember, I was caring for myself instead of everyone else. I went for walks, did yoga, painted, took candlelit baths, listened to music, and generally enjoyed myself. It was like a huge burden lifted off my shoulders and, for the first time I could ever remember, I felt free.

I lay on the grass and watched clouds. I sat for hours watching birds. I sat with my back up against old oak trees and listened to their messages. I had been so busy in my life that I had forgotten to listen and to drink in the wisdom of the earth, the trees, and the sky. As I listened, this book gestated within me. I thought about what I wanted to say to you and what results I hoped you would gain from reading it. I really hoped that it would make a difference in your life and increase your understanding of yourself as a woman.

In my seven weeks of solitude, I began to feel the emergence of a passionate and powerful wild woman rising from somewhere deep in the murky waters of my soul. I caught glimpses of her in my dreams. I heard her song in the rhythm of my beating drums. She cascaded over my body during the spring showers. This erotic, strong, sumptuous, and sacred part of my personality—the Goddess part of me—yearned to be born. But like a long labor, it wasn't easy.

When I was giving birth to my daughter, and the shock of the first strong contraction ripped through my body, I said: "That's it. I'm not going through with this." I told everyone to go home . . . and meant it. Despite my hesitation, and with a fierce insistence, my uterus continued to contract, and I gave birth to a beautiful baby girl.

Giving birth to the glorious Goddess part of myself, in some ways, has been like giving birth to a child. It isn't without effort. Sometimes I want to quit, but the desire to change my life is stronger than the pull to continue living in a comfortable, yet uninspired, manner. Slowly but surely, the Goddess within is emerging as I delve even deeper into the secrets, mysteries, and magic of being a woman.

Searching for the Goddess Within

I believe that a Goddess lives in all of us. She is the part of each of us that is beautiful, outrageous, and remarkable. She knows how to relax and cherish herself. But she isn't always easy to find. We have been brought up with the idea that to do things for ourselves is selfish. We have been conditioned since early childhood to put the needs of others ahead of our own needs. Somewhere along the way we have lost our inner, sacred, wise woman.

If you feel this way, you are not alone. For the past thirty years, I've taught in nineteen countries, and I have met many different kinds of women through my seminars. Sometimes my courses have been small, but more often the audiences have been large, up to a thousand or more participants. Most of the people who attend are female. In my workshops, I have met women from all walks of life: young punk rockers with tattoos, suburban mothers with kids in tow, Rastafarians, doctors, homemakers, veiled Muslims, traditionally dressed Africans, grandmothers with tinted blue hair, Native Americans, Gucci-dressed lawyers, tie-dyed hippies, belly dancers, artists, and computer programmers. They have been single, married, divorced, widowed, gay; females of all ages, and so many different countries, professions, religions, and lifestyles.

Over the years, I've listened and learned from these women. One idea that continues to surface, no matter whom I am speaking to, is that today's women are overcome by stress, time constraints, and overexertion. Many of them feel a need to realign their physical, emotional, and spiritual lives. However, in order to do this, every woman must first discover the deeper meaning of her life.

Many women are currently on an immense spiritual quest that springs from an urge to live purposefully and in harmony with the rhythms of the earth. There is a common feeling that there has to be more to life. It's like somehow we don't quite fit in today's world. We are round pegs trying to fit into square holes. We yearn for sacred places that nurture the soul. We are often so busy that we don't stop to wonder about the way we are living. We crave the solace of having time to ourselves to relax and take pleasure in life, yet instead we find the speed of life ever-increasing.

Rising in many women, however, is a yearning to return to the vanished womanly values that existed during the Goddess era; before female history was distorted and ancestral wisdom lost. There is a deep desire to reclaim the parts of our collective psyche that have been lost, and thus, once again, to be whole.

There are many paths to self-discovery and wholeness. I have outlined a number of them within this book. Some are steeped in ancient mysticism and lore, and some are more practical and everyday. In my life, I have had the honor of participating in many secret and mystical traditions, as well as spending time within native cultures throughout the world. So I have included ancient woman wisdom that I have learned through the years as well as modern insights.

All the information in this book is aimed at developing a deeper sense of self-esteem. At a certain level, you and I share the same quest, the same challenges, and the same yearning to live a life that is meaningful. No matter what your lifestyle is, no matter who you are, or where you live, I feel that on some level, we know each other. And I'm glad that we are on this journey together.

EMBRACING THE GODDESS

WE were four friends on a mission. Our four-wheel-drive Jeep bumped up the dirt road as evening approached. As we got closer to the top of the mountain, the road got steeper and more difficult to maneuver in the darkness. We felt an urgency to make it to the open vista at the top of the mountain. Our goal was to watch the full moon rise over the distant snow-covered peaks and call forth the energy of the Goddess.

We reached the summit just seconds before the moon rose. We jumped out of the Jeep and raced to a viewpoint. Suddenly, the earth seemed to stand still. The air was crisp and cold. It was so silent. Like a primal force being born, the golden moon silently slipped up over the far mountain ranges, giving the snow an amber glow.

Spontaneously, piercing the silence, one woman began to howl at the moon. Without hesitation we all joined her. Like four female wolves, we howled wildly at the moon. Later that night, around the fire in our cabin, we talked about how we had each experienced the energy of the Goddess swirling in and around us. We had felt her divine power and wisdom.

Establishing a connection to the Goddess is something any woman can do. It's easy and fun and it can be the beginning a wonderful odyssey into the forgotten crevices of your soul. When you adopt or claim a particular Goddess (or aspect of the Great Goddess), a rich fullness begins to unfold in your life.

When I claimed my Goddesses, I felt like a flower that had just started to bloom. There are a number of Goddesses with whom I feel a strong connection, but the one who helped me through a listless period was Artemis, the Greek equivalent of the Roman Goddess Diana. She is the Goddess of the hunt and of nature and wild, untamed things.

Seattle winters are renowned for being dark, gray, and wet. I had spent much of the winter in front of my computer. Every day brought rain and more rain . . . damp, soggy, dreary rain. Lethargy had sunk into my bones. The weather was so dismal. The idea of getting out and going for a walk seemed to be too much effort.

Early one morning, I decided to light a candle to Artemis and called upon her spirit to bless my day. It was the first time I had ever focused on her. As I lit the candle, I thought of her magnificent qualities as I asked for her guidance. At first, nothing seemed to be changed. I sat at my computer and Artemis slipped from my mind as I immersed myself in the magazine article I was writing. An hour later, without warning, I began to feel a warmth fill my body. It started at the base of my spine, moved to the top of my head, and radiated throughout my entire body. I looked around my office: although everything looked the same, the room seemed to have a warm glow. An urge to be outdoors engulfed me. I grabbed my shoes, put on a coat, and raced outside.

The winter wind whipped my jacket around my body, but the growing warmth enveloped me in a cocoon of safety. The wind, wild and untamed, seemed to be a sign that Artemis had heard my prayer. I walked to a small lake near my home. Suddenly, the wind receded and everything became very still as I found myself standing on the shore. A mist hung low on the surface, ducks floated on the lake with heads tucked into their wings, and tree branches were silhouetted dark against the gray sky. The world felt soft, serene, and wondrous. For a moment it was so quiet that even the distant din of traffic subsided. I could feel the depth of sacredness in all life. I breathed deeply and thanked Artemis.

Something magical had occurred. I felt a spark ignite inside me, and I was stronger and clearer than I had been in weeks. This is the power of connecting to a Goddess. Calling forth Goddess energy doesn't necessarily always bring dramatic changes: it works in mysterious ways. You may find that after putting out the call, you're overcome by a feeling of tranquility, vitality, or strength, or you may just feel as though a bad day starts to look a bit brighter.

At the Dawn of Religion, God Was a Woman

To understand about the Goddess we need to go back to a time thousands of years ago when it was believed that the soul of the earth was female. Life depended upon living in balance with the land, and insight into the workings of nature was not phrased intellectually, but distinguished in images. Springing forth from every archeological find around the world, even artifacts from 30,000 years ago, the image of the Goddess has been found again and again—the oldest and most revered of recorded deities. She was the primary symbol for an unseen world that manifested itself in the visible form of the sky, the moon, the sun, the stars, the flowing rivers, the morning dew, and the fertile earth. Ancient people revered the Goddess. To them, her invisible forces were very real, and they felt that adherence to those cosmic laws that were the domain of the Goddess was necessary to maintain a balance of life.

Perhaps it was natural to have a female deity in those early days, because women's bodies, which had the ability to give birth to another human being, were considered sacred. As a result, women were the first guardians of the inner realms, just as priests were in later centuries. The earliest religions were founded on the worship of a single deity—the Great Goddess—who later evolved into various Goddesses in different cultures throughout the world.

In recent years, as archeologists have amassed research from various sites around the world, they have agreed more and more with renowned art historian Merlin Stone, who states that "at the very dawn of religion, God was a woman." "Goddess worship can be traced from the Palaeolithic period, as early as 2,000,000 B.C.E., until less than 5,000 years ago, when God became a man.

In other words, *God has been a male for one quarter of one percent of human history, and God has been female for 99.75 percent of the rest of the time.* A male God is a relative newcomer on the divine scene. Yet, in modern culture, there is an ingrained belief that God is, *and always has been*, male.

Living in a society with a male God can have a powerful subliminal effect on a young female as she grows and begins to define herself as a human being. It can also have far-reaching effects on women of all ages and of all religious backgrounds, from the very devout to those most removed from religious institutions. It is impossible to separate the forces that have shaped us personally from the forces that shape humanity. The religious beliefs of a culture cradle the entire fabric of society.

Our culture believes, in general, that God is male, and this creates a subliminal belief that males are superior. Today men have the great advantage of having a God that validates them, simply by being the same gender. It is empowering to believe that the supreme deity in the Universe is of your sex. Although we have gone through an enormous revolution of the sexes in the last 50 years in the Western world, we are still in a strongly patriarchal time that has a male God at its core.

How did it happen that for most of human history, God was female and now God is male? It didn't happen overnight, or even in several generations, but slowly and surely the connection to the spirit of the earth and a mothering, nurturing divine spirit that dwelled beneath our feet was replaced by a governing presence who judges and views us from high above in the heavens. Many bloodlines that used to be traced through the female are now traced through the male. We moved into a culture where a person who is logical and has mastered facts and statistics is often revered much more that someone who is intuitive. We have moved out of the mystical realm, where dreams, intuition, and the magic of life reside, and into a realm that is more analytical and rational.

Life always moves in cycles, and perhaps the pendulum had swung so far into the mysterious and earthy realm of the Goddess that it was natural that it would swing toward a patriarchal time where the male force reigned supreme. Since the decline of Goddess religions, however, women have lacked the spiritual systems that speak to female needs, and they have not been taught to explore their own spiritual strengths. But the ancient feminine principle is beginning to reassert its power, and that power is beginning to be felt in the hearts of women—not so much as a religious tenet, but as an incredible inner force, with the power to reshape our view of ourselves as women.

Although the majesty of our female history has been distorted over time, and in many ways we have been dispossessed of our spiritual identity as women, I believe that locked in each woman's genetic structure is a subconscious memory of a time when there was a powerful and benevolent female deity. Like a great tide rising, this ancestral cellular memory is beginning to resound in our soul. Many women desire to return to the spirit of the divine feminine. In the deepest place within the female soul, we yearn to reclaim not only the part of our history that has been vanquished and the womanly traditions that have been expunged, but also the corresponding missing part of our psyches . . . and until this reclamation is complete we are not whole. Thus, it is immensely valuable that we begin to awaken the mysteries of the Great Goddess that dwells within us.

Goddess symbolism offers a solution for life's frenetic pace because it inspires us to see ourselves as unique and wondrous, while cherishing our bodies and encouraging us to understand that every cycle within our life is sacred. By aligning ourselves with the Goddesses, we can find our strength, discover our primal birthright, and activate the sheer intoxication of being alive.

When you open your heart to the Divine Feminine, you deepen your understanding of yourself as a woman. Unlike a male God, the Goddess does not govern the world from the outside—she *is* the world within each of us, and thus we can know her very intimately.

Great Mystery

Adhering to the tenets of the Goddess does not mean that you need to repudiate a male God. Since each person has male and female energy within them, you do not betray a female Goddess by having a male God and vice versa. God and Goddess are two aspects of the universal creative force. Embracing the Goddess can enhance your connection with all aspects of the Creator.

Many women find that even though they have a strong yearning to embrace an earth-centered, Goddess-inspired spirituality, in their heart, God remains male. The old images embedded in their childhood remain ever present in spite of a conscious desire to cherish the Goddess. You can be nurtured by the energy of the Goddess and still honor a male God.

Ultimately I believe that God is beyond the confines of male and female, but since we live in a dualistic, male-and-female universe, it is often easier to think of God in our own image as either a man or a woman. I find, however, the Native American tradition of calling God "Great Mystery" very appealing because it denotes neither a male or a female. It attests to the fact that God's true essence and magnitude are unknowable and unfathomable.

Even though I follow the tradition of my Cherokee ancestors and pray to Great Mystery, I also call upon the Goddess, because I realize that I have different associations for the words "God" and "Goddess" and "Great Mystery." I feel different when I say "Goddess" rather than "God." Goddess represents the female power within things, mysterious and wondrous. It is an image that allows me to touch areas deep inside myself, rather than traveling outside for answers. The image of a female God also connects me to nature and to the earth herself, much in the way that I became acutely aware of nature and my environment after calling upon Artemis.

As a result of my childhood associations, I think of God as a patriarchal authority figure who rules with a loving but firm hand that at times can be comforting. However, sometimes when I think of God, I see myself as a little girl hoping to win the approval of her father. This image can be disempowering to me as a woman. It can make me feel the victim of forces outside myself, whereas the image of the Goddess calls forth a genuine, powerful, and compassionate womanly response within me. Focusing on the Goddess makes me feel connected to all things, rather than aligned with one point of view. It gives me a sense of power over my destiny and my life.

I sometimes will interchange the words "Goddess" and "Spirit" because for me they both convey a sacred connection to all of life and a oneness with the earth and the universe in an internal and much more personal way than a male God. I passionately believe that the Goddess image is for both men and women. Men can benefit from an exploration of the Goddess, for within each man there is a feminine spirit, just as there is a masculine energy within each woman.

Calling the Goddess into Your Life

When you begin to understand, and honor, the Goddess, you can reach the magical realm inside yourself. Goddess qualities will begin to bloom within you. Your creativity, magic, mystery, passion, serenity, self-esteem, dreams, and visions will expand. Your self-confidence as a woman will grow. You will discover that you indeed possess the passionate and wondrous soul of a woman. Life doesn't need to be a struggle, and as you embrace the Goddess qualities in your life, everything will become easier. Opportunities will begin to come toward you rather than your having to work hard to attain what you desire.

There are numerous ways to claim your Goddess: research, meditation, keeping a journal, dreams, or prayer. You can research the mythology of various Goddesses to find the one(s) that feel most suited to you and your life (you could begin your search by looking over the list below). When researching Goddesses, I suggest you take your ancestry into consideration. Connecting to the Goddesses of your foremothers can ignite a powerful genetic memory. For example, women who have Scandinavian or northern European ancestry can benefit from connecting to the Norse Goddess Freya. If your ancestors were from Africa, you might want to invoke Yemaya. It is also helpful, especially in Europe, to look to your local landscape, which may well have Goddess associations—for example, pre historic monuments, holy wells, or church dedications. The most important thing to remember, however, is to find one that resonates with you. Although I do not have any Greek blood, I connect strongly with Artemis.

Choose a Goddess who has the qualities that you want to expand in your life. For example, if you need to release old negative habits and addictions, Kali, from the Hindu tradition, is an excellent choice because of her fierce quelling of impurities. Or if you desire to call love into your life, you might choose the Roman Goddess Venus.

You might also feel drawn to the oldest Goddess, who existed in almost all matriarchal cultures, known nowadays as "the Great Goddess" or simply, "the Goddess." In the furthest reaches of history, prior to the time when the Goddesses were divided into various aspects and functions, there was the most ancient of Goddesses . . . *the One*. She had different names in different cultures, but she was the one deity of all beings. You might find that you relate better to this very ancient Goddess rather than a specialized one. The Great Goddess is everything . . . nature . . . the earth, grass, mountains, trees, animals. She is Gaia, Mother Nature, Earth Mother . . . the omnipresent spirit of the earth and nature.

Trace back through time and you will find an abundance of Goddesses in every ancient culture. I have listed a few of them, with some of their associated qualities, below. It was difficult to choose only a few, because each Goddess carries her own majesty and particular, unique qualities. I chose some of the Goddesses who—due to our culture's strong roots in Ancient Greece and Rome, for example—are better known in our Western society and also some who are less widely known, but who carry particular potent qualities. Although several of the Goddesses have an equivalent in another culture (Aphrodite and Venus; Athena and Minerva; Artemis and Diana), in some cases I have chosen to include both because of their slightly different, yet important, emphases and associations. For example, even though they are essentially the same Goddess, many people have different associations for the name Venus than for the name Aphrodite.

Aphrodite (Greek)—pleasure, creativity, marriage, femininity, sensuality, love, inner beauty, awakening inner passions, attracting lovers.
Artemis (Greek)—connection to nature, independence, courage, determination to reach goals, childbirth, new projects.
Athena (Greek)—intelligence, strategy, art, inner wisdom, creativity, protection.

Bast (Egyptian)—sensuous feline energy, focused and yet playful; celebration, self-containment, joy, ecstasy, your wild nature.

Black Madonna (Christian, but thought to be originally an African Goddess)—primordial strength, passion, power.

Brigit (Celtic)—protection, gardening, fertility, healing.

Ceridwen (Celtic)—harvest, abundance, death and rebirth.

Corn Woman (Native American)—abundance, grounding, earthiness, fertility, deepening your connection to the earth.

Demeter (Greek)—nurturing of self and others, maternity, abundance, harvest, material riches, new possibilities.

Diana (Roman)—connection to nature, independence, bravery, standing on your own as a woman, reaching your goals, primal instincts.

Durga (Hindu)—great fortitude to overcome any and all obstacles, fighting spirit of a mother who protects her young.

Freya (Norse)—new directions in life, being grounded, sexual love and fertility, turning challenges into opportunities.

Hathor (Egyptian)—beauty, power, wisdom, fertility, abundance, prosperity, productivity, passion for life.

Hecate (Greek)—mystical experiences, ancient wisdom, healing abilities, inner magic, invisible realms.

Hera (Greek)—protection, material prosperity, the comfort of possessions, confidence, self-esteem, honest expression.

Hestia (Greek)—creating a home of beauty and grace, spirituality, enjoying solitude, being at home with yourself no matter where you are.

Inanna (Sumerian)—fertility, abundance, passion, self-sufficiency, accepting all aspects of yourself with compassion.

Ishtar (Babylonian)—forging forward with power, courage, joy, and passion; sexuality, sensuality, voluptuousness, passion.

Isis (Egyptian)—mystical experiences, self-assurance, lifting out of negativity, mystical realms, intuition, inner light.

Kali (Hindu)—courage, releasing negative patterns, overcoming fear, indomitable spirit.

Kuan Yin (Asian)—compassion, mercy, tranquillity, serenity, repose, tenderness, receptivity, forgiveness.

Lakshmi (Hindu)—inner wealth, abundance, material prosperity, pouring out abundance to the community.

Lilith (Sumero-Babylonian)—unbridled passion, indomitable spirit, sexual pleasure, unabashed sexuality, taking a stand in life.

Mary (Christian)—compassion, intercession.

Medusa (Greek)—wild, untamed, unabashed vital life force; regeneration, healing abilities, breaking through personal barriers.

Minerva (Roman)—intelligence, wisdom, strategy, arts and crafts, wise choices in life, healing abilities, intuition.

Nut (Egyptian)—acceptance, death and rebirth, overview of life.

Persephone (Greek)—deepest inner realms, harmonizing inner life with outer life, maintaining hope amid despair, balance.

Rhiannon (Celtic)—inner wisdom, reaching into your depths.

Sarasvati (Hindu)—insight, healing, musical abilities.

Selene (Greek)—dreams, the moon, divine feminine spirituality, receptivity, inner magic, receptivity to the gifts of the universe.

Sophia (Greek)—kindness, peace, joy.

Tara (Tibetan)—compassion, mothering skills, liberation.

Tlazolteotl (Aztec)—dissolving impurities within yourself, forgiving yourself, releasing guilt and shame, absolving the past.

Venus (Roman)—romantic love, connection to springtime, new growth, blossoming into womanhood, sacred sexuality.

White Buffalo Calf Woman (Native American)—connection to the earth, dignity, grace, balancing male and female energies.

Yemaya (African): nurturing, abundance, protection for journeys across water, expanding your prosperity consciousness.

The Invitation

There are many ways to activate Goddess qualities within you. One immediate way is to simply invite a Goddess into your life. The invitation can take many forms. Simply studying or thinking about a particular Goddess, or saying, "I invite you, Isis [or Medusa or Corn Woman], into my life," will begin to bring that Goddess closer to you. You can write your Goddess's name on a piece of paper that you place under a candle that you light every night. You can also look for pictures or icons of her to put up around your home, or make your own.

Sarah, a woman who attended one of my seminars, had been through a traumatic breakup. She wanted to connect with a Goddess who could help her feel empowered again. She lived near the ocean and felt drawn to Yemaya, Goddess of the Sea. When I suggested drawing Yemaya to bring forth her energy, Sarah said, "But I don't know what she looks like—how can I draw her?" I told her that the only thing that is important is the feeling that you have as you draw. I suggested that Sarah focus on her sense of Yemaya—almost as if she was breathing in the Goddess—and then choose colors and movements that reflected what she was feeling.

After closing her eyes and being silent for a moment, Sarah picked up a paintbrush and began to paint. I watched Sarah's body. She started to sway, and every part of her seemed to grow in stature and strength as swatches of purple, blue, and green were lavishly layered on the canvas and large rounded shapes began to emerge. Sarah was beaming when she was complete. "I could feel it, Denise! I could feel the spirit of Yemaya fill me as I painted. I haven't felt this good or this strong for a long time!" Painting her Goddess was a turning point for Sarah in her process of healing her broken heart.

Additionally, consider invoking your Goddess during the full moon to increase the potency of your link with her. You can do this as I did with my friends, by going to a place in the country where you can watch the rising moon. Alternatively, the power of the full moon is such that you can have equally good results at that time from the comfort of your living room, as long as you hold a strong intention to connect with the Goddess.

As you focus on a particular Goddess, her energy will flow to you. When you begin to think about her, the veil between her dimension and yours begins to thin. Sometimes the invitation is subtle, yet the response is immediate and profound. For example, just saying to yourself, "Please, Durga [the Hindu Goddess that overcomes obstacles], I need help to push through some of these challenges in my life" could begin a process in which your difficulties begin to lessen.

As the spirit of a Goddess becomes alive within you, you will actually begin to demonstrate and exhibit her qualities. You will become more magnificent, magnanimous, intuitive, and powerful. A remarkable transformation will begin, and you will find that you are less bothered by trivial irritations. Even the smallest amount of interest in the ways of the Goddess can bring generous rewards.

Inner Journeys into the Mysteries of the Goddess

I stand naked on a great plain. Around me tower great boulders, silent witnesses to primeval history. Each one looks like the giant fist of some ancient god, turned to stone as it broke through the red earth to reach to the heavens. Twilight swirls around me and darkness descends quickly. Nothing stirs in the stillness of anticipation. Golden and glowing, a hammock moon hangs low on the horizon. Slowly and majestically a luminous woman strides towards me. Her skin glows with the intensity of a full moon. Her full, pendulous breasts and voluptuous hips sway. Her presence is at once immediate, yet whispers of faraway places and ancient secrets.

I can feel her eyes reach into my soul. Gentle tendrils of energy reach into the deepest and darkest recesses of my being. Old wounds are healing, shame and guilt, anger and resentment melting away under her gentle touch. I can feel her spirit flowing through me. At my depth, her primordial waters ebb and flow inside me. Her winds billow in my soul, her great mountains soar in my being, and her fires replace darkness with light. I know I am a part of all things. I am a part of the wind, the sky, the earth, and the heavens. The Great Mother dwells within me and around me.

This experience, which touched me deeply, occurred on one of my meditative journeys. At the conclusion of this inner sojourn, I found that a sense of grace and peace filled my body. I noticed that when I stood and walked, I felt a dignity and pride unlike any I had ever felt.

An inner journey can be as powerful, moving, and life-transforming as any physical experience. In fact, in some ways it can be more powerful because in the stillness of meditation, your spirit can open to other dimensions. It is a powerful way for you to tap into the Goddess realms.

This kind of meditation can be a potent way to call the spirit of the Goddess into your body and life. In past times, women's inner journeys were traditionally accompanied by drums and/or chanting. They were often done in the wild, as that was where the Goddess energy could be felt deeply and fully. This type of inner pilgrimage, where she became still, closed her eyes, and went into a meditative state, allowed a woman to reach into herself and tap into the Goddess mysteries. Her world was never the same afterwards.

Suggested Goddess Journeys

To embark on an inner Goddess journey, simply find somewhere comfortable to lie down. Play some soothing music (or, you could have a friend gently drum with a sonorous, even cadence). Having chosen one of the following scenarios to focus on, allow yourself to become very relaxed and then imagine that you are traveling through time and space to the realm of the Goddess.

- Imagine that you are climbing a mountain to speak to the old, wise crone who lives in a hut right at the top.
- Visit an ancient temple to connect with the spirit of the Goddess to whom it was dedicated.
- Go deep into a cavern to find the Great Goddess, whose spirit is especially strong in the deep, dark places within the earth.
- Travel to the seashore to call upon the Goddess Yemaya, who rises majestically out of the sea to greet you.

The earliest worshippers of the Goddess perceived that life was made up of patterns of swirling energy fields. Every tree, cloud, river, stone, and living creature was comprised of flowing, spiraling flows of energy. Drawings of spirals in archaic cave paintings throughout the world are thought to be renditions of this early perception of reality. The concept that all life was comprised of flowing energy forms was one of the most basic insights into the nature of life.

The current Western view of the universe, consisting of objects fixed in time and space, is a deviation from long-held human perceptions of existence. Those who gained wisdom from the earth experienced all things, from the Great Lakes to the Great Pyramid, as being in constant motion, and that underlying this motion was order and harmony. Modern physics now supports that ancient view, by saying that matter is indeed made up of vortexes of currents in an ever-changing sea of energy.

Ordinary consciousness sees the world as solid and immutable, comprised of separate objects isolated from their surroundings. However, the non-ordinary, Goddess-perception of life is to see patterns and intimate relationships between people and things.

Seeing the World Through the Eyes of a Goddess

Sit quietly in a natural setting. (If you have no countryside nearby, find a quiet place in a park.) Start by looking around and focusing on one object at a time. For example, first look at a tree, then a squirrel, then a stone. This should feel quite normal, as this is the way we are trained to view the world. Now allow your eyes to go soft and begin to perceive everything at once. Of course you won't be able to "see" everything at once ... but allow yourself to "feel" the environment around you.

As you quiet your mind, begin to sense the rhythms within your environment. The earth may have a slow and sonorous cadence. A young birch tree may have delicate, rippling energy, like water cascading down a mountain stream. Now imagine that you are aware of all of these rhythms merging and melding together, the way the sounds of the individual instruments of an orchestra blend to create beautiful music. Be especially aware of yourself and your own rhythms within this great symphony of energy.

Doing this exercise periodically will begin to create a connection between you and the natural world. You will find your inner wisdom and intuition growing.

Dreaming the Goddess

If you want to invite the Goddess into your waking life, you can also call upon her in the night through your dreams. Cultures that honored the Goddess often used dreams to connect to her, for the night was her realm. Before you go to bed, affirm over and over again: "Tonight I am embraced in the arms of the Goddess," "I invoke the spirit of the Goddess to watch over me and to inspire me through the night," or "With gratitude and blessing, I invite the Goddess to visit me in my dreams tonight." Use words that feel right and comfortable to you and say them over and over with the intention that you will indeed connect to the spirit of the Goddess during your dreams.

Upon waking, if you can recall a dream, immediately write it down. Take time to dwell on your dreams to see in what ways the Goddess may have communicated to you. If you don't recall a dream, notice what you are feeling emotionally . . . often the feelings that we have upon waking are indications of the timbre of our dreams.

As you continue this technique, you will find that the depth and breadth of your Goddess dreams expands.

Tools to Help "Dream the Goddess"

- Keep a piece of the mineral selenite next to your bed. Selenite is a soft, translucent mineral that is associated with the Goddess Selene, but can be used to invoke any Goddess.
- Place a small sachet pillow filled with dried lavender by your head. This has been shown to help relaxation and assist the ability to dream.
- Create a Goddess altar in your bedroom where it can be seen from your bed. This will help focus your dreams on the Divine Feminine.
- Drink moon-water just before you go to sleep to invoke the Goddess. To make moon-water, leave water in an open vessel in the moonlight overnight.
- If possible, wake up naturally, as the jarring sound of an alarm clock can make it difficult to remember dreams. If you need to set an alarm, tell yourself before falling asleep that you want to wake up naturally. Often you'll find that by preprogramming yourself, you'll wake up before your alarm rings.

Goddess Ceremonies

A ceremony or ritual is a formalized act performed with an intrinsic purpose. For example, lighting a candle with the intent of activating the quality of love within yourself is a simple ceremony. As the Goddess realm is invisible and mysterious, a ritual offers a vehicle to reach that realm. Ceremonies provide a bridge between outer worlds and inner dimensions and can be used to invite divine feminine qualities into your life. In ancient times, Goddess ceremonies allowed mortals to literally enter into the sacred realms. They even sanctioned the quickening of Goddess qualities within the mortal.

We can use these same methods in present times. Your Goddess ritual can be very simple or it can be elaborate and involve many people. To create it, there are several steps that you might find helpful:

1. Become clear about your intention

It is essential that you have a clear vision of the results that you want from your ceremony. This is the most important step. Perhaps you want to leave a destructive relationship or to purge negative patterns, so your intent might be to begin your life anew. If you feel overwhelmed by the struggles in your life, your intention for the ceremony might include becoming a stronger and more confident woman. If you have a project that is lagging, your intention might be to garner the strength, courage, and focus to complete it.

Perhaps you want to create a Goddess ceremony to bless your new home. You will first need to become clear about what kinds of experiences you desire to have within its walls. For example, you could say, "I desire that my home is a safe haven, a sanctuary for myself and others. It is a place where I feel completely at home with myself."

2. Choose a Goddess

Choose a Goddess to focus on who both inspires you and who best represents your intention. For example, if you desire to bless your home, you might choose Hestia. The ancient Greeks said that a house or temple is just a building until it receives its Hestian soul. Hestia was worshipped at the fire at the center of the home. Before moving into a new home, she was summoned to bring her blessings to the home and to all those who dwelled there.

3. Preparation

As simply, concisely, and eloquently as you can, decide what tools you will have present, what actions you will perform, and who will be present. Pay attention to details. It is easy for the grandeur of the event to overwhelm your original pure intention. Remember that *every* aspect of the ceremony must be directed toward your intention. A precise and dedicated lighting of a single candle with the intention of opening your heart to the compassion of Kuan Yin can be more powerful than lots of elaborate words and actions that are unfocused.

When you are planning your ritual, write out what is needed: your shopping list, who needs to be contacted, what preparation needs to be done, dates, times. Then map out the event in advance. It's valuable to have some structure in your Goddess ceremony, and it is also important to use your intuition. In the middle of a ceremony, you may have a spontaneous idea about your ritual—such premonitions are often Goddess-inspired (the Goddess rules your intuition), so, it's important to follow them, if possible.

4. Purification

Prepare and purify the space for your ritual. If it's going to be performed indoors, sweep the floor and wipe the counters. If it is going to be outdoors, ready the area by removing clutter and raking up any fallen leaves. After an area has been prepared, you may consider doing some space clearing.

Space clearing employs ancient methods to clear and remove negative or stagnant energy from a location. For example, take a burning bundle of sage and waft or "smudge" the smoke throughout the ceremonial area. The purifying qualities of the smoke permeate the area and help to neutralize any stagnant energy. Another technique is to circle the ceremonial area while ringing a bell. With each chime of the bell, hold the intention of creating a sparkling energy in the environment. After the area has been thus restored to harmony, proceed with your ceremony.

5. The ceremony

Your ceremony can take many forms. It can be a simple one that you do for yourself, or you may involve other people. For example, if you are creating a ceremony to bless your home, you may decide to gather your friends together for it. Ask each friend to write their wishes for you in your new home on a piece of paper. While everyone stands in a circle and offers up their wish for your home, you can call upon Hestia to bring her blessings.

> May the Great Goddess within all things bring blessings and peace to us all. May the spirit of Hestia bring blessings to this home and to each person who enters here.

Walk around the circle holding a small ceramic pot or basket in front of you as you stand before each friend. Each person places their piece of paper in the pot. Complete the circle by placing your paper with your own wishes for your home in the pot. Once the ceremony has begun, let go of expectations . . . ceremonies often have a life of their own, and the result is often better when you can allow it to progress without judging the form.

6. Invocation

At the apex of the ceremony, invoke or call upon the Goddess and be open to receiving her blessings. This can be done silently or out loud. Your prayers do not need to be eloquent or long. Usually a simple prayer from the heart is most effective. For example, if you have collected prayers from your friends for your house blessing, take the pot into the center of the circle. Burn the papers in a fireproof vessel (a large ashtray will work) and invoke Hestia, saying:

> Hestia, Goddess of hearth and home, I invite you into this home and give thanks for all that is received from you. As our prayers travel upward on the smoke to you, may your blessings travel downward through the smoke to us. May this home truly become a sanctuary for all who enter here.

7. Be still

After an invocation, it's always important to take time to be still so you can listen to any inner messages that may come as a result of the ceremony. It is often in the stillness after a ceremony that you can feel the spirit most strongly.

8. Integration

This is an important step. At the completion of the ceremony, give thanks for blessings received. Clear the area to transform sacred space back into normal space. Take time to integrate your experience by asking yourself, "How can this ceremony inspire me to change, and what actions can I take to manifest the insights of this ceremony in my life?" By taking time to integrate your Goddess ceremony, you will find the results deeper and more lasting.

The Glory of Goddess Circles

The consciousness-raising and sometimes vehemently feminist environment of women's circles and groups of the late sixties and early seventies has grown and changed through the years. The anger and rage that was sometimes shared in them was necessary at the time to break through old stereotypes and repression. However, it has been necessary for the form to evolve, because feminism not based on spirituality becomes just one more form of politics, and this doesn't feed the soul.

Most women's circles now focus more on the inner process rather than outer life, and I have found that the time I have spent in them has provided some of the deepest and richest experiences of my life. Many women in today's world could gain a great deal from participating in a Goddess circle; for the gathering of women in a circle is an archetypal practice that nourishes our souls. It can be a place of mutual trust, where each woman can reclaim her spirit.

A Goddess circle begins with an idea, an intention, and a yearning to be in community with other women. It recalls women in ancient times, who gathered in sisterhood around the sacred fire to rekindle wisdom and compassion, and to connect to the spirit of the Goddess. The following suggestions are intended to help you start your own circle.

The first step is to become clear about why you want to have a Goddess circle. What kind of results do you want from it? Will the circle be a place of mutual support for life issues? Will it be a study group to understand more about women's history? Or will it be a place to activate creativity?

Visualize who might be the potential members of your circle. It's valuable to get together with two or three friends to discuss the formation of your circle and decide whom you will invite into it. You can also be daring and announce your intention through a bulletin board, a newsletter, or even through the Internet and just see who comes. It is never an accident who answers your call.

It's valuable to choose a specific, regular time and stick to it—once a week, every two weeks, or once a month. It can be a good idea to have a time limit for each session, too—say two hours. Time constraints offer a structure that makes it easier for everyone to schedule the time into their busy lives.

You can meet anywhere that is fairly quiet and feels safe. You do not want to be constantly invaded by other people. It's also worth finding a place where women can laugh with abandon without worrying about disturbing the neighbors. Someone's living room, a kitchen table, even a space that you rent can all work well. Or you could use a chat room and have a cyber circle on the Internet.

Plan on beginning each session by quieting the mind and taking time for centering. This can be done via a silent meditation, a song, a guided visualization, or by simply holding hands together in silence. This is a time of gestation where energy, love, and wisdom are forming and maturing. You could perform a simple ritual at the beginning, such as lighting a candle or ringing a bell and saying the words, "May the light of the Goddess fill our hearts and this circle."

It's a good idea to take it in turns to lead the opening ceremony. Sitting in a circle also demonstrates the fact that every woman is equal to every other woman there. (This is a different premise than the one created by the priest and congregation, where the priest is elevated higher than everyone else, and all are facing him, suggesting that one individual is wiser, smarter, and holier than the others.) The format that the Goddess circle takes after this initial centering is highly individual. I enjoy circles that start with each woman taking a short amount of time to share about her life at this moment . . . both her triumphs and her challenges.

A Goddess circle isn't a therapy group. It is a place of trust and safety where each woman has equal voice and is free to share herself honestly and openly. It is not a place to fix people, but a place to share each woman's journey to wholeness as she expresses her pain, her joy, and her love.

I continue to be amazed at the phenomenal synchronicity that occurs in Goddess groups. If one woman comes who has had a rough week, perhaps dealing with authority issues, almost always other women in the group have had similar experiences. It seems that in the compassion that is shared, all are healed in an organic way.

How a gathering is closed is just as important as how it is opened. Take the time to honor the sacred and holy nature of that which has been created together. I believe that the healing and gathering of wisdom that occurs in Goddess circles has powerful ramifications outside the circles themselves. Margaret Mead, the renowned anthropologist, said, "Never doubt that a small group of thoughtful, committed citizens can change the world." The energy created in your circle will be like a pebble thrown into a still pool. The ripples of love and compassion that are created will radiate in all directions.

We are at a crucial time in our history, and the rising feminine principle is needed to harmonize the imbalances that have circled the planet. Women are natural healers, and as we embrace the Goddess within, we activate the spirit of healing inside ourselves. Thus, we become a potent force for healing ourself, others, and the planet. This is needed. You are needed. Embracing the spirit and qualities of the Goddess in your life will contribute to your becoming a healing force on the planet.

YOUR 3 ALLIES

FEMININE power is mysterious, healing, serene, and mystical. A woman who has accessed her quintessential womanly wisdom has no need to speak of it, for her inner strength radiates out from her in all directions and touches everyone around her.

There are many ways that you can access your feminine power. One time-honored way is to claim your spiritual allies and understand how to use power objects. When you open yourself to guidance, protection, and support from the realm of Spirit, you are embarking on an ancient tradition that generations of women before you have accessed.

No matter what your life circumstances are, there is a vast store of spiritual help available to you at any time. The inner realms have a multitude of helpers, guides, and guardians just waiting for you to call upon them. Even if you don't believe in them, they can help you. They can come in the form of angels, guides, nature devas, ancestors, or even animal and plant allies. You may find that you resonate more with one kind of ally than another. The secret is learning how to connect to these realms and becoming familiar with your allies. Inner wisdom and power are available to a woman who understands this.

Angels As Allies

I squeezed my eyes shut in extreme pain. It was the middle of the night. The slightest exertion seemed to tear me open as I lay in the intensive-care unit at the hospital after I'd been shot, aged seventeen. I couldn't get away from the pain; it rolled over me, wave after wave. I silently pleaded for someone to help me.

I felt a hand gently slip into mine. Immediately the pain subsided. I opened my eyes expecting to see a nurse or doctor who had kindly come in to comfort me . . . but there wasn't anyone there!

I looked at my hand. I could feel the warmth and texture of someone's hand, but I couldn't see anyone! Although I was completely astonished, suddenly I couldn't keep my eyes open. A deep feeling of peace and drowsiness washed over me, and I fell into a sound sleep. Every night after that, whenever I was enveloped in pain, comforting hands would come to hold mine. Sometimes the hand felt male, sometimes female, and once it felt like a child's hand. I was so grateful for their presence. I now believe that these midnight comforters were angels.

Since that time, many years ago, angels have come into my life in many forms. Usually they come invisibly, as they did when I was in the hospital, but sometimes they have come in a physical form, looking human but with a heavenly presence. Mostly they come as a sudden insight or intuition.

Angels are real. Every culture throughout history and mythology is replete with references to angels. They are messengers from Spirit. You have angels that are available for you. We all do. They are associated with beauty, peace, joy, fulfillment, laughter, and love. Your angels can help you to lay down your burden of fear, uncertainty, guilt, and worry. Communing with your angels can help replace feelings of unworthiness and insecurity with joy and belonging. They can enable you to live with joy instead of fear.

There are different kinds of angels, and they each serve a different purpose in your life. Guardian angels are beings who are personally connected with you and your evolution. They can assist you in creative endeavors, protect you, and help you to achieve your dreams. There are also nature angels or devas, each one being the spiritual custodian of a particular area such as a mountain or lake. Places in nature that have a very special feeling are most often under the protection of an angel.

Most people picture angels as they are traditionally shown in church windows, with wings and a halo. Almost every culture throughout the world has spoken of winged angels. Native Americans, for instance, sometimes call angels the "winged people" or the "bird people." Encounters with winged angels are rarely reported anywhere nowadays; however, more common are reports of angels appearing in human form. They appear as both male and female, young and old, of all different races and in all kinds of clothing. They take a form that is comforting and pleasing to the person to whom they appear.

When I was eighteen years old, I lived in a small trailer near a busy freeway. During the day, I washed dishes and worked as a waitress in a café that was frequented by truckers and tattooed bikers. I felt so alone. Since I desperately wanted to go to college, I worked long hours and hoarded every penny. To save money, I even tried eating cat food.

At night, the penetrating coldness of winter and the constant noise of the freeway seeped in through the metal seams of my trailer. The nights were the hardest. The trauma of my childhood, the drama of being shot, the humiliation of the subsequent trial—in those days, a major defense in a jury trial was to show that the victim deserved to be shot—and the harshness of my job, seemed overwhelming, and I would often fall asleep in deep despair.

One chilly November night, at three in the morning, I woke up gravely despondent. I had had enough. I wanted out of my life. A dead calm came over me. I knew what I had to do. There was a large river in town. I could jump off the bridge and drown myself.

With grim determination, I walked out of my trailer, down the road, and eventually across a large park toward the bridge. The ground was covered with patches of dirty snow. As I walked through the park, I saw a young man about my age sitting on a park bench with his head hung low. Normally I would have never approached a lone male in a park in the middle of the night, but now I thought, *What does it matter if he tries to hurt me? I'm going to be dead in a few moments anyway.*

I walked over to him and asked, "Are you okay?"

He said, "No, I'm not," and then he proceeded to tell me about some troubles in his life and said that *he was on the way to the bridge to kill himself.* (At the time, I didn't realize what an amazing coincidence this was.)

I sat down next to him and said, "Hey, you're young. You're going through a rough time, but things will get better."

We chatted for a long time. He perked up, told me how much I had helped him, and profusely thanked me. I felt so good that I forgot about drowning myself, and I turned around and went back home. As I walked back through the park, the sun was rising and the patches of snow that had previously looked so dingy and sullied, glowed pink and looked beautiful against the dark earth. As I stepped into my trailer, I knew that although I was going through a rough period, things would get better . . . and they did.

Years later, in a moment of clarity, I realized that my encounter wasn't by chance. I knew that on that freezing November night, I had met an angel . . . and it made all the difference.

Usually, however, angels are not seen but only felt. Often the wonderful smell of flowers accompanies their presence. Sometimes they announce their arrival with a slight breeze, even if the windows are closed. Occasionally, you will hear the subtle sound of bells or chimes, or you may see a flash of blue or golden light, which can indicate the arrival of an angel. The most usual way that you know that you are in the presence of an angel is that you feel a wash of love flow over you. If you think an angel is near . . . usually there is. As you trust in them, they will pour their blessings on you.

Calling Angels into Your Life

The angelic dimension is only a thought away. I believe that all prayers are heard. As you focus your awareness on angels, they will make their presence known to you in a myriad of ways. Meditation upon angels, spending time in nature in places that feel holy or sacred, and thinking about angels are all ways to call them into your life. To deepen the connection, you can also place pictures or statues of angels throughout your home. Allow your home to be a sacred space that welcomes spirit protectors into your life.

Ancestors As Allies

A year ago, my husband, David, and I had spent an hour and a half trying to fix the plumbing on the kitchen sink. "Damn!" he yelled. "I hate plumbing! We're going to have to get a whole new sink and fixtures!"

"Wait just a minute," I said. "When my dad was alive, he was good at plumbing. I'm going to call upon him to help me."

David looked at me a little dubiously but stepped back and watched me.

"Dad, if you can hear me, could you help me with this sink?" I was quiet for a moment and then took the pliers and reached up under the sink and turned. It was fixed! David cheered and grabbed me and swung me around! "Hey, I didn't do it," I said. "Remember, we both tried to fix it and we couldn't. Dad just guided my hands."

Your ancestors are physically a part of you; they are present in your genes. Within each cell in your body is a microscopic trace of every single one of your forebears. Your predecessors are also available to you on a spiritual level to act as your allies. Numerous cultures throughout the world continue the ancient practice of communing with their forebears. While most people in Western cultures discount the power of their ancestors, your forefathers and foremothers can offer you an untold wealth of advice and guidance. All you need to do is ask, and their love, guidance, and wisdom will be made available to you. If you are adopted, you have the advantage of having both biological ancestors and spiritual ancestors from your adopted family.

Even if your family was dysfunctional and you want nothing to do with them, if you trace your ancestry back far enough, you will find those beings in your family lineage who were noble, strong, loving, and kind. You will gain by calling upon them.

Your ancestors do not just dwell in the past, they dwell inside your brain as well as residing in every cell in your body. By giving your predecessors a place of honor in your heart, you acknowledge the gifts that have been given to you by them. Finding ways to honor them can empower that place in yourself where their spirit dwells.

Asking Your Ancestors for Guidance

Traditionally, ancestral altars were created for the purpose of communing with those who had passed on. It may very well be that the practice of placing a group of photographs together on a piano or shelf is a remnant from this ancient practice, a subliminal ancestor altar. However, even just asking for their help can be valuable. For example, say: "Ancestors, please help me with my project" or "I ask for guidance and assistance from my ancestors for the safety of our children today." Remember to give thanks whenever you feel that you have gained their support.

Animal Spirit Allies

In history and mythology, it is not uncommon to see women pictured alongside animals or mythological creatures. The Greek Goddess Athena, for example, is always accompanied by an owl, and the Norse Goddess Freya is often pictured riding in a chariot pulled by cats.

Emissaries from Spirit can arrive in many forms. The use of animal allies (also called totems, power animals, spirit animals, or animal guides) is a well-documented and long-standing tradition all over the world. In the distant past (as well as in many contemporary non-Western cultures), it was believed that the physical and spiritual worlds overlapped.

Personal spirit animals come with messages during dreams, in visions, and during meditation. Animal totems (this includes birds, fish, reptiles, and even insects) play a significant role as guides and helpers in all indigenous cultures. As a result of my Cherokee heritage, I revere and embrace Native American culture and the understanding that each animal brings its own "medicine" or healing power and will often appear in various forms as one goes through transitions in life.

Just as you have angel allies and guardians, you also have an individual animal ally that can provide you with guidance, strength, and protection. A woman who knows and communes with her totem animal deepens her understanding of herself and expands her power. Though an individual can have more than one totem, usually there will be one that is predominant at any given time. Anyone from any culture can benefit from accessing their totem animal.

Working with an animal ally will help you to be aware of what is really occurring around you. Most animals are highly instinctive, and when you access your animal allies, you'll find that your instincts and intuition intensify. Even if you are not consciously aware of the energy undercurrents in people, places, and situations, your instincts about them will be good and you'll find yourself more and more often at the right place at the right time.

In historical metaphysical traditions, it was not uncommon for a woman to have a "familiar," or a pet that served as a connection to the spiritual realms. Often this was a cat, but it could be any animal. Adopting an animal as your ally and familiar elevates your relationship beyond that of mere pet and owner. It creates a deeper sense of connection between you.

Communing with Your "Familiar"

Sit quietly with your pet and imagine that you can hear its thoughts and feelings. Ask if it has any information or wisdom that it would like to share with you. Imagine that you can hear the response.

In the beginning, this exercise may feel like you are making up the communication, but almost always you will begin to discover that your animal has a way of giving you information that you couldn't have possibly known otherwise. An acquaintance, Gabrielle, did this exercise with her dog and "heard" the dog tell her that there was a carbon monoxide leak. Gabrielle said that she felt like she was just making it all up and she couldn't smell anything, but she called the gas company anyway. They came to her home and discovered a leak. She credits her dog with saving her life.

Wild animals can also be allies. I am fortunate to live in the country, in an area with abundant animal life. On our land we have seen bobcats, mountain lions, coyotes, foxes, deer, wild turkey, great horned owls, and numerous other types of birds and wildlife. When I take the time to be still and listen, I can hear the messages from the animals. For example, last spring the coyotes were constantly playing in the meadow. In the early morning and late evening, we would see coyote families tumbling, prancing, and howling together. When I listened to what the spirit of the coyote had to tell me, I "heard" the message that I needed to play more and have more fun. This was a message that I took to heart, and I began to be less serious and more playful.

In the past two weeks, a number of very large bobcats have come close to our home. They sit as still as Buddhas on the green hills behind our home and just look down at me. It's quite amazing to see them so close and so seemingly serene. It has been a really busy time in my life, and I haven't really stopped much to rest and unwind. Every day as I look at the bobcats, they seem to say, "Denise, be still. Slow down." Yesterday I took their advice and took time to breathe and relax. It will be interesting to see if they return, now that I have received their message.

Finding Your Animal Ally

In many native traditions, finding one's animal ally often involved a vision quest in nature. However, as we don't always have the opportunity to go on a vision quest, there are a number of other ways that you can find your ally.

You may find your power animal by noticing the animals to which you feel irresistibly drawn. It could be your favorite animal since childhood. Perhaps you loved stories about cats, and have always felt allied to them. A totem may also appear repeatedly in a dream or meditation. If an animal manifests itself a number of times, especially in unusual ways, this most likely is one of your allies. For example, you receive a card with a horse on it in the mail. Then you begin seeing horses on posters and billboards. There's a song playing on the radio about a horse as you're driving by a field full of horses. If everywhere you turn, you see horses, then it's a good possibility that the horse is your totem.

Discovering the Qualities of Your Animal Ally

Different cultures assign varying meanings to totems. I suggest that you trust your intuition to find the significance of yours. There are also many books that list power animals as seen in different cultures and what they represent. Though these can be very useful, it is important to remember that this is only one person's interpretation. Read the definition of your *animal ally* in the book and see if it *feels* right to you. Your own sense of what a particular totem means is unique and is certainly as valid as anyone else's opinion.

The owl spirit ally is a good example of these varying definitions. When I was in Western Australia, discussing totems with Aboriginal male elders, I was told that men feared the owl, for it was woman's totem and it represented the darkness and the unknown. They said that as men were afraid of the power of women, they also feared the owl.

In Greek mythology and in many cultures throughout the world, the owl represents feminine wisdom. In New Zealand, I discussed animal allies with members of the Terinaki Maori tribe (which I was "adopted" into) and asked about the owl. I was told that it was a sacred bird to the Maoris. It was so sacred that its name was never spoken. In my own Native American culture, some tribes revere the owl, saying that it represents deep wisdom, yet other tribes consider it the harbinger of death and darkness. The meaning for each ally can vary dramatically; therefore, it is crucial that you find the meaning of your ally for yourself.

Another way to discover what your totem represents is to read wildlife books, nature magazines, and encyclopedias. Research the habits and habitat of the animals with which you feel a special kinship. For example, if you feel that the wolf is your ally, by researching their habits in the wild, you will discover that they have a strong sense of family. Thus, having a wolf for your ally may increase your connection to your family.

Here is a brief list of animal totems and some of the meanings with which they are sometimes associated:

alligator—formidable strength, power.
ape—primitive power, intelligence.
bat—ancient wisdom.
bear—mother earth, healing.
beaver—hard work, prosperity through your own efforts.
buffalo—abundance, harvest and plenty.
bull—great strength, force, power.
camel—endurance, getting through a difficulty.
canary—harmony.
cat—intuition, feminine essence.
chameleon—adaptability, flexibility.
cobra—life-force energy.
deer—fertility, grace, joy.

dog—faithfulness, loyalty, friendship.
dolphin—playfulness, spontaneity, intelligence.
dove—peace, freedom.
eagle—spirituality, farsightedness.
elephant—power, mindfulness.
elk—power, beauty, dignity.
fish—emotional flow, feminine energy.
fox—intelligence, physical attraction.
frog—abundance, prosperity.
horse—freedom, movement, beauty.
leopard—prowess, sensuality.
lion—majesty, power, bravery, leadership.
otter—capriciousness, playfulness.
owl—wisdom, feminine power, transformation.
peacock—confidence, celebration, pride in oneself.
polar bear—healing, strength.
rabbit—prosperity, abundance, fertility.
ram—masculine strength, pioneering spirit.
raven—wisdom from unseen realms.
rhinoceros—male sexuality.
robin—harbinger of good tidings, new beginnings.
salmon—being in the flow, moving ahead against all odds.
seal—grace, emotional balance, curiosity.
snake—womanly power, healing, spiritual awakening.
swan—beauty, strength, gliding to new heights.
tiger—prowess, power, strength.
turtle—grounding, abundance.
vulture—ancient Goddess, purification.
whale—perception, intuition, power.
wolf—community, social connection, family support.

Plant and Mineral Allies

In addition to your animal totems, you also have specific herbs, flowers, trees, and stones that are your allies. When you connect with these totems—growing your flower allies, spending time sitting under the boughs of your oak tree ally, or carrying your jade stone ally in your pocket—you gain access to remarkable sources of wisdom and information. Additionally, using drops of environmental essences (from flowers, trees, or minerals; see Resources) can also allow you to connect with and expand the qualities of your ally inside yourself.

Tree Allies

On our land is a 300-year-old oak tree I have named "Geronimo." Although the tree is scarred and twisted, he continues to stand tall and strong like the famous Apache warrior. I sit with my back against his rough bark and imagine that I am talking to him. I feel comforted by his steady advice and support. (Even if you live in a home that doesn't have trees, you can adopt one in a local park, or visit your ally tree in nature in your meditations.)

Trees have souls. My Cherokee ancestors, as well as other American Indian tribes, considered trees to be holy. They called them "tree people." The Druids (Celtic religious leaders) also revered trees and believed that each tree expressed particular spiritual qualities. In worldwide shamanic traditions, trees are also mystic passageways for earth-dwellers to enter into other worlds. While in a trance state, a shamaness can travel down through the root system of a tree to gain insight and wisdom from the underworld.

Honoring tree spirits opens up a wonderful connection to spiritual realms while staying very grounded and focused. It is particularly valuable to meditate with trees in wild places. Choose a tree that feels welcoming. Sit with your back against it and open your heart. You may feel energy running up your spine, and feel renewed and energized afterwards.

Although the meanings of your own allies will be very personal, here is a list of some of the common meanings of tree allies. It is by no means comprehensive, but should give you a starting point. The best way to discover the meaning of your tree ally, however, is to ask it.

alder—awakening courage to move forward.

almond—abundance.

aspen—overcoming fear, protection; in mythology, Greek Goddesses protected those who had aspen leaves.

apple—healing, love, symbol of the Goddess Aphrodite; the mystical Celtic Avalon means "island of apples."

ash—balance, order, guardian; to ancient Celts, this tree represented balance and was the guardian of the order of the universe.

bamboo—good luck, prosperity.

birch—new beginnings, renewal, the youthful aspect of the Goddess.

cedar—detoxification, purification; Cherokees believe this tree provides powerful strengthening.

chestnut—fertility, great strength.

elder—moon energy, grace, honor; associated with the Goddess.

elm—feminine power, love.

eucalyptus—renewal, purification.

fir—cleansing, renewal, releasing stagnant emotions.

hawthorn—love, healing negative emotions, birth; associated with Blodeuwedd, the Welsh Goddess of spring.

hazel—inspiration, communication, knowledge.

holly—regeneration, female blood-of-life.

juniper—protection, purification; in the Himalayas, Sherpas bless and purify their ropes with the smoke of juniper boughs.

maple—prosperity, ability to adapt to new circumstances.

oak—strength, fortitude, courage, faith.

olive—peace, healing.

pine—purification, cleansing negative emotions.

plum—love, protection.

rowan—protection, strength, magical realms; sacred to Brigit, the Celtic Goddess of protection.

sandalwood—wisdom, spirituality.

sycamore—strength, vitality, feminine energy.

willow—moon cycles and water, emotional healing, intuition, divine feminine spirit.

yew—regeneration, rebirth, letting go of the old and embracing the new.

Flower Allies

Discovering your flower allies is a wonderful way to ignite joy and beauty in your life. They can inspire you to greater heights of awareness. To connect more deeply with your flower allies, grow them in your garden, visualize them in your meditations, keep photographs or botanical prints of them in your home, take flower essences, or have them as cut flowers in your home.

anemone—fertility.

bluebell—good luck.

daffodil—joy, success in business.

daisy—innocence, joy.

dandelion—strength, fortitude.

gardenia—self-esteem, love.

geranium—endurance.

hibiscus—passion.

honeysuckle—prosperity, abundance, joy.

iris—feminine spirit.

jasmine—sensual love.

lilac—abundance, harmony.

lily—divine femininity, purity, rebirth.
marigold—protection, honoring the sacred.
morning glory—joy, spiritual attunement.
orchid—fertility, stamina.
peony—longevity.
rose—love, emotional healing, angelic kingdoms.
sunflower—prosperity, fertility, success.
tulip—abundance, sensuality.
violet—spirituality, psychic healing.

Plant and Herb Allies

Each woman has particular plants and herbs that are her allies. Take time to find your plant allies and you will find your healers. For example, goldenseal is one of my plant allies. This bitter herb was used by my Native American ancestors for healing. When my body is out of balance, I ingest goldenseal powder or take the extract, and immediately feel the medicinal as well as the healing spiritual qualities fill my body.

basil—blessing, purification.
chamomile—calm, relaxation.
dill—wealth, success.
fennel—healing.
foxglove—protection, emotional balance.
garlic—protection, healing.
ivy—protection, abundance.
lavender—calm, relaxation.
marjoram—marriage, love.
mint—cleansing, refreshment.
mistletoe—love, protection.
mugwort—focus, healing.
nettle—protection.
rosemary—purification, stimulation.
sage—cleansing, renewal.
thyme—health, healing.

Mineral Allies

Minerals have been used by women as special allies for thousands of years. Throughout history, gems and mineral stones have been associated with special powers. When you wear or hold a mineral that is your ally, or place it in your home, you will feel stronger and more vital. If it is not your ally, when you hold or wear it you will either feel nothing, or possibly feel weaker.

Every rock has a story waiting to be heard. When you train yourself to listen to these stories from the mineral kingdom, you will find a wealth of information and guidance available. Here is a very limited list of some stones and their symbolism.

agate—stability and balance.
amber—absorbs and neutralizes negativity.
amethyst—feminine energy, calm.
aquamarine—relaxation, calm.
aventurine—healing, freedom.
bloodstone—detoxification, strength.
carnelian—motivation, confidence, action.
citrine—confidence, communication, decision making.
coral—physical strength, determination.
fluorite—creativity, spiritual awareness.
garnet—activates passion and life force.
jade—healing, soothing, abundance.
lapis lazuli—spiritual awakening.
malachite—calm, physical healing, peace.
moonstone—feminine energy, love.
pearl—love, femininity, moon, water.
obsidian—masculine energy, groundedness.
rose quartz—love, children, family, creativity.
smoky quartz—abundance, wisdom.
sodalite—spiritual awakening.
sugalite—inner vision, meditation.
tiger's-eye—groundedness, focus.
tourmaline—neutralizes negativity, psychic protection.
turquoise—strength, success, fulfillment, protection.

Strategies for Finding Your Allies

There are a number of ways to find your ally (whether it is animal, stone, plant, elemental, devic, angelic, a guide, guardian, or ancestor). In addition to watching your dreams, you can also go on a meditative visualization journey where you imagine yourself standing in a circle of stones and calling your allies to you. Additionally, as with finding an animal totem, be aware of pictures, photographs, and conversations where a particular ally is repeatedly mentioned.

Let your allies find you
Be still
Be silent and empty
Say nothing
Ask nothing
Be quiet
Open your heart
They will find you
They will help you
You are not alone
Love and guidance is all around you
Be ready to receive

Once you have discovered your allies, take time to listen to their advice. Meditate upon them and imagine that they are each giving you guidance and love. A woman who knows how to access her allies will find a well-spring of insight available to her.

For many, the greatest spiritual ally is the Goddess/God/Great Mystery/the Creator; all different names for the sacred divine spirit within all things. Having spirit allies does not disassociate you from God; in fact, allies are all aspects of the divine. Simply being grateful, and speaking in a personal way to the living spirit in all things can create miracles. Saying, "Creator, thank you for this day. Help me to love and appreciate myself and others even more," will help you to access the greatest ally of all.

SECRETS 4 OF THE
SHAMANESS

I WAS twenty years old and very upset. One of my best friends had been diagnosed with tuberculosis. I didn't know what to do, so I went to my spiritual mentor for help. My teacher was a Hawaiian kahuna—a shamaness—in a long line of shamanic healers. As far back as she could track her lineage, her female ancestors had been healers.

She said, "Denise, bring me your friend's x-rays."

I brought her the x-rays and watched as she carefully traced her fingers over the film. She began chanting and talking to an unseen presence. Then, placing both of her hands over the film, she became silent. Slowly she handed the film back to me and said, "Your friend will be fine now."

Ten days later, my friend went back in for more x-rays. The doctors were astounded to find that her lungs were almost completely clear. When I told my teacher, she didn't seemed surprised.

In my life I have had the honor of meeting and learning from some remarkable female shamans and medicine women in various cultures throughout the world. They have the ability to reach into hidden worlds to gain insight, strength, and healing. Although there are differences depending on the culture and local traditions, there are also similarities between them. These special women share an intimate awareness of nature, an understanding of a woman's connection to the earth's cycles, an ability to take inner journeys, and a realization of the power of one's spirit name. Even though we live in a modern, Westernized society, these are all areas of wisdom that can empower our present lives.

We can each activate our inner wise woman. When we embrace our inner shamaness, our instincts become highly attuned, and this helps in every aspect of our lives. For example, when this ability is awakened, you may spontaneously take a different road home and thus avoid a traffic jam or accident. Or you may intuitively feel that your child needs you and arrive just as he is trying to get down out of an apple tree. In ways that cannot be numbered, your inner shamaness can help your intuition and assist you in making good choices in life for you and your family.

There *is* an inner shamaness within you. She is mystical and wondrous. She knows how to listen to the messages in the clouds, gain energy from walking barefoot on the earth, and watch for signs in her dreams. She understands her own internal cycles, the art of shape-shifting, and the power of her spirit name. She is your inner healer, visionary, and medicine woman . . . and she waits inside you to be called forth.

Divine Feminine Cycles

To begin your journey to awaken your inner shamaness, it is valuable to be aware of Earth wisdom. Female shamanic traditions around the world vary according to local customs and beliefs, but one thing that they all have in common is a deep connection to nature and to the cycles of the earth. As a woman, your body rhythms are closely connected to the cyclical energy shifts of the planet. Your body chemistry is affected by the daily sun cycle of day and night, the cycle of the stages of the moon, and the rhythm of the seasons. A shamaness's secret energy source is her ability to attune her body with these cycles. As you draw upon your inner shamaness and learn to be in harmony with these cycles, you will experience more energy and balance in your life.

One of the earth's most potent cycles, for a woman, is the cycle of the moon. Its potent gravitational pull affects the tides and the surface of the earth, as each month it actually slightly distorts the earth, pulling one side toward it. This cyclical pulling dramatically affects our energy, our body fluids, and our menstrual cycles.

To primitive people, the moon was a visible and revered symbol of the very essence of womanhood. The sun represented the male principle, and the moon portrayed the female principle. As their monthly cycles coincided with lunar rhythms, women were considered the moon's earthly representatives. They were called upon to become the priestess and prophetess of the moon. In their ancient moon rituals, visions, and intuition were valued as absolutely necessary to daily life. In fact, without these states, it was thought that a balance of life was not possible and that understanding of the universe would dwindle.

These early emissaries of moon wisdom taught the importance of a woman honoring the great moon cycle within herself by moderating activity with rest. They used the example of the lunar cycle as the basic pattern for renewal. Rest, meditation, and gestation were revered as much as productivity. There was equal respect for all parts of the cycle. In the present we have forgotten this. We spend so much time being productive that we have forgotten the need for an equal amount of time for regenerating and reflection.

For every full moon there is also an equal amount of dark moon, so allow the moon to be your guide and know that a few minutes of doing absolutely nothing is as valuable as busily achieving. Have a gestation period, such as a "stay-in-bed" day, and read to your heart's content without guilt. This is your still time, and it's valuable. Or sit in the grass, lean your back up against a tree, and watch the clouds. Take time to relax. Your value as a woman doesn't come from what you do. It comes from who you are. Please listen to the wisdom of the moon and take time to rest, be still, and cherish yourself.

A woman who pays attention to the cycles of the moon is more in touch with her own rhythms and cycles. She knows when to expend energy and when to rest, when to party and when to ponder. Each cycle of the moon is divided into four phases—new moon, waxing moon, full moon, and waning moon. Each lasts about seven days. There are no set moments when one ends and another begins; they just flow into each other, as does our own energy. Here are their traditional meanings:

New moon: In astronomy (and as marked on calendars), "new moon" begins with the dark of the moon, the sky being moonless for about three days before the new moon is actually visible. This is the time for deep inner reflection and introspection. It is the time to be still and listen to your inner voice. Then, as the visible new moon approaches, it is the time to plant seeds for new ideas and new projects. It is the time of birth and renewal. This is a great time to visualize your life for the next moon cycle and focus on an energy that will see you through the month. During this time, rest, be still, and meditate. Feel that deepest and most internal movement of your inner self. In this stillness, allow the seed of the coming weeks to be planted in you.

Waxing moon: This is the time when the light reflected from the moon is growing. When the moon waxes, or enlarges, start acting upon the revelations you received during the new moon. It is a time for the growth and energizing of your new ideas. If there is something that you want to manifest in your life, this is an excellent time to put the wheels in motion.

Full moon: This is a time for the culmination of projects, and celebration. It is traditionally a time when a woman's power is at its peak. If you are planning an activity that requires a lot of energy, aim to do it, if you can, near a waxing full moon. The full moon is the culmination of the seed that you planted in the new moon. Let loose your creative forces. Be alive and animated. Participate. Celebrate. Spend time with friends.

Waning moon: This is the time when energy is receding, a time to release and let go of what isn't needed. It's also a great time to do clutter-clearing in your home. The waning moon is a time to assimilate and absorb what you have learned in the previous weeks.

Eons ago, when people slept under the stars, most women had their monthly cycle during the new moon. An old Chinese maxim was: "Women who have their cycles at the new moon are in correct balance with nature." The full moon was the time of fertility. During the expansive energy of the full moon, ovulation was usually at its height. Women thus moderated their activities with the phases of the moon.

Women's bodies naturally harmonized with the phases of the moon. Menstruation (also called "moon-time") was a time of powerful community among women. During it the females in a tribe would gather in what was called a "moon lodge" in Native American traditions, or "the red tent" in Middle Eastern traditions. They didn't forage, cook, or prepare food. They allowed themselves time for rest and renewal. As they gathered together, the women pulled their energy inward and rebuilt themselves, in preparation for the month ahead.

Since we have become separated from nature and we no longer sleep outdoors under the night sky, our body rhythms and our moon-times no longer correspond so exactly with the lunar rhythms, and we are out of balance with nature. However, there is a way to help harmonize your body rhythms. During the dark of the moon, make your bedroom as dark as possible, and during the three or four days of the full moon, sleep with a small night-light. There is a place inside you that will respond. Although this is not ideal, women who have done this report that it feels like something inside of them that was out of sync has moved back into balance.

Women subconsciously harmonize their menstrual cycles with close friends and/or female family members. This phenomenon also occurs when women live together, for example in a boarding school. Have you ever had the experience of having your period at the same time as a good friend, sometimes starting within hours of each other? This could be the result of pheromones, but there are also invisible yet nevertheless very real lines of energy that connect us to those we love.

When you walk with a friend, you both adopt the same walking rhythm, so you are both in harmony. When women are emotionally or physically close, their bodies subconsciously adopt the same rhythm, and often their periods will occur at the same time. It's also not uncommon that when two women who have always had their periods at the same time begin to move apart emotionally, their moon-times will suddenly cease to synchronize. (Of course, this can happen for any number of reasons, such as stress, or a change in sleep patterns or food intake.)

The moon is one of a woman's most powerful allies. To understand the mysteries of the moon is to understand your own deep inner mysteries. One of the ways to integrate your cycles with the moon's rhythms is to create a moon ritual. This kind of ceremony uses the moon as a focal point to move into a more expanded level of consciousness. It is a sacred way to experience connection with the whole universe.

You do not need years of training to create a ritual. It is a symbolic event, and the best ceremonies come straight from the heart. A moon ritual is a stylized series of actions that is used to bring about change. It comes from deep in the psyche of all women. Therefore, you have within you the ingredients from your own unconscious to trigger the experiences you desire. So look within, and create a moon ritual that speaks of your life and your needs. Use symbols and artifacts that represent the qualities of the feminine spirit to you.

When you have created your own moon ritual and begin to do it, you may feel foolish or awkward. Persist past that point and you will feel the sacred enter you. At the start of the ritual, your emotions will be buried under layers of linear and rational thinking. Continue, and eventually the majesty of the ceremony will come through.

Moon Rituals

The best ceremonies are often the ones you create for yourself. Here are some simple modern-day rituals that you can do:

- Stand at a window, or outdoors, during the full moon. Lift your arms to the moon, as women have done centuries before you. Feel the energy of the moon surge and fill you.
- Take a moon bath. Allow the light of the moon to bathe and cleanse you. Dance in the light of the moon. Let yourself move with abandon.
- Create a circle of stones to sit inside. Decorate each stone as a different phase of the moon. (This can be done indoors or outdoors.) Call upon the Goddess of the moon to bless you and fill you with grace.
- Leave water out in the moonlight and then drink it, knowing that it is activating your dreams, intuition, and femininity.

The Worlds of the Shamaness

A shamaness understands the power of the inner journey, which expands awareness far beyond the boundaries of normal reality. To embark on a mystical inner journey takes courage, for we are taught to think in terms of linear time and space. This type of experience isn't just an occurrence that takes place in the mind. You literally have the opportunity to step beyond your body and your normal perceptions of life, to enter into a sacred realm.

Your inner journey can be as simple as closing your eyes and imagining that you are traveling to other realms. This ability can help you in every-day life. For example, if your boss is being particularly irritable, a journey to the lower world may reveal that he is having difficulty in his marriage or with his health. This understanding may help you to be less sensitive to his mood swings.

There are three worlds that are traditional to shamanism: the upper world, middle world, and lower world. These worlds roughly correspond to the higher self, conscious self, and the base or subconscious self. The shamaness knows how to travel to these realms to gain answers for herself and her people. You can also use the three worlds for your inner explorations; simply enter into a relaxed state and imagine visiting them.

The upper world: This is the dimension of the higher self. It is also the realm of angels and guides. Go to this realm when you need inspiration or spiritual assistance. To journey there, go into a meditative state and imagine climbing a mountain, scrambling up a tree, ascending a stair-way, or even taking a magic carpet ride. At the end of your journey, meet a guide, guardian, or wise being to ask for guidance.

The middle world: The middle world is the realm of present time and of your conscious self. To enter this world, go into a meditative state and imagine that you are walking through a forest or boating across a lake to a sacred island. Here you may find animal allies, as well as the energy of friends and family members, offering you assistance. It is also in this world that you can communicate straight from your heart. For example, if you had an argument with your son, you could visualize the two of you in the middle world and imagine conversing with him and telling him how you feel and also really hearing how he feels. Often this kind of inner work eases tension and creates understanding without confrontation.

The lower world: To enter the lower world, the shamaness travels in spirit through the trunk of a tree and out through its roots, or else she enters a crystal cave or a deep tunnel, or voyages under the sea. This is the place of your ancestors and the deep energies of the earth. It is the place to release wounds from the past. Imagine that your pain, trauma, negative habits, and addictions have a physical form. Meet and medi-tate with them in the lower world.

Shape-Shifting

"Shape-shifting" is a type of inner journey that most shamanesses practice. It is the metamorphosis of a person into an animal or other form. Historical records and literature are full of accounts of this phenomenon. It is still practiced today in many traditional cultures.

One warm autumn afternoon, I sat by a river that flowed through the mountains of New Mexico with my friend and teacher, Dancing Feather. He was an exceptional Tewa Pueblo Indian elder. In passing, he mentioned that sometimes he became a fox. He said his father and his grandfather could do it, too. Although I have Native American blood, I was raised in a Western culture, so I was a bit skeptical. I said, "Dancing Feather, you mean that you go into a trance and then *imagine* that you are a fox?"

He looked at me and was quiet for a long time. Finally he said, "No, I actually become a fox."

I was taken aback. I knew that Dancing Feather always told the truth, yet my Western upbringing made me uncertain that one could actually turn into a fox. So many questions filled me. What actually happens during a shape-shifting experience? Why have so many people from the earliest times believed that a person could change shape? And what is the value of such a metamorphosis?

There are many theories about shape-shifting. Some scientists believe that there is a neurological basis for it in the mammalian brain that sits at the top of the spine. (We share this primitive core with other species such as the ape and the prairie dog.) Some believe that this part of the brain conceals primal powers that our ancestors knew how to tap into but we have forgotten. Carl Jung postulated that there was a collective unconscious shared by all humans, a repository of all wisdom contained in archetypal images. This also could explain shape-shifting.

I have met other elders in native cultures who attest to the fact that shape-shifting is not just an exercise in creative visualization, it is an actual metamorphosis. However, even if your journey is only in your imagination, there is great value in employing these techniques in modern life.

When you imagine that you are an animal (or plant or stone), you can begin to experience your life from a different perspective. Seeing the world through the eyes of a sparrow, or through the experience of a pebble, will expand your boundaries, and this in turn allows you a wider world-view. When humans become myopic and can only see the world through the narrow and limited perspective of their own experience, they fall prey to prejudices and judgments (which are as damaging to them as to the universe around them).

Shape-Shifting Exercise

- Close your eyes and allow yourself to become deeply relaxed. As a suggestion, have a friend with you who is drumming a very steady, continuous beat. Or, play some music designed for relaxation, which can help you to enter into altered states of consciousness.
- Imagine that your body is metamorphosing into another form. It can be anything you choose. Take time to experience fully how that other being feels.
- With your eyes closed, allow your body to move while feeling yourself changing into another shape.
- Really imagine that you have become that animal, plant, mineral, or person. Involve all your senses. Imagine what you would smell, taste, hear, and feel. For example, if you become a wolf, imagine having an acute ability to smell. If you become an eagle, imagine your eyesight to be very sharp and far-seeing.
- Afterwards, while it is still fresh in your memory, make notes about your experience.

When you can see the world through the experience of another, it deepens your compassion for the world. For example, if you have had a terrible argument with your husband and you shape-shift to see the world through his eyes, you might find that your anger subsides. Or if you are depressed because you were passed over for a job promotion, you might shapeshift to see the world through the eyes of a robin, and realize that the world is much more vast and wondrous than the arena of your job. Your job depression pales in comparison to the joy of flight and the exhilaration of bursting into song.

Sometimes I imagine myself seeing through the eyes of another person. When I can see the world through his or her eyes, it allows me to have compassion and understanding for them. I have found this particularly helpful when I have been having a hard time with someone. When I see the world through their eyes, I'm usually no longer critical of them.

The Power of Your Spirit Name

A shamaness always knows her spirit name. The vibration and sound of it allow her to call forth her inner power. It is the name that she uses to activate her connection to the world of nature. In shamanic tradition, you have a family-use name and you also have a spirit name. This name represents your essence and your power. Sometimes it is a sound that has a feeling rather than a word with a specific meaning, but most often it is a name from nature.

During my life, I have had the opportunity to spend time in a number of earth-based cultures. In some of these native cultures I have been given a name. This is an honor and it connects me to the people of the tribe or culture. To the Zulu I am "Nogukini." To the New Zealand Maoris, I am "Whetu-Marama-Ote-Rangi." Thirty years ago when I studied the ancient Hawaiians' traditions with a kahuna, I was given the name "Maileonahunalani." I cherish these names; however, I had a desire to have a name that came straight from my soul and straight from the earth. A number of years ago, I gained my spirit name in a most unusual way.

It was a hot summer afternoon in the Cascade Mountains in the northwest of the United States. All day I had been thinking about how to find my spirit name. To escape the heat, I decided to take a walk into the coolness of the woods near our small mountain home. I loved walking in the forest. It was peaceful and quiet. Long rays of light filtered through the canopy of leaves overhead. I stopped under a large old tree and closed my eyes. It was so still. There wasn't even the normal hum of insects or the chatter of birds.

When I opened my eyes, a few feet in front of me, on a branch, was a great horned owl, so close that if I had reached out I could have touched him. He hadn't been there when I closed my eyes, so he must have landed in those few seconds. He looked straight at me. All I could see were his enormous eyes. It seemed like such a long time passed. Then, with a blink, he lifted his massive wings and silently glided away into the forest.

After a moment, the afternoon sounds of the forest returned. I looked at the branch where the owl had landed. Three small, downy feathers were caught on it. I picked them up and held them in my hand. They were so soft and white.

Suddenly, I heard an inner voice say, "Put the feathers in your medicine bag." The words puzzled me. I had a beautiful medicine bag, but it wasn't with me. Again I heard the voice. "You are your own medicine bag," the voice insisted. "Put the feathers in your medicine bag."

The invitation seemed clear: I was being asked to take the feathers into my body. Without further thought, I put the feathers into my mouth and swallowed them. (I don't recommend this. Feathers are *very* hard to swallow and probably not sanitary at all, but that didn't occur to me at the time.) The inner voice continued, "As you have taken owl feathers into your body, the spirit of the owl has permeated your being and shall always be with you."

Gradually, I came back to the reality of the woods around me, with a feeling of serenity and strength. This experience precipitated the awareness that my spirit name was "White Feather." (My husband, David, who still can't believe that I actually ate feathers, jokes that my true name is "Eating Feather.")

Once I acquired my spirit name, I felt like I'd come home. Every time I said, "I am White Feather," I felt a sense of peace wash over me. There is great power in a name that is in alignment with your essence. Every time you are called by that name, or you think of yourself in that way, it reinforces your spirit.

Not everyone needs to seek a spirit name. Sometimes it is the one you already have. My daughter, Meadow, came back from a vision quest and said, "Mom, I found my true name. It is the one that you gave me when I was born." Your present name may be your spirit name. If your name feels that it represents who you are and who you are striving to be, then it is perfect just as it is. If your name doesn't feel like a good fit for your soul, you may want to acquire a spirit name.

In some ancient mystical traditions, a person's spirit name was kept secret. In these traditions, such a name was thought to carry a person's power, so if someone knew your true spirit name, they had power over you. In other traditions, a person's spirit name wasn't secret, but it wasn't the name you used every day. And in yet other cultures, once you gained your true name it also became the name that others called you. In many native cultures, when a child was born, they were given a birth name. Then during a vision quest or an initiation experience, they received their name from Spirit and that became their name for the rest of their life. After you gain your name, you need to decide whether it's to be kept secret, it's not a secret but it isn't the name you use every day, or it will be the name you use.

Your name is important. It is how you are known to the world. It has an energy or feeling associated with it. The name "Edith" has a different feeling from the name "Bunny." One name elicits images of someone who is responsible and practical, while the other suggests a woman who is fun, gregarious, and light-hearted. This doesn't mean that someone named Edith isn't playful, or someone named Bunny isn't serious and pragmatic. However, research has shown that people relate to you differently as a result of your name. More important, you will feel differently about yourself. One name isn't better than another one, they just have different energies. And it's important to find a name that matches your essence.

Below is an exercise to help you begin to be aware of how you feel about your name. There are no right answers to this exercise; it is aimed at allowing you to understand your relationship with your name.

The Meaning of Your Name

- Do you like your name?
- What does your name mean to you?
- What associations do you have for your name?
- Are you named after anyone?
- How do you feel about that person?
- Do other people think that your name suits you?
- If it doesn't fit you now, will it fit you in the future?
- What is the meaning or origin of your name?
- Is there a correlation between the meaning of your name and you?

On a spiritual level, the name you were given at birth is not an accident. Your name has a vibration that was necessary for you at the time you were born. It might have provided you with the opportunity to grow, or it might have formed an important energy connection with the person you were named after. Even if it doesn't suit you, there is great value in finding the meaning and the reason for your name.

Growing up, I never really liked the name "Denise"; it didn't feel like me. When I was young, someone said the origin of "Denise" was Dionysus, the god of wine. This didn't sound very good to me. I had images of orgies and drunkenness. (It was interesting that I learned this fact in my late teens when I was drinking way too much.) As I embarked on a more spiritual path, I did some research on my name and found that the god Dionysus was also the god of ecstasy and joy. The mystery cults of Dionysus thrived in the ancient Mediterranean world. Their festivals of initiation went on for days and culminated in a drama of death and rebirth. During the festivals, dancers entered into states of ecstasy and joy through trance-like dancing. This was a revelation to me, and I began to understand why my name was Denise.

Your last name also has an impact on your energy fields, though not as potent an influence as your first name. My maiden name had the word "fort" in it and it seemed right because I felt that so much of my early life I had put myself in a fort and barricaded myself away from everyone. (The symbolism of names isn't universal. A name is what it is to you. Someone else with the name "Fort" might feel that it means "fortress" or "fortify." Or, as in French, "strong.") I was at the point in my life when I was going to change my last name, as I felt it no longer suited me, when I met and I married a wonderful man with the last name "Linn". It was only after we had gotten married by a waterfall that I found that "Linn" is a Celtic word meaning "waterfall" or "flowing waters."

My grandmother (on my father's side) was an astrologer and a numerologist. She calculated the vibration of names based on a Pythagorean system that equated each letter of the alphabet with a partic- ular number, and each number had a specific type of energy. She shared many stories with me of people who changed their names and then their life changed. She believed that every name had a spiritual vibration that deeply influenced each person. When they changed their name, its energy changed and hence the person's vibration changed.

Maril is a friend of mine who claims that changing her name changed her life. She and three friends, who were all in mid-life, decided that they were ready for a change. She told me, "We knew that our names had power, so we decided to change them to honor and recognize the new cycle in our lives."

Maril had always been Marilyn, and she decided to change her name to "free herself from her childhood and come into power." Judy decided that this name no longer reflected who she was, so she decided to revert to "Judith," the name on her birth certificate. Donna had gone through a divorce and decided that it was a great time for a change so she also reverted to her birth name, Eldonna—a name originally given to her by her father, who was dying and whom she wanted to honor.

These three women invited forty friends to join them at a park on May 15. They asked each person to bring something to the gathering that represented the three women's new path. The women said the event felt like a "birthing." Before the event, they each took herbal baths, purified themselves, and put on the new clothes that they had bought for the event (even new underwear). Everyone danced and celebrated. This was fourteen years ago, but every year on May 15 they contact each other to wish each other a happy day of birth. Each of these women felt that changing her name started a new energy in her life and truly was a rebirth.

If you feel ready for a new name, as a suggestion, spend time with friends. Work out how you would like to perceive yourself. Find a name that supports your new identity and then co-create a naming ceremony.

Discovering Your Spirit Name

Try one of the following:

- Pray, meditate, and ask your allies and spirit helpers for your name.
- Spend time in nature, lie on the earth, and ask Mother Earth for your true name.
- Take pen and paper and free-flow lots of names; try a name out for a day or two to see how it feels.
- Before sleep, ask that your true name appear in your dreams, and every morning write about your dreams in your journal.

There are several other ways that you can use the magic of the name. These methods have been used for generations by shamanesses who understood the value of names for invoking power. You can use these techniques to call forth various aspects of yourself as you need them. One method is to call yourself by the name of a Goddess to invoke her grace. For example, saying the words "I am Shakti" can allow the incredible vitality of the Goddess Shakti to fill you.

Another method is to create a secret name for yourself that contains the qualities you need at this time. For example, if you want to call indomitable strength and fortitude into your life, you might say over and over to yourself: "I am Amazon Queen." Go for a walk and continually repeat, "I am Amazon Queen." Each time you say it, imagine yourself filled with the courage, physical prowess, and ferocity of an Amazon queen.

If you are feeling uninspired and stagnant, you can call forth the part of yourself that is wild, juicy, and creative. Jump on a mini-trampoline and say over and over to yourself, "I am Juicy Wild Woman" or whatever words invoke the feeling of unleashed power in you. Each time you repeat the words, imagine vitality pouring through you. If you want to elicit your innate, inner wisdom, use a name such as "Wondrous Wise Woman." Say it with passion and intensity, and the power of the name will bring forth the qualities that you desire. Be creative in the names that you devise for yourself—for example, if you want to be joyous, open, spontaneous, and delight in every moment, you might name yourself Enchanted Fairy Child. If you want to be feminine, soft, dreaming, spiritual, and visionary, you might call yourself Moon Goddess.

When you use this technique, allow your body positioning to reflect the name. For example, as you state to yourself, "I am Amazon Queen," throw your shoulders back, stand tall, and hold your head high.

Shamanic Symbols and Power Objects

Throughout history, there have been objects, symbols, and aspects of nature that have been associated with the shamaness and with female wisdom. Becoming aware of these can help you activate your feminine power.

In the ancient past, caves were thought to be the womb of the Great Earth Mother. In cultures throughout the world, the Goddess was honored and worshipped in caves. Sacred subterranean chambers were considered her shrines. To enter a cave was to enter into the deepest secrets of the Great Mother, and female religious and initiation rites were traditionally performed in there.

One day I was hiking alone, in the dry heat of the day, across the red sand and rock of the Utah sage lands. I had heard of a secret cavern high in one of the rocky cliffs surrounding the desert, and I felt a compulsion to find it. The heat seemed to penetrate to my bones as I scaled the cliff. I kept asking my allies, "Which way now?" and then following my instincts to guide me to the cave. Around one large boulder I finally saw an opening into the side of the rock. As I peered in, I felt frightened. I had come so far to enter this cave, yet it looked so dark and forbidding. What if there were snakes, scorpions, or mountain lions in its depths? I closed my eyes and asked my guides and allies. "Is it right for me to enter?" I received the answer, "You are invited to enter."

Cautiously climbing through the opening, I found myself in a large cavern. My eyes adjusted to the darkness. The cool temperature was delicious, and a small crack high in the rock ceiling allowed filtered light to illuminate the walls. The floor was soft sand. It was so still, sacred and holy. I slowly lay down in the sand. As sensuous and as palpable as my heartbeat, I could feel a rhythm emanating up from the earth. "Ahh, this is the heartbeat of Mother Earth." I felt cradled and loved. It was as if she had reached up and surrounded me with tentacles of feminine energy. I left the cave feeling refreshed and renewed.

At least once in your life, enter a cave in silence and darkness. Sit in the stillness and listen to the beat of your own heart. If you are still enough, you will begin to hear the rhythm of Mother Earth. If you cannot do this, travel in your meditations into a sacred cave. It is here that your deepest womanly wisdom can begin to awaken.

In Goddess-based religions, another symbol of the womb of the Great Mother was the cauldron. In Egyptian hieroglyphics, the Great Goddess was represented by three cauldrons. In India, the Goddess Kali kept her life-giving ambrosia in three cauldrons. In Celtic tradition, the Goddess Branwen maintained a Cauldron of Regeneration where the dead could be resuscitated. Repeated throughout history, this holy vessel was the womb-like receptacle of the regenerative powers of the Goddess. It was only when Goddess religions were displaced by a patriarchal god that the cauldron was associated with negativity and witchcraft.

Creating a sacred cauldron of your own can be an act of power because the human psyche responds magnificently to symbolic acts. Your cauldron can be a symbolic womb that is gestating and giving birth to new aspects of your life. When you create your own cauldron—symbolically filling it with your intentions—its energy will radiate in all directions, enveloping your space with life force.

To make a sacred cauldron, obtain a bowl, ceramic pot, or even a large basket and carefully put it in a place of honor in your home. Within it, place items that are symbolic of what you desire to energize in your life. For example, if you want your body to strengthen, then you might place a beach stone that resembles a strong female body in your cauldron, together with any other items that represent strength to you. If you want to bring more love into your life, you might put into it hearts, photographs of loved ones, or cards on which you have hand-drawn hearts and have written the word "love."

The image of the womb repeats itself again and again in shamanic Goddess traditions. Another venerated object from earlier times is the chalice. Although the chalice is usually associated with the lost cup from which Christ drank at the Last Supper, historians agree that this is a thinly veiled Christian interpretation of a primarily pagan and feminine symbol. Over the centuries, Christianity adopted many ancient Goddess customs. During the reign of Goddess religions, the chalice symbolized the womb and resurrection. Wine was considered to be the blood of the earth, and thus found a symbolic home in the womb-like chalice. Drinking wine from a chalice was holy, and the custom of raising your glass before drinking was originally a gesture to honor the divine.

You can recreate this ancient act by cradling the bowl of a wine glass in your hands and imagining that energy and love is flowing from your hands into the wine. As you drink, give thanks for the blessings in your life. If you do not drink wine, grape juice or non-alcoholic wine can serve the same purpose. The important thing is the intent with which you drink from the chalice.

Another womb-like object that was used traditionally by a shamaness was a medicine bag or pouch containing special objects that symbolized and magnified her power. For example, a Native American medicine woman carried a medicine bag with small objects that each had importance to her, such as a special stone, fur from a bear, or strands of hair from her favorite horse. These items were thought to magnify qualities that she desired to achieve: for example, bear fur might help her to activate the strength and courage of a mother bear within herself.

Creating a Medicine Bag

Using cloth, felt, or leather, make a simple bag, or choose a large piece of fabric or leather that you can roll items in to create a medicine bundle. The fabric can be painted with magical symbols or beaded: decorate it in a style unique to you. Fill the bag or bundle with your power objects, which should be things that make you feel confident and strong. They can be an heirloom from your great-grandmother, a shell you found at the beach, or your child's first tooth. Keep your medicine bag in a safe place, close to you. If it is small, it can be worn around your neck (usually under your clothes), or it can be kept near your pillow at night.

Fire, especially in the form of candles, is another shamanic tool. Although fire has often been thought of as a masculine principle, it was first and primarily the domain of women. It was the woman who tended the hearth in the cave or hut. She kept the flames going through the cold of winter, cooking food and drying clothes by its warmth. The original altars were in the home next to the fire, since fire sustained life, and women were the keepers of the fire. The shamaness would use fire as a focus point to peer into the future and also to send healing energy to others.

To use your candles as a shamanic tool, dedicate them. For example, as you light one say, "I dedicate this candle to the health and well-being of my family," or "I dedicate this candle to love and light." To send healing to someone else, focus on the flame and at the same time visualize that person absolutely healthy and strong. The pure light of the candle can serve as a focus point as well as a connection to the natural life force of fire.

A shamaness has an intimate connection to all aspects of nature and understands the energetic power of herbs, plants, and flowers. One flower that is closely connected to the feminine spirit is the rose, and it can help you in your ventures into spiritual realms. In the Far East, the rose was called the "flower of the Goddess." In Europe, Aphrodite was addressed as the "Holy Rose." The formation of the rose creates a natural pentagram, which is a Goddess symbol. Arabian mystics spoke of a paradise they called "the rose garden," which was the dwelling place of the Babylonian Goddess Gula.

The rose was also associated with the mysteries of female sexuality. The rosary was originally known as the "flower of Venus" and was the badge of the sacred prostitutes of Rome. These women were initiated into the sexual mysteries of Venus and gave their bodies in honor of the Goddess. Red roses were the sign of maternal sexuality; white roses were the sign of the Virgin Goddess. The rosary was borrowed by early Christianity, and the Virgin Mary was called the Holy Rose, thus the rose became pure for the Church despite its earlier sexual symbolism.

Whenever you desire to activate your feminine spirit and intuition, surround yourself with the spiritual energy of the rose. Take a rose-scented bath. Use an atomizer to mist yourself with rose essential oil. Have cut roses in vases. Decorate your home with photographs or paintings of roses.

Earlier in this book, I described how I learned an important truth about myself through the snake. The snake is the oldest symbol of shamanic womanhood. From Palaeolithic caves in Europe to rock art in Africa and Australia, to Greek and Roman Goddess temples, the womanly symbol of the serpent appears throughout the world. Serpents were associated with women for many reasons. They lay close to the Earth Mother, and thus it was felt that they were psychically sensitive to her messages. They were kept in temples to assist priestesses in prophecies because of this psychic link to the Great Goddess. The divinatory Delphic ("womb") oracles were called serpent priestesses. In the Middle East, the snake was the feminine embodiment of enlightenment and wisdom. In Tantric traditions, the female kundalini life force lies at the base of the spine in the form of a serpent of light and energy. Mystical exercises allow the serpent to rise up the spine, contributing to healing and rejuvenation.

The snake was also connected to female mysteries because it sheds its skin just as a woman sheds her uterine lining. This cyclical shedding of both snakes and women was seen as being tied to the rhythm of the moon and represented the mystery of transformation: thus, the serpent has long been a symbol of the healing power of transformation. So watch for the snake in your dreams and meditations, for it will often come as a secret and important sign that you are in a period of transformation and healing.

Becoming Your Own Inner Shamaness

In this chapter, I've described many tools common to shamanesses throughout the world; however, sometimes the most powerful gateway into your inner mystical wisdom is a shift of perception.

I had been camping with friends on Vancouver Island in British Columbia. We had completed a week studying with a medicine woman and were breaking down our camp. The two poles that formed the center of my tent were stuck together and I couldn't get them apart. I pulled, twisted and yanked but they were stuck. I went to some of the men and said, "You guys are strong. Can you pull these tent poles apart for me?" They tugged, wrenched, and yanked, but the poles remained stuck. As this was occurring, the medicine woman sat nearby serenely beading a medicine bag.

I went up to her and said, "I can't get my tent poles apart."

She looked at me steadily for a moment and then reached up and touched the poles. They fell apart like butter melting on a hot day. I stood shocked, with both poles in my hands. She beckoned me to come closer and quietly said, "Did you think the men were more powerful than you?"

Nothing else needed to be said. With a swift stroke of her shamanic force, she cut through my illusion that my power lay outside me. I felt as if she had reached into my core and reminded me that I was not separate from the world around me. The knowledge that I was a part of all things showed me that it was possible to tap into a universal life force rather than using my individual energy. It was a subtle shift but a potent one.

Releasing the two poles wasn't a miracle, but it was the result of aligning with the rhythms of the earth. We each have a deep well of inner wisdom and strength within us. It is our birthright as a woman. When we take the time to align our natural cycles with the flows of nature and listen to the earth, our perceptions transform. This in turn allows us to begin to step into the realm of the shamaness.

AWAKENING YOUR WARRIOR WOMAN

A POLL of students was taken at my high school every year. The categories were things like: "most popular," "best dresser," "most likely to succeed," and so on. Everyone eagerly awaited this annual tradition. When the results were posted in the main hallway, everyone gathered around the list. The news of who won spread quickly through the school. Right after the results were posted, a friend ran up to me as I was stepping out of history class. She was out of breath with excitement. "Denise! Guess what? You won! You've been voted *nicest*." I was thrilled! I thought it was the best thing that had ever happened to me.

Years later, I realized what it really meant to be voted *nicest*. It meant that I was always trying to please everyone and I never said how I really felt. It meant that I did things I really didn't want to do, and accepted responsibilities I neither wanted nor enjoyed. It also meant that I went along with other people's wishes and points of view without taking into consideration my own needs. Being *nice* had long-range damaging effects on my self-esteem and integrity.

Now I no longer try to constantly please everyone, and because of this, I'm much happier and stronger. I have a glorious Warrior Woman arising within me. She encourages me to say "yes" when I mean yes, and "no" when I mean no. She propels me to give with no strings attached. (In the past, sometimes I gave gifts with a subconscious desire for the recipient to like me in return.) My inner Warrior Woman invites me to speak and to live my truth with courage and grace.

You have an inner Warrior Woman within you. She is a victor, never a victim. She's strong and confident, a natural leader. She is rarely resentful or bitter. Although she can be fierce, her actions always come from the heart; they are an assertion of power rather than anger. When your Warrior Woman is awake within you, you do not continually get mad or hurt because life is not to your liking; you simply develop a strategy to change the situation or your attitude.

When someone cuts in front of you when you're waiting to pay in a store, the path of your inner Warrior Woman is clear; there are two choices. You can either completely let it go without harboring any resentment, or you can take action. If you choose to take action, clearly state to the offender that you were ahead of him. You can communicate either in a forthright manner or lightly with humor; either way your intentions will be clear. The perpetrator may or may not yield or step back, but what you have accomplished is infinitely more important. You have removed yourself from the role of a passive victim who allows resentment to fester. You have asserted yourself without being aggressive, in a manner that empowers you but does not disempower other people.

The Warrior Woman is never a victim of life. Even when it looks to the world like she is the victim, in her heart she recognizes the potential for spiritual growth in every situation. When I was shot by a gunman during a random act of violence, it seemed to everyone, including me, that I was a victim. On one level of reality, I really was a victim of life circumstances. I was innocent of any wrongdoing, yet a horrible thing happened to me. For many years I maintained that role and felt sorry for myself. It's an easy role to fall into, since most people feel sympathy for a victim.

When I first heard the expression, "There are no victims, only volunteers," I became enraged. How dare anyone suggest that I chose to be shot or chose the trauma of my childhood? I was a victim! I had done nothing to deserve what happened to me! I was vehement in my rage. Finally, when my ranting had exhausted itself, I became very quiet and the small voice of truth inside of me began to speak. It began to wonder if, on some subconscious level, I really *did* choose my experiences. I began to think about my life and realize that I *had* grown spiritually through all the things that had happened to me; I was stronger and wiser because of those events. My inner voice reasoned that even if the universe is completely random and sometimes bad things just happen, it might actually *feel* better to carry the mantle of a woman who chose her destiny rather than a woman who was always at the mercy of the whims of fate.

I began to imagine how I would feel if everything that happened to me really was a choice I had made for my highest good. It was an amazing concept that completely changed the way I viewed my past. I realized that if there truly was a greater reason for all the challenges and disappoint-ments in my life, then I could accept my life more readily Envisioning myself acting as a victor rather than a victim felt really good. That was the moment the Warrior Woman inside me was born.

Your inner Warrior Woman is the voice within you that encourages you to leave a damaging marriage, even if it means a loss of friends, prestige, and security. It is also the part of you that knows when to stay in a challenging marriage because it will ultimately be worth the struggle. It is your inner strength to resign from a job that you've outgrown, and embark on a career for which you have neither talent nor credentials but which is your heart's desire. It is the part of you that has the courage to ask for a raise when every cell in your body is terrified to make the request. Your Warrior Woman helps you dream big and know that you can achieve your goals, even if no one believes in you. This is what she can help you achieve. If she isn't already awakened within you, isn't it about time?

Although you have a Warrior Woman within you, sometimes this gallant, noble, and powerful being is hidden beneath years of denial and suppressions, smothered by the "good girl." Nevertheless, she is within you. If you haven't claimed her, let this be the time. It can be as simple as making a declaration: "I am now awakening the Warrior Woman that dwells within me." Or, you may find that it takes a journey of self-dis-covery to allow her emergence, but there is power in your intent. Where your intention goes, your energy flows; so intend to change from being a victim of life to a woman who creates her own destiny . . . and so it shall be.

The Disease to Please

One of the blocks to discovering your Warrior Woman is needing to please everyone. Being nice is often a subconscious strategy to survive in the world. It's not uncommon in women who have had a dysfunctional childhood to develop this strategy as a survival mechanism. The subcon-scious mind believes that being acquiescent can mitigate being abused, molested, or hurt. The problem with this strategy is that it leaves a woman feeling powerless, and often filled with resentment.

Growing up, my home life was a shambles. I experienced harsh emotional, physical, and sexual abuse. Every child develops their own survival strategies; for example, they might become aggressive or withdraw into themselves. I subconsciously developed the tactic of trying to please everyone. And it seemed to work. People did like me because I was so nice. I often felt, however, that I was taken advantage of and not appreciated, and this led to resentment. Thus, my childhood strategy became a lifelong pattern. I would try to please someone, then I would feel unappreciated and eventually become resentful. I repeated this pattern over and over again with different people and situations. It's called the "disease to please," and it eats away at health and well-being as surely as any other disease.

Shedding my "nice" persona has not been easy. Old habits often die hard, and vestiges of the past still remain with me. There are times when being nice is gracious (if it's authentic); however, "nice" is not always genuine or sincere. A "nice" person often has low self-esteem and puts others before herself to gain their friendship. For example, the "nice" woman sends a birthday present because she wants the recipient to like her, whereas the Warrior Woman sends it because she feels compelled to give. If there is no thank-you note, the "nice" woman says, "Oh well, they are too busy," but inside she feels resentful and hurt. Whereas the Warrior Woman calls up and says, "Hi! I didn't hear if you got the gift I sent. Did you like it?" By asserting herself and communicating, she is not embittered by this situation.

At some point in each woman's life, she needs to stand up and cry "Freedom!" This is the battle cry of her inner Warrior Woman. She needs to declare to herself as well as to the world, "This is who I am, this is what I stand for. This is my truth." Until she does that, there will always be a place inside her that feels empty, no matter how much material comfort and acclaim she has received in her life. Your cry of "Freedom!" can be a quiet, internal declaration that grows over time, or it can be a ferocious roar. The shell has to break before the bird can fly.

Sometimes it takes an act of power to awaken your inner Warrior Woman. Rosa Parks, the African-American woman who refused to surrender her bus seat to a younger white person (as was expected in those days), activated her inner Warrior Woman. Her intention was so strong that her cry of "Freedom!" became the catalyst for the bus boycott in Montgomery, Alabama, in the early 1950s, which eventually resulted in racial integration on buses. Rosa's cry was an important turning point in the move toward racial equality in the United States.

My own cry of "Freedom!" has occurred in increments in my life. The day I left an emotionally difficult relationship and didn't look back was a cry of "Freedom!" The time the doctors were about to try what I considered an invasive procedure on me, and I rose from the surgery table and walked out, was also a cry of "Freedom!" Telling the therapist who said I would never get better without his services that I didn't need therapy anymore was another. Even returning a defective article to the store for a refund can be a kind of cry of "Freedom!"

Holy Bitch

I love my women friends. They comfort me during the hard times and celebrate with me during the splendid times. They are wonderful, passionate, compassionate, and kind . . . and some of them are also occasionally considered "bitches." People have said to me, "Denise, you are so nice. Why do you have friends that act like bitches?" After hearing this comment, a number of times, I realized that I was subconsciously drawn to strong women who spoke their truth and weren't afraid to speak up for themselves. As I desired to become more genuine, assertive, authentic, and forthright, I subliminally chose a peer group of strong women . . . who were sometimes considered bitches.

The word "bitch" has an interesting history. It became a derogatory term in early Christendom because it was one of the most sacred titles of the Goddess Artemis, who led a pack of hunting dogs. When Athena assumed her death-Goddess form, her priestesses filled her temple with dogs who howled at the moon. Holy bitches are also found in ancient India as the revered Great Bitch Goddess Sarama, who led the sacred Vedic dogs of death and rebirth. In early Christianity, the term "son of a bitch" was an insult not because it meant the person was a dog, but because it implied that the man was the son of a pagan Goddess. I have grown to cherish the word "bitch," and I even use it as an acronym for a woman who is "Being In Total Control of Herself."

Of course there are nasty bitches, but the woman I'm describing is a "holy bitch." She is self-assertive while at the same time maintaining her humor, dignity, and grace. I cherish my strong women friends. From spending time with them, I have learned that self-assertion is a positive quality that people admire. A holy bitch speaks up for herself, yet she still has love, joy, and creativity in her life. The greatest thing I learned from these friends is that you can communicate your truth clearly and compassionately, without having to package it with a pink bow and "niceness."

There are a number of things that can act as barriers to uncovering your inner Warrior Woman. As strange as it may sound, positive thinking can sometimes be one of these blocks. It can be a remarkable tool to replace and overcome negative thinking, but many people do not use positive affirmations in the way that they are intended; instead, they use them to deny and suppress a problem. Although saying an affirmation over and over again such as, "I'm strong and powerful" can help you feel stronger, sometimes it can have the opposite effect. For example, saying, "I'm happy; I'm happy" over and over again as away to suppress a lot of anger and rage can be damaging because *your soul loves the truth*. It's usually better to experience and examine your anger, rather than deny and suppress it with a smothering layer of positive thinking.

A problem can be compared to weeds in your garden. Affirming over and over, "There are no weeds; there are no weeds" doesn't get rid of them. The weeds keep pushing through the earth. You can also complain about the weeds and resent the fact that they are growing in your garden. You can even become resigned to being a victim of the weeds, but this also doesn't get rid of them. Denying and resenting them doesn't make them go away. Just notice that they are there and then pull out the damn weeds! Upon seeing weeds in her garden, the Warrior Woman acknowledges their presence and pulls them up by the fistful. She removes them and gets on with her life.

How to Activate Your Inner Warrior Woman

1. **Acknowledge that a Warrior Woman dwells in you:** The first step to awakening your inner Warrior Woman is to acknowledge that she exists. In nature, there is nothing more ferocious than a mother defending her children. Even if you don't have children, you are still genetically programmed to be capable of intense ferocity; the spirit of the mother bear dwells within you. No matter how unsure, timid, peace-loving, mild-mannered, shy, and uncertain you are, you still have a wild, ferocious spirit inside you.

2. **Act "as if"**: Act *as if* you are a powerful, magnificent, and strong Warrior Woman *even when you are not feeling it.* To do this, imagine yourself feeling invincible and stalwart, the way a warrior might feel, then change your body positioning, until you are in the stance of a warrior. Just as slumping your shoulders can make you feel depressed or meek, you can feel the powerful mind-set of a warrior woman by standing tall, squaring your shoulders, lifting your head, dropping your chin, and breathing deeply and fully.

When you dare to act *as if* you are powerful and unstoppable, you will start to feel that you are. When you dare to act powerfully, commit to taking action, and use your strength in support of your truth, it becomes less and less important whether you are afraid. The momentum of your intent and actions will carry you forward.

3. **Find a role model**: When confronted with a seemingly impossible dilemma or situation, imagine how your role model would react. For example, think how Eleanor Roosevelt, Mother Teresa, or Artemis would respond to the same situation. Your role model can be someone in history, a mythic heroine, or a friend you greatly admire. Children use role models to help acquire positive qualities such as wisdom and courage. You can use one for similar results.

4. **Take action**: The fourth step is to take action, even if that action is small. The Dalai Lama says, "It's not enough to be compassionate, you must act." Until you have committed yourself to action, it is difficult to change the circumstances of your life. The moment that you absolutely commit yourself, magic happens. A whole stream of events will flow from your commitment.

In one of the *Star Wars* films, Luke Skywalker hesitantly says he will "try" to complete a task. Yoda, the warrior mystic, replies, "No! Not 'try'! Do, or not do." Anytime you say that you will *try* something, your words imply a lack of commitment. They suggest that you feel that you won't be able to keep your commitment. Do it or don't do it, but don't just *try*. When you are willing to boldly take action, remarkable things will happen for you. Begin now.

Celebrate Your Worthy Opponents

A measure of the Warrior Woman's success is her capacity to recognize and honor her opponents. In mythology, a hero is defined by the size of his or her opponents. The bigger, meaner, and tougher the dragon, the more courageous and admired is the hero. The bigger your adversary, the stronger you become. It can be said that you are defined and strengthened by your willingness to face and conquer sizable problems. Give thanks for your problem, no matter how big it seems. Say, "Aha! I must be growing in stature and majesty because I now have a worthy opponent!"

In the beginning it may feel strange to celebrate your problems, especially if you are used to getting upset and depressed about them. Even if it feels uncomfortable in the beginning, try it! Changing your attitude about your problems and celebrating each one can change your entire life.

A Warrior Woman does not seek adversity, but she understands that she is strengthened by it when it appears in he life. A bodybuilder sculpts her muscles by pushing against resistance. The Creator gives us problems to sculpt our soul. When I was going through really rough times in my childhood, my grandmother would whisper to me, "Denise, the roots of the tree grow deepest when the wind blows the hardest. The winds of your life are blowing hard right now, but as a result, you are going to be strong in the future; you will have a deep foundation for the rest of your life." I've never forgotten her words. They echo in my soul during distressing times. A Warrior Woman knows that the difficult times in life are shaping her soul and allowing her spiritual roots to sink deep.

Another measure of a Glorious Warrior Woman is that she picks her battles with care. Not every grievance in life is worthy of her prowess and skill. Here is an example of a woman who didn't pick her battle with care.

I was having breakfast in a hotel restaurant in Europe. There was a very cultured-looking couple seated at the adjacent table. I watched as the wife's face became more and more distorted and upset. Her husband leaned forward and said, "Darling, what is the matter?" She whispered in a whiny voice, "They forgot the spoon for my tea!" The gentleman looked at her place setting and then looked up, horrified. "You're right. They didn't bring spoons for our tea. I'll call the waiter!"

The waiter was busy that morning. I watched as the couple tried to get his attention. They sighed and rolled their eyes and shared disgruntled comments with each other about the service when he wasn't quick to respond. I looked at their place settings and saw that they each had a spoon at their table settings, presumably for their cereal. I wanted to shout, "Hey! Have fun! Live on the wild side! Stir your tea with the cereal spoon, it will taste just as good . . . maybe better!" But I was quiet. After they got their teaspoons, they complained to each other about how the tea had grown cold while they waited for the spoons.

This is an extreme example, but it is so easy in life to get upset about stupid, inconsequential things and not experience the joy available in every moment. There is nothing wrong with going to battle for something you believe in, but choose your battles wisely. Put your energy where it can do the most good.

The Warrior Woman is able to distinguish small grievances from larger ones. For instance, if her toast burns, rather than being annoyed, she shrugs it off and makes herself another slice or finds a way to take pleasure in eating it as it is. If something on the news upsets her, she either changes the way she feels about it or she does something to help change the situation. She might write a letter to her senator, donate money, join an action group, or work on raising public awareness. She also knows the power of her intent and her prayers, so she may pray and meditate to focus positive energy to the situation. The Glorious Warrior Woman is never helpless.

When you find yourself getting upset, ask, "Is this a battle about which I am passionate?" If it is, jump forward with fierce intensity. If it is not, let it go. It is not worthy of your attention or your energy.

Warrior Woman Mantras

One valuable tool that you possess, when confronted with life's irritations, is the power of your thoughts and words, which you can use to shift your emotional state. Although we all occasionally encounter what we feel are Joan-of-Arc-size battles, usually it is small grievances that eat away at us. Every time you allow the slings and arrows of life to penetrate your core, you lose power. For example, in a typical day, someone might cut you off on the highway, another person might ignore you at a social gathering, your car gets a scratch on it, a flower in your garden is eaten by slugs. And finally, you turn on the television and you hear about some faraway tragedy. These are common everyday occurrences in life, but if you get upset at each one, your emotional and physical health suffers.

In order to combat these small annoyances, I developed simple mantras to say out loud or silently. For example, sometimes I repeat, "I am relaxed and serene" or "I release this, it is not worthy of my anger." These mantras tell my subconscious mind that I refuse to be thrown into a negative emotional state about events over which I have no control.

Any time you are in a situation where you feel the need to activate your inner Warrior Woman, you may find the use of a mantra that you have created to be helpful. I know a woman who silently chants to herself anytime her boss is in an irritable mood, "Your words roll off me like water off a duck's back. I am a powerful woman." When she repeats this mantra to herself, her boss can say anything to her and she doesn't get upset. When life seems most difficult is when a Warrior Woman mantra is most needed.

There are times in life when you are bound to fall flat on your face. It's the nature of being human. You also will have times when you feel depressed, angry, hurt, or lacking in self-esteem. However, you are not a failure if you fall down . . . only if you stay down.

When life gets me down, I remember the Japanese proverb: "Fall down seven times, get up eight." When you feel that you have been knocked down by circumstances, brush yourself off, get up, and affirm to yourself over and over, "I am a strong and powerful woman. No matter what knocks me down, I will continue to get up!"

If you allow yourself to get upset by a word or a look, then you have given someone power over you. If this does occur, acknowledge that you are upset, then let it go, affirming to yourself that you are not the type of person who gets upset about small things. Although you've been knocked down for a moment, you will soon be on your feet again.

You can tell when you have truly awakened your inner Warrior Woman, because you will rarely need her. When you are confident of your ability to stand up for yourself, you usually don't have to do so. In the ancient samurai tradition, you were thought to have lost as soon as you drew your sword. The most powerful samurai had so much inner strength, skill, and confidence in their ability that they never needed to draw their swords.

When it feels like the world is turning upside down, remember the only thing worthy of you is compassion—infinite, eternal, unconditional compassion. Face the challenge with courage, kindness, and a smile because you know that beneath the surface is a wild, outrageous, powerful Warrior Woman who can conquer anything.

FACING YOUR SHADOW

As a child, I was afraid of so many things. I was terrified during my parents' violent arguments. I was afraid of my mother's rage and my father's simmering undercurrents. I was initially scared at every new school I attended. (We moved nine times during my childhood.) I was afraid that no one would like me and that I wouldn't have any friends. And I was frightened that there was something under the bed that would grab me in the night. My childhood was defined by my fears.

As I grew up, I suppressed fear and denied its existence. But it shaped my life in hundreds of ways. For example, as a teenager I applied for jobs that were mediocre because I knew they would accept my application. I was afraid that if I tried for jobs I wanted, I wouldn't get hired, so I never even tried. I didn't usually date guys I was really attracted to because I was worried they might reject me, so I dated guys that I wasn't drawn to but who were comfortable.

Looking back, I can see that most of the major decisions I made in my youth were based on fear. Now, in my adult years, I still feel fear. I'm afraid of lots of things such as rejection, humiliation, both failure *and* success, and something happening to my loved ones. But now I'm unraveling my fears, understanding my shadow self, and learning about the woman who exists beneath the fear. It is a journey well worth taking.

What Is the Shadow?

On your journey to discover your inner secrets and mysteries, you may find it valuable to explore the dark, hidden crevices within your psyche. The renowned Swiss psychologist Carl Jung called this place the "shadow self." It is also called the lower self, animal nature, the alter ego, or the inner demon—the place where the unowned side of your personality lives. Your shadow self is the part of you that stays unknown, unexamined, and out of the light of your conscious awareness. It is the part that is denied or suppressed because it makes you uncomfortable or afraid. Whatever doesn't fit your image of your ideal self becomes your shadow.

Jung asked, "Would you rather be good or whole?" Many women choose goodness, and as a result, are fractured. It is especially important to explore your shadow as you strive for the light, because this often increases its density. This occurs because what you resist in life tends to persist and even become stronger. If you resist your dark side, it becomes more solid.

I've noticed a high proportion of light-seekers have been abused or severely traumatized as children. I believe that a number of women are drawn to light work, such as angel studies, because it makes it easier to suppress the pain of the past. Focusing on higher realms can make it easier to deny the pain of the darker inner realms. Many women who are "striving for the light" deny the existence of their dark side, and thus it can eat away at them and be damaging in many ways. Research confirms that women who get cancer tend to be much nicer than average. I believe this is because they subconsciously repress their shadow self. Also, research shows that a woman who rages at her cancer situation heals faster than a woman who is a people-pleaser and doesn't want to bother anyone. When you own and accept your shadow, you will be healthier and happier.

Where Did Your Shadow Come From?

You weren't born with your shadow. Babies love and accept themselves; they poop all over themselves and then laugh with glee. They don't judge themselves harshly and think some parts are good and some parts are bad. There are only two natural fears—fear of falling and fear of loud noises. All other fears are learned or conditioned by your family, culture, and upbringing; and what you have learned, you can unlearn!

From our earliest years, we build belief systems about ourselves based on our childhood experiences and things we were told about ourselves. For every positive statement a child receives, they receive, on average, twenty-five negative statements such as "You're always so clumsy" or "You'll never learn." A child doesn't have the protective shields that an adult has. They haven't learned how to filter and discern the information they receive, so they accept negative statements about themselves as true. A child who is told that she is unlovable will believe this to be true. As that child grows, these beliefs will become overtly obvious, or they will become masked in the form of a shadow self.

The more hidden your shadow is, the more covert an influence it will have on you. Once you are prepared to shine a light on the darker parts of yourself, you must be prepared to be honest about what you uncover. I believe that you will never be completely fulfilled as a woman until you look in every corner of yourself to reveal what lies deep within. Until the moment that you face your fears and honor your shadow side, there will exist a depth inside you that you cannot fathom.

Facing Your Shadow

When I lead seminars I'm blessed to have people come up to me afterwards and say, "'Oh Denise, you are such a wonderful, compassionate human being!" When this first started, I was really uncomfortable. I wanted to shout, "If you really knew me and knew my background, you wouldn't say that." But I would nod and smile, and hope like hell that they didn't find out who I really was. As some well-wisher would speak to me in glowing terms about how they perceived me during the seminar, images from my past would flood my mind: memories of panhandling on the streets of Chicago; sleeping overnight on a park bench in Yugoslavia (which landed me in jail for a few hours); working for a dating escort service in Hawaii; the suicide attempt that landed me in a hospital; hitchhiking alone through Europe; and getting so drunk every weekend in college that I couldn't remember what had happened the night before. I would think of all the unacceptable and disgusting parts of myself—lies I had told, injustices I had perpetrated, my rampant lack of self-esteem—and I would feel like such a fake. I would then bravely tell the seminar participant about some of these unlovable parts of myself so they wouldn't think I was fooling them. They would say, "Denise, you're so humble!"

I felt caught in a pretense of trying to hide what I couldn't accept about myself. And even when I confessed my "sins," expecting that others would judge me as harshly as I judged myself, they didn't. It took a long time before I could see the wonderful qualities which so many people perceived in me.

Over the years, I have begun to heal the split between my conscious self and the other parts of me. I am integrating the aspects of the shadow into my whole. It has taken courage for me to face myself exactly as I am, without illusion or self-deception. It isn't always easy, because the shadow self can be so difficult to find and accept, but it has been well worth the effort.

Exercise to Help You Uncover Your Shadow Self

Relax. Imagine yourself on a boat approaching an island. As you pull the boat to shore, the first person you meet says, "Hi, I am part of your shadow self." What does she look like? Ask her what she is called. How do you feel toward her? What is her mood and body language telling you? What is her gift to you? Is there anything that she desires to tell you? Allow the next shadow self to appear.

When you are complete with this exercise, write your experiences down in a journal. When you know your shadow, you know yourself.

"Projections": Casting Your Shadow into the World

Sometimes the shadow self is so well camouflaged that it can take a profound effort to discover it. We are so disconnected from our darkest inner realms that it would be impossible to discover what lies there if it weren't for our "projections." These occur when we subconsciously cast our shadow on to the world around us, which then reflects it back to us. If you always see angry people all around you, your shadow self has suppressed anger, *even if you don't feel angry*. If everywhere you go, you are aware of sad people, then chances are that you are suppressing grief. Your shadow self will draw to you people who share the same shadow.

A woman who attended one of my seminars matter-of-factly stated, "All women resent their father." I was surprised by her words and asked her about this. She said, "Well, everyone knows that women resent and hate their fathers. Every woman I know resents her father." I asked her about her relationship with her father, and she said that she was the exception to the rule because her relationship with her father was really good. This seemed to me to be a very obvious case of someone who had suppressed hatred and anger about her father. Expression of emotion probably wasn't acceptable in her home, so she consciously thought everything was fine in her relationship with her father. Subconsciously, however, she projected her shadow feelings into the world, and they were reflected back to her by all her friends who "resented their fathers."

If you want to see the nature of your shadow, be aware of your judgments about others. If you *observe* something it is not a projection, but if you *judge* it, it is. If you observe someone throw litter out of their car but you don't react emotionally, it's an observation. If you get upset and think, *What a disgusting, selfish pig!* then you are probably projecting. What you judge in others can be a reflection of qualities that you possess, but deny, within yourself. If you are always judging others, then it is likely that your own shadow self is quietly screaming at *you*.

We are repelled by our own negative projections. If I am unreasonably upset and offended by someone's whining/rudeness/selfishness, etc., it's because I am not embracing these qualities in myself. I need to look carefully within to see if I have exhibited these qualities in the past, am doing so now, or have the capacity to demonstrate them in the future. If, when I've acknowledged their existence within me, I accept these qualities, I won't be deeply offended by someone else who has them.

Finding Your "Hot Buttons"

To begin to be aware of what's held in your shadow, make a list of the qualities that you vehemently dislike in others. When I first did this exercise, the trait I disliked the most was condescension and arrogance. Of course there were lots of qualities that I generally didn't like in other people, but condescension was the quality that was the biggest button. For example, if someone acted condescendingly toward me, it was like they pushed a "hot button" and I would see red. But I couldn't see anything that I had in common with this quality. . . . I thought, *I don't condescend to others. I genuinely feel equal with everyone I meet. That can't be me!*

I remembered meeting a woman who was condescending; and I swore to myself, "I'm not anything like her! I'm not!" I had met her a number of years ago, on a speaking tour. She was well known in her field of spiritual awareness, and we shared the stage. On the surface, she was "love and light," but at every turn she made me spit nails.

Before one talk, where I was scheduled to go first, she turned to the promoter and said, "Everyone is here to see me, so I should go before Denise so they don't have to wait" . . . and then smiled sweetly as she went on stage. I was so out of touch with what I was subconsciously feeling that I didn't have any reaction at the time, for I also was "love and light." Later, in my hotel room, I felt depressed. (When you are depressed, it is because you are suppressing some kind of emotion.) When I looked beneath the surface, I realized that I was angry with her for condescending to me.

Another time we were at a book signing, and someone came to get her autograph. She smiled in a sugary way and introduced me, saying, "You probably haven't heard of Denise. She's not very well known, but some people seem to enjoy her books." I smiled wanly, as I raged inside. Then I sternly chided myself for reacting to her words. I said to myself, "Denise, you have no right to be upset over something so trivial. You're selfish for being upset!" (This is the kind of self-talk that can occur when people suppress their shadow self.)

The images of her faded away and I thought, *No, I'm not anything like her. I treat everyone equally. I don't condescend to anyone. That isn't my shadow self.*

Not long after that, we hired several people to do gardening. One man was of Hispanic origin. After several months, he wanted to leave. When I asked him why, he said it was because *he didn't feel that he was being treated equally.* He said he had left his last two jobs for the same reason; he felt he was condescended to because he was Hispanic. I was really upset that he would think we were condescending to him. We weren't like everyone else. We were different. In fact, I had just given him one of my computers so that he could go to college because he wanted to become a lawyer. I had loaned him money, and done so much for him and his family. Certainly he couldn't think I was condescending! I was indignant.

Suddenly, in horror, I realized he was right. I recognized that I had given special privileges to him that I hadn't given to the other workers *because* he was Hispanic. He was right. I *had* treated him unequally. As I began to examine all my relationships, it was gut-wrenching to acknowledge to myself that I actually didn't view all people as equal. My identity as a woman who treats everyone with equality was shattered. It felt like part of myself was dying.

I had to face the hard and very uncomfortable truth about myself: there were some people I placed above me and some I placed below. There had been some people in my life to whom I had acquiesced and others to whom I had been condescending. The shame of this realization was horrible.

I knew enough about shadow work to know that I needed to own this "ugly" part of me, so I said over and over to myself, "I am condescending." I felt sick every time I said it. Images from my childhood surfaced. I remembered a time I was with my mother, who is of Cherokee heritage, when we tried to check into a motel and were condescendingly told that there were no vacancies. Then a white family came in after us and they were told that there were spaces available. It was so humiliating. I was in anguish. Had I unknowingly treated others in a similar way?

The more I acknowledged the part of me that was condescending, the easier it was to accept. I knew I was beginning to love the condescending part of myself when I ran into the Hispanic worker in our small central Californian town. He beamed at me. *"Hola,* Denise!" *"Hola!"* I replied. As we chatted, I could feel love, clarity, and *equality* flowing between us. It was a wonderful moment.

Exercise to Find Your Projections

List the qualities that you disdain in others. Take each trait and see if that is a quality that you have demonstrated in the past, are exhibiting currently, or are capable of manifesting in the future. You don't necessarily need to do anything with this information. Just examining and owning these parts of you allows an integration to begin to occur.

Understanding and Releasing Fear

One bold aspect of the shadow is fear. Beneath every conscious apprehension is a wellspring of subconscious fear. Each fear is like a small sub-personality inside of you demanding to be heard. One "fear-being" might chatter, "Don't go outside. It's raining. You'll catch a cold." Another might be constantly whimpering in your ear, "Don't fall in love. You know you'll get hurt. It's better to be alone than be hurt!" No wonder it's hard to move forward in life when you have all these frantic voices jamming your thoughts.

Each fear-being will act as if it needs attention, and as if, if you don't listen to it, terrible things could happen to you. When you allow fear-beings to dominate your life, you live in reaction rather than living by choice. Sometimes, even if you don't think that you have any fear, your life is still being dominated by it. For example, "stress" is just a codeword for fear. Anytime you're "stressed out," you have been listening to the fear-beings. If a woman is stressed out about not finishing her project on time, at a deeper level she's probably afraid of being rejected by her co-workers, of receiving a poor evaluation report, or of letting people down.

When you clutch your fears tight to your breast, suppressing them with bravado or denial, they become stronger. We cling so closely to our fears that they begin to become part of our identity. It becomes scary to let them go because it can feel like part of us is dying. We hold our fears captive and even justify them, declaring, "That's just who I am." Remember this: *you have fears . . . but you are not fear.* You are larger than your fears.

The road to releasing your fears is to first acknowledge that they are there. "A fear named is a fear tamed" describes what happens when you begin to face fear. If you can name it and understand its effect on you, it becomes manageable rather than wild and unwieldy.

Begin by taking a huge piece of paper and writing down every fear you have. Big ones. Little ones. Everything. Even some that you are not sure of but which you might have. Be specific. Keep writing until you are exhausted and then find some more. As soon as you can see them listed on paper, they will begin to lose some of their hold on you.

Once you have listed your fears, take one and examine it. As you examine each fear, ask yourself if it is a fear that serves and supports you. For example, if you are afraid that you will get out of shape if you don't exercise, then this fear-being has some value in your life. You can thank it for its presence but ask that it doesn't judge you so harshly on those days you don't exercise. Your fears need your love. The more you acknowledge and embrace them, the less they affect your life.

When you discover a fear on your list that does not serve you, allow yourself to feel it. For example, if you are terrified of public speaking, imagine that you are in front of a group of people who are waiting for you to speak. Feel the fear and at the same time observe yourself. Notice what you feel physically in your body. Be aware of any emotions or memories from the past that come into your consciousness. The more you resist experiencing your fears, the more they will dictate your life.

The next step in this process is to intensify your fear. I mean *really* feel it. For example, imagine that the people in the audience are laughing at you and nothing is coming out of your mouth. Some of the people are rolling in the aisle laughing at you, and you can't move or speak because you are so frightened. Imagine feeling your fear as fully as you can. An amazing thing happens when you do this. The more you try to intensify your fear, the more it diminishes. When you stop resisting your fear-beings and give them expression, they begin to dissolve.

An exercise that I have found to be extraordinarily helpful is to imagine the worst that could happen in a worrisome situation and see how I could gain value from this potential future. This simple act has helped me overcome some hefty fears. For example, many years ago I had financial problems and was in serious debt. I was so scared. Then I thought, "Hey! What's the worst that could happen here?" I have a pretty active imagination, so I imagined that I got thrown in prison for years for not paying off my debts. (I didn't realize that in the United States, we don't send people to prison for debt.)

Then I thought, "Okay, if that is the worst that could happen, how could I gain value from it?" I'm a good teacher, so I thought, *I could give classes to the other inmates. I could even write about the experience of being in prison.* I discovered all kinds of ways that "the worst that could happen" wasn't so bad. I felt more relaxed and less stressed about my financial situation. As outrageous as this exercise sounds, when you can really confront and accept the most terrible outcome, your fear will subside. Fear paralyzes you and limits your ability to see other possible answers for your problem. When I let the fear go, I found a multitude of creative ways to change my financial situation. I was then able to get out of debt fairly easily.

To release a specific fear, begin by taking "baby steps." For example, I used to be afraid of heights. Whenever I was on a cliff, hill, or mountain I would get vertigo and feel faint. I wanted to overcome this fear, so I started by visualizing myself standing on a cliff. It took a while until I could actually visualize this, but I just did it in small chunks. First I imagined myself near the cliff, then closer to the top, until finally I could envision myself right at the edge. Then when I was in Australia for a few weeks, I actually went to the top of a cliff near Manly Beach in Sydney. Every day I would walk to the top of the cliff and go a little closer to the edge, until one day I stood near the precipice railing without fear. Since that time, I am no longer afraid of heights, and just a few weeks ago, on another trip to Australia, I climbed to the top of the Sydney Harbor Bridge. It was exhilarating!

Fear occurs when you don't feel that you have the ability to cope with a situation. The more means you have to deal with fear, the less impact it will have on your life. Be willing to take action to minimize your fears. For example, if you are a single woman living in a dangerous neighborhood, it is justifiable to feel frightened walking alone at night. But don't allow your fear to overwhelm your life. Take action to minimize your fears. Take self-defense courses. Learn to walk boldly, with confidence. Pray, meditate, and ask your allies for protection. Get a friend to walk with you. Take steps to cope with the situation and your fear will lessen.

Walking confidently through a dangerous area is *acting as if* you weren't afraid. Some people might call this "faking it until you make it." No matter what saying you use, this technique works. If you act as if you are courageous, strong, and powerful in a fearful situation, you will become so. I have often felt shy and nervous when meeting new people. To overcome this fear, whenever I am in a new social situation, instead of trying to be invisible and hiding in a corner, I act as if I'm not afraid. I courageously introduce myself to strangers and get to know them. And after a while, I don't feel fearful at all. Not only is it satisfying to get over an old fear, but I have met some wonderful people this way.

Whatever you focus on will expand in your life. If you focus on what you love, you will have more love in your life. If you focus on what you fear, then your fears will expand. I knew a woman who was frightened that her young son would fall. She was constantly saying, "I'm so worried that he is going to fall," and warning her son, "Be careful that you don't fall down." One day this child took a frightful fall off a neighbor's veranda and was unconscious for a number of hours. This event only justified his mother's fears. She focused even more on her fear of her son falling. As her son grew, he was constantly falling. He fell off his bike numerous times; he fell out of a tree and broke his ankle. I believe that the mother's extraordinary fear actually precipitated some of his accidents. A better strategy would have been for her to focus on her child's grace and balance.

The Effects of Fear

Whenever I am irritable with someone who is acting less than nobly, I remember that all bad behavior comes from fear. If someone you know is being selfish, rude, boorish, unkind, angry, bitter, or any other negative emotion, it's because they are afraid. They might be worried that they are not lovable, or frightened of not being accepted, or concerned that they won't have enough. The individual motivating fears may be different, but whenever someone acts badly, it's because they are afraid. The man who looks down on others does so because he is afraid that he isn't worthwhile and valuable. Realizing this helps me have compassion for others, rather than becoming upset with them.

We get upset and frightened when we think that we don't have any options. *You always have options.* Sometimes your option is to change your point of view about the situation. Even if you can't change the situation, usually there is another way to look at it. Shift your perspective of the situation and you can shift your fear.

Sometimes the best option is to leave the situation. You do not need to stay in a situation that does not empower you. When my daughter was young, I told her, "Meadow, if you are ever in a situation that doesn't feel right, get out! Say to yourself, 'This sucks. I'm leaving.' Trust your intuition. If you are with a group of kids who are going to do something that doesn't feel right, leave. If someone asks you to do something that you don't want to do, get out of there." I had her repeat the words "This sucks.

I'm leaving" until I knew that they would come to mind whenever the need arose.

Fear isn't necessarily always a bad thing. Sometimes it acts as a warning system. It is true; females do have intuition. It is one of our gifts. If you are in a place that doesn't feel right, leave immediately. If you step into an elevator and it feels strange, get out! Forget about being polite or nice. Female victims when telling their stories usually say that they could sense something was wrong beforehand but didn't act on that feeling because it wouldn't have been polite. Always listen to your gut instincts. Your fear can be a warning system giving you immediate information about a situation or person.

Roberta is a strong and capable woman who leads hiking treks in the lower Himalayan mountains. One morning, as her trekking group started out, she began to have an uneasy feeling, which expanded into a full-blown fear. Rationally there was no reason for her anxiety. The skies were clear, the mountain reports were good. Instead of listening to her mind, though, she listened to her fear. She took an alternative route to their destination. When they arrived, they heard that another group had been caught in an avalanche *on the trail they had intended to take,* and several people had been killed. This is a dramatic example of listening to your fear; there will be times when you'll never know the reason why you chose one road instead of another in life, but have confidence that there is always a reason.

Facing Old Age and Death Without Fear

Hattie Linn, my husband's grandmother, was a role model for me. She was independent, fun, and feisty and lived to almost a hundred years old. She loved to travel and have adventures. When she was in her nineties, she found herself close to the epicenter of a huge earthquake in California. When it hit, she was standing next to a door in her home; she grabbed on hard and thought, *I'm going to hang on for the ride!* The earthquake whipped her body back and forth, but Hattie staunchly hung on. When the shaking stopped, she yelped for joy. The earthquake had thrown her back *in*, and it felt great. The earthquake had been like an enormous chiropractic adjustment that had released the pain in a chronically troublesome back. If her attitude had been different and she had thought the world was coming to an end during the earthquake, I don't think that she would have had such a positive reaction.

I want to be a glorious older woman. I want to be willing to take risks, learn new things, and dance with abandon under the stars no matter how old I am. But I know that being a glorious older woman starts with being a glorious younger woman. It starts here and now. We are all getting older every day. One day you and I will both be old women, if it is our destiny to live that long. It is our choice whether we live in fear and act according to other people's expectations of what an older woman is or whether we allow ourselves to be authentic and real. Start now; you are an elder in training. The more you experience joy, satisfaction, and fulfillment in the present moment, the easier it will be to have these qualities in the years ahead.

As we age it's important to find the joy in the present moment rather than clinging to what we once were. On the day I turned forty I was lamenting growing older. Meadow, who was twelve years old at the time, said, "Mom, it's true that you're not as young as you once were . . . but you're certainly not as old as you're going to be. Enjoy forty." And she was so right. It's all perspective. I'm fifty-two now, and forty seems young to me.

My mother is eighty-four years old and lives in a Veterans of War nursing home. She stays in bed most of the time. I was feeling sad about this, but she said, "Actually, it's great to be in bed all the time. I love to read and now I can read to my heart's content. And on top of this, my meals are brought to me!" I was impressed with her ability to find joy in the present, rather than clinging to what she once had. If you cling to what you once were or what you once had, you will be miserable. If you find joy where you are, your life will blossom.

I don't know what I'll be like when I face my death. I'd like to think I will be noble and gracious. In my wishful imagination, my death will be a spiritual experience. But most deaths are painful, messy, unpleasant, and accompanied by fear. I don't know how or when I will die. I do know that my willingness to accept it will make death easier and will make me live more fully until that time.

In Native American culture, there is an expression that I love. When it is a beautiful day, we say, "It's a good day to die." To me this means that I am ready to face death today because, right now, I am complete and whole; therefore, I am ready to live fully this day. A woman who recognizes and accepts her natural cycles—including death—experiences an unparalleled depth of life. For as long as you fear death, your fear hovers over every moment of your life and filters every experience.

Are you ready to die? If not, why not? What is incomplete or undone in your life? With whom do you need to communicate? Whom do you need to forgive? Whom do you need to tell that you love? If you aren't ready, get ready. A Glorious Woman is prepared and ready for her death whenever it might be. You might die in sixty years or thirty or ten or next month or tomorrow. When you live as if every moment were your last—your last sunset, your last rainbow, your last kiss—then life becomes so much more precious.

One of the best ways to prepare for your death is to be genuine and authentic. Dr. Elisabeth Kübler-Ross, a powerful advocate for dying with dignity and who has been with thousands of people as they died, says that people who are "wishy-washy Protestants, or wishy-washy Catholics, or wishy-washy Jews" have a terrible time dying. She claims that people who are "solidly something or solidly nothing, die with more peace." If your beliefs are half-hearted and merely intellectual, they will fall apart at the approach of death. Whoever you are and whatever you believe, be solid in it without hesitation or remorse; be all of it.

It's comforting to think that we can die with dignity and grace, but death isn't always neat and tidy. Sometimes it's hard to maintain our sense of self and authenticity when we are faced with fear, suffering, and pain. However, as you begin now to rid yourself of anger, fear, and resentment, you'll be more prepared for death. This way, whenever it's time for you to cross over, it will truly be a "good day to die." Acceptance is the key to dying well. When that day is upon you, accept yourself in whatever emotional state you are in. If you are afraid, accept that. If you are angry, accept that. If you are whining, accept that. Acceptance and authenticity is the key to stepping through the veil with grace and ease.

Your Faults Can Be Your Virtues

Here is a great way you can begin to love your shadow. Look on your so-called faults and all the things that you don't like about yourself as your assets. When you accept these qualities and learn how to moderate the amplitude of each "fault," they can serve you.

Your weaknesses can then become your strengths. For example, instead of condemning yourself for being so stubborn, think of stubbornness as overamplified determination. This is a wonderful quality that you can call upon when you need to complete a project or get through a challenging time.

If you judge yourself for coming on too strong, this same quality, toned down just a bit, could also be a trait of leadership. Or, if you smother people, turn it down a few notches and you have wonderful mothering skills: from "smother" to "'mother." Do not disown or repress your "negative" qualities; just use them in a different way. Learn to be appropriate with those qualities and each one will serve you in a positive way.

Faults to Virtues

List your so-called faults and then next to this list find ways that each one be viewed in a positive manner. For example:

stubborn	*toned down becomes:*	determined
flighty	*toned down becomes:*	spontaneous
silly	*toned down becomes:*	joyous
shy	*toned down becomes:*	pensive
penny-pinching	*toned down becomes:*	thrifty

The key to being whole is to be utterly honest with yourself and to face all the deep hidden parts of your shadow. This means facing the parts that you want to pretend aren't there or that you don't want to see. When you do this, you become genuine, and authenticity is the gateway to unconditional love of yourself and others.

7
CHERISHING
YOUR BODY

E SALEN is a renowned personal growth center on the Pacific Ocean in Big Sur, California. It is famous for its natural hot spring tubs, which perch along the rocky coastline. At any given time, there are a number of self-help programs and activities occurring there. I once went there to teach a five-day feng shui workshop. When I first arrived, I was told that the tubs were for both men and women, and most people who used them went nude. "This is no big deal," I kept saying to myself. When I keep repeating "no big deal," I know that actually it is a big deal. I was a bit nervous about being nude because I had become self-conscious about my body over the years. I asked about wearing towels to the tubs. The assistant kindly explained to me, "You get one . . . and they're small."

"Oh," I meekly replied. *Darn*, I thought. *One towel can either cover my breasts or my buttocks . . .but not both!* I was in a dilemma about what to cover and what to leave exposed.

At first I used the tubs only at night. I would slip from the changing rooms into a hot tub under the cover of darkness. I wasn't quite ready to sally forth across the deck in my full glory in the bright light of day. However, as the days passed and I became less self-conscious, I ventured into the hot tubs in the daytime.

On the last day, I was trying to discreetly undress in the corner in the changing room (men and women shared the same dressing room and the same showers!). I was taken aback when a naked man innocently came up to me in the dressing room to ask me a question about feng shui. It was a weird experience talking with a nude stranger about the correct placement of the front door of his new house. I kept trying not to look down. And it was even weirder when, after a while, it wasn't two naked people of the opposite sex talking to each other . . . it was just two people talking. It's on days such as that, I realize that life is a great and grand adventure!

Esalen is famous for its massages. You soak in the hot tub until your masseuse or masseur comes to escort you to a massage yurt. My masseur's name was Paolo. I was horrified when I first saw him. He was young, gorgeous, and Italian. I would have been so much more comfortable with someone older rather than a handsome young man. Rather than spend the entire massage feeling embarrassed as he kneaded my well-endowed body, I took a breath and said, "I'm really self-conscious about my body." He smiled gently and replied, "I'm Italian. We love womanly bodies." With these six kind and loving words, I felt completely comfortable within my body and safe with him. It was a great massage.

One late afternoon at Esalen while taking a quick dip in the hot tubs, I chatted with a woman in her fifties who was in the communal tub. After a while she said she had to go. When she stood up, water dripped off her body, which was silhouetted against the Pacific Ocean and the golden setting sun. She looked so glorious . . . and she only had one breast. On her chest was a long scar where her other breast had been. As she dried off, she continued to casually chat with me. There was no sense of shame, embarrassment, or insecurity. She didn't try to hide her body. Instead, she exuded a strength and serenity that were inspiring. She was so confident within herself and her body. There is nothing as beautiful as confidence.

Esalen is an amazing place to work through insecurities and hangups about your body. After you have seen dozens of people of all ages and all shapes who are unself-conscious about their bodies, it begins to feel that it is *really* no big deal.

Many Western women are dissatisfied with their bodies. In my travels around the world, I have found that this phenomenon is almost universal.

Women often find it difficult to accept and love the way they look. Unfortunately, studies have shown that this feeling of dissatisfaction is growing. I met a woman when I was in Brazil whose mother sent her to a diet doctor who gave her diet pills when she was five years old!

Our ideal of beauty is shaped and influenced by airbrushed magazine covers and actresses who have had numerous "nips and tucks" from their plastic surgeons. We are supposed to—or at least think that we have to—measure up to this fantasy. Yet this "ideal" is impossible to attain. In many ways, natural inner beauty has been suppressed by this Hollywood and Madison Avenue view. However, this wasn't always the case. Renaissance paintings not only depicted women in their natural state, but also glorified how voluptuous and sumptuous they truly were.

In subtle, yet powerful, ways we have been programmed to believe that our bodies aren't beautiful, fabulous, and glorious. We aren't aware of our true beauty, because when we gaze in the mirror, we see what we are not, instead of reveling in what we are. Shame and anxiety about our bodies puts barriers between us and other people. When we are preoccupied with our image, it's difficult to let anyone else intimately into our lives. Since we don't know how to love our bodies, it's difficult to love ourselves. We have lost the ability to celebrate how exquisite and unique our bodies are.

The truth is . . . you have an amazing body. Your heart beats without your conscious effort, your brain stores and organizes a phenomenal amount of information that even the most sophisticated computers haven't been able to duplicate. Your digestive system discerns what nutrients are in your food and absorbs what it needs. If you injure yourself, hundreds of healing mechanisms are activated to repair the damage. Your body is so remarkable that even if you judge or abuse it, it continues to function in wondrous ways.

No matter what shape your body is in, there are many reasons to love and cherish it. To truly love and accept yourself, you must love every aspect of your being, including your body, for it is the temple that houses your spirit. I believe that the reason we are on the planet is to learn to love, and we can only love others as deeply as we can love ourselves . . . and our bodies.

Anything you love, grows in beauty and power. A plant that is loved and nurtured grows strong and beautiful, while a plant that is neglected withers. As you cherish and listen to your body, it will become more and more beautiful.

You Have the Body of a Goddess

It is time for all of us to reclaim our bodies. Goddesses in times past were presented in a multitude of ways. Some were very plump and voluptuous, some were elongated and thin; some were tall and some short. The portrayals of Goddess bodies are just as different as the wonderful variety of women's bodies today. The truth is, you do have the body of a Goddess.

There is no universal ideal in bodies. In fact, to this day in a remote area of Nigeria, before they marry, women spend months in a special "fattening room" where they pack on pounds eating nothing but starchy foods. If a Nigerian village girl is told she looks thin, it's considered an insult. Fat is a sign of good health and prosperity. No matter what shape your body is in, at some time in our history, your body was the ideal.

Fabulous Affirmations for Your Body

One of the ways to deepen your appreciation of your body is to do affirmations. These will help diminish negative self-talk.

Repeat them as you go about the normal business of life—walking, swimming, or meditating. Sense and feel the truth of the words sinking deep within you. Don't just say the words. Really feel and believe them. If you say you are strong and healthy, put your body in a position where you feel strong and healthy. If you affirm your radiance, imagine it exuding from every pore in your body. Choose one or two of the following affirmations to work with—go for the ones you find most exciting.

My body is beautiful, supple, and graceful. I have a gorgeous, fabulous body. My body is strong and healthy. I have a remarkably healthy body. My body radiates light and vibrant energy. I enjoy my body. I experience pleasure through and with my body. What a splendid body I have!

My body exudes sensuality and radiance. Through my body I experience ecstasy more and more. My body is beautiful inside and out. With every passing moment, my body is becoming healthier and healthier. I take pride in my body and nurture it. I do things that are good for my body and I nourish it with food and drink that strengthen and heal it.

My body is the body of a Goddess. My body is a sacred vessel for the creative spirit within all things. My body is beautiful . . . I am beautiful. I LOVE my body. My body is lovable and I am lovable. I am so grateful for my body. I am filled with gratitude for my body.

Whenever I start to judge my body or feel ashamed and embarrassed by my scars, lumps, and fat rolls, I think of the one-breasted woman in the Esalen hot tub. I remember her poise and grace. It's great to have a body role model, since it will allow your self-judgment to diminish. Find someone who has a good attitude about her body, or who has a body similar to yours that you admire. It can be a friend, acquaintance, or someone in films or on television. It can even be a representation of a mythical person, such as a Goddess statue or figurine from antiquity. I once met a very large woman who told me that she was "wonderfully Rubenesque." When she said those words, she was glowing. I could feel her love and appreciation for her body. She would make a great role model for any full-sized woman.

The Joy of Exercise?

I know it's good to exercise. I believe in it. I can tell you all the reasons why it's imperative. However, exercise has not been easy for me. Here is an entry from one of my journals to give you an example of what my attitude to exercise used to be:

> I signed up for an aerobics class today. It said "all levels" but after I arrived I realized it should have said "all levels except for flabby, overweight, middle-aged women." Those prancing, pumped up, high-tone, young cheerleader-types drive me crazy. I felt so clumsy and awkward trying to keep up with everyone else. I hate exercise.

So, as you can see, exercise, especially aerobics, hasn't been on my top list of pleasurable experiences. There is nothing wrong with aerobics; it just isn't right for me. Since I really wanted the benefits of exercise, I figured there had to be another way. I thought about what it would take for me to exercise on a consistent basis, and my bottom line was "fun." It has to be fun. I love dancing. So I decided the best kind of exercise for me was to put on rock and roll and just dance. I dance through the kitchen, jump up on the couch and boogie, career across the dining room. It's joyous! I feel exhilarated and alive.

I believe the more joy you feel when you exercise, the more benefits your body will receive. If you hate doing exercise, think of it as punishment, and only do it because it's good for you, there's no doubt that it will still have some benefit to your body. However, the value multiplies if you really love what you are doing. Find some kind of exercise that makes you happy—the kind where when you are done you can't stop smiling—and every cell in your body will respond positively. Your immune system will soar. Walk, swim, canoe, bicycle, dance, play tennis, take a jitterbug class. Have fun! The type of exercise you do is less important than actually doing it and enjoying yourself. The truth is you have only one body and it has to last you for a long time. It's a lot easier to feel good about yourself and life when your body feels good. There are thousands of courses, books, doctors, and gurus who will tell you what you need to do to stay healthy. Here are a few things I think are important:

1. **Movement:** Your body needs to move. (Hey, I'm talking to myself here.) Do some kind of movement or exercise. Have fun doing it!

2. **Get a health routine:** It's easy to get caught up with life, so have an "hour of power" first thing every morning (or at least ten minutes of power) where you meditate or pray, visualize good things for your day, and do some kind of movement or exercise. The secret is to make it routine.

3. **Get to know your body:** Learn about your body and its secret signals to you. For example, if there are dark circles under your eyes, your adrenal glands are under stress. Cut back on coffee and get more sleep. Licorice root tea is good for the adrenals. If your face is puffy, your kidneys are under stress. Cut back on salt and increase your water intake.

4. **Eat well:** We are so fortunate to be living in a time when we have access to excellent food and the finest nutritional supplements. Research nutrition and health. Find out what is best for your body. Dr Christiane Northrup has a great website (www.drnorthrup.com). It gives health information from a holistic perspective as well as a medical one.

5. **Drink water:** Drink water. Drink water!

6. **Be consciously aware of your breathing** for at least three minutes every day. Sit quietly and just inhale deeply and exhale deeply. We often get so busy that we forget to breathe properly.

7. **Only have mirrors in your home that make you look great:** Get rid of "fat" mirrors that distort your image. When you look in a mirror and look good, you will feel good.

8. **Walk like a Goddess:** Throw your shoulders back, put your head up, and breathe deeply. Stand up straight and tall. Carry yourself as if you were the guardian of a powerful secret.

Loving Your Body As It Is

What is it about those Frenchwomen? During my visits to my daughter in France, it has been especially inspiring to observe the way Frenchwomen relate to their bodies; they seem comfortable and accepting of them. They tend to think of themselves as sexy, no matter what age they are. It's not uncommon for older Frenchwomen, in their fifties and sixties, to play erotic leads in French movies. This is in direct contrast to most American women, who have been culturally conditioned to equate beauty with youth.

As a Frenchwoman ages, rather than covering up her body with loose clothes or long tunic tops, she is likely to wear something that shows off her plump belly. In France there doesn't seem to be such a desperate need to have a flat stomach. Whenever I find myself caught up in the beauty myth generated by the media, I think of those Frenchwomen who often feel sexy and sensual into their elder years.

Chakras: Subtle Energy Centers of the Body

When I was in my early twenties, I had a kundalini experience. It occurred spontaneously as I was on a plane flying over the Pacific Ocean from San Francisco to Hawaii. I had been looking out of the window at some clouds when I felt a rush of energy like molten lava move up my spine. It felt like the top of my head was exploding out into the clouds. By the time I was picked up at the airport, I was having trouble talking or comprehending what was happening to me. My spine felt like a hot iron poker, and the top of my head felt as if a volcano were erupting through it.

I was taken home, and a perceptive friend arranged to have a Tibetan lama, who was visiting Hawaii, come over to examine me. "Oh," he said, "it's nothing to worry about. You've just had your kundalini rise." (Kundalini is a vast store of energy that rests at the base of the spine. In India and Tibet this energy is symbolized as a coiled serpent.) He told me to rest for a few days and I would then feel better. He explained that life-force energy was moving up my chakras (the subtle energy centers in the body) and I was going through a spiritual purification. He explained how every chakra has an effect on the subtle energy of the body. When energy flows through the chakra system, we are in balance. He said in my case, Shakti (the female universal life force who dwells at the base of the spine) was rising up through the chakras to meet Shiva (the male life force that resides at the crown of the head), and this was why I felt so much heat in my spine. He explained that this does not usually occur without substantial spiritual preparation. However, in rare cases, kundalini rises spontaneously, which is very disconcerting for someone who isn't prepared for it.

This experience precipitated a strange occurrence, for it had an effect on my physical weight. Although I weighed about 150 pounds at the time, scales only measured me as weighing 50 pounds! I was a local attraction, and lots of friends and acquaintances came around to lift my body up because it was so light. My body looked the same, but somehow it was almost weightless for a week. It was a disturbing and very strange week, but eventually the flow of heat up my spine stopped and my weight returned to normal. To this day I don't know exactly why it happened.

Your body has centers of energy or power points. They are each hubs for the body's vital energy. Practitioners of yoga believe that prana (cosmic energy) enters the body through our breath and then travels through a network of channels. The energy centers or chakras are the main intersections for this unseen energy flow. When these areas of the body are balanced, you will feel strong and full of vitality.

Some spiritual traditions suggest meditating on the upper chakras and closing down or ignoring the lower ones. This comes from the idea that the lower chakras represent a person's lower nature and the higher chakras represent one's higher nature. In my experience, when you focus solely on the upper chakras, you become ungrounded and sometimes "so heavenly you are no good on earth." Every chakra is important. Allow the energy to flow freely through each chakra and your life will be in balance.

Chakra Meditation

Sit still with your spine straight and imagine an energy cord coming up from the earth through your feet, up through your spine, out the top of your head, and into the stars. As energy moves up your body, imagine each chakra opening like a flower to the sun and then spinning. When you are complete, imagine the cord moving back into the earth and each chakra closing like a flower closes at the end of the day. This exercise activates your chakras but allows you to not be too open during a busy and hectic day.

Base Chakra

This energy center is found at the base of your spine. It is associated with the vibratory energy of the color red, and with physical energy, survival and sexuality. Although modern interpretations of this chakra are conflicting with regard to its connection with sexuality, ancient tradition states that this is the chakra of physical sexual energy.

Symptoms of base chakra imbalance: Are you feeling tired or physically weak? Do you have sexual problems? Are your periods irregular or painful? Has your Warrior Woman taken the month off? Are you overcome with assorted fears and worries? Are you having trouble taking action?

Chakra solution: Pull out the red! Wear a red dress. Accessorize your home with red. Paint your lips bright glossy red. Eat red cherries by the handful. Any kind of red food from apples to cranberry juice to rare meat will help activate this chakra. Put on the sexiest music you have and dance with power and passion. Shout "Yes! Yes! Yes!" as loud as you can. Sleep in red sheets for a few nights. Wear or carry a red stone such as ruby or red jasper.

Second Chakra

Located in the abdomen, a few inches below the navel, the color associated with this center is orange. This area governs social encounters, sensuality, and pleasure.

Symptoms of second chakra imbalance: Are your social interactions at a stalemate? Are you forgetting to take time for pleasure and enjoyment? Have you forgotten how long it's been since your home was filled with friends, family, parties? Have you been tackling problems on your own and now are ready for some company?

Chakra solution: Oranges! Eat them. Place orange-scented aromatherapy candles everywhere. Spray orange perfume throughout your home. Throw an orange shawl over your shoulders. Paint a wall pumpkin color. Wear or carry orange calcite (you could even tie it round your waist so it hangs over the second chakra).

Solar-Plexus Chakra

Self-esteem, self-confidence, personal will and the ability to assimilate information are connected with this center. The color that symbolizes it is yellow.

Symptoms of solar-plexus chakra imbalance: Has your confidence been sagging? Have your mental processes been fuzzy? Are you having difficulty knowing your own value? Are you afraid that you are not good enough for a situation, project, or person?

Chakra solution: Sunshine, glorious sunshine! Get out in the light of the sun. Fill your home with daffodils or dandelions—it doesn't matter what kind of flower as long as it's yellow. Play "Here Comes the Sun" over and over again. Eat lemons. Smell lemon-scented anything. Wear or carry citrine.

Heart Chakra

This area, which is in the center of the chest, rules love, compassion, relationships and community sharing. Both green and pink are used to harmonize it.

Symptoms of heart chakra imbalance: Are you looking for love? Are you having trouble loving yourself? Have you experienced heartbreak? Do you feel separated from your community? Do you need to activate more compassion and kindness in your life?

Chakra solution: Hearts everywhere! Wear heart-shaped jewelry, especially if it comes in rose quartz, emerald, or green turquoise. Sleep with rose quartz next to your bed. Wear a pink nightgown and sleep between pink sheets. Put green plants throughout your home. Roses of any kind or color, but especially pink, activate this chakra. Eat lots of greens! Eat any kind of green food.

Throat Chakra

This is located in the throat area and its color is brilliant blue. It is associated with communication, sound, and self-expression.

Symptoms of throat chakra imbalance: Are you having trouble expressing yourself? Do you mean to say one thing and another just jumps out of your mouth? Are there things that you have been meaning to communicate to others but have been afraid to?

Chakra solution: Place a blue scarf around your throat. Wear a choker set with blue stones such as lapis lazuli. Wear blue colors, especially a clear deep rich blue such as cobalt. Eat blueberries. Lie on your back outside on a clear day and imagine that you are breathing in the beautiful blue sky.

Third-Eye Chakra

This is located in the area between and slightly above your eyes. It rules intuition, insight, and clairvoyance. Its color is indigo.

Symptoms of third-eye chakra imbalance: Has your intuition been off lately? Would you like to be more clairvoyant than you are right now? Are you having trouble being at the right place at the right time? Are you feeling fidgety rather than peaceful and serene?

Chakra solution: Be the lady who wears purple. Eat grapes, plums, and eggplant. Meditate upon your third eye. Imagine your breath entering and leaving your body through a small portal on your forehead. Wear or carry amethyst.

Crown Chakra

In Sanskrit this chakra is called the thousand-petal lotus; it is associated with higher thought, spiritual knowledge, enlightenment, and bliss. Its colors are violet and white.

Symptoms of crown chakra imbalance: Is your spiritual connection closed off? Do you yearn for higher thoughts, yet find yourself mired in earthly concerns?

Chakra solution: Light a candle and focus on the part of the flame that is closest to the wick, where you can see a violet light. Meditate on this light and then imagine that it is filling and consuming your entire body. Wear pearls, opals, clear quartz or moonstones. Listen to Schubert's *Ave Maria*.

*

Your body is your temple. As you love, honor and cherish your body, it will become your friend and confidante. The more love you lavish on your body, the more you will love yourself. And the more you love yourself, the more you can love the world.

Secrets of Feminine Radiance

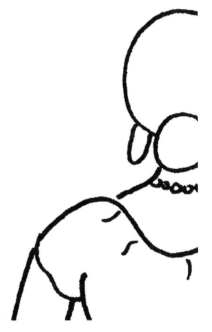

Aix-en-Provence, France: I got up early to go to the open-air market. Even as the sun peeked through the canopy of trees overhead, the market was filling. As I perused the goat cheese, out of the corner of my eye, at the adjacent vegetable stall, a full-bodied woman captured my attention. She was holding a fig in her hands as if to gauge the weight of it. She held it to her nose and inhaled. It seemed as though the scent of the fig filled her so thoroughly that she disappeared into it. Holding the fig in one hand, as if it were a precious jewel, she handed the stall holder the payment with the other. Their eyes met for a moment. The faintest and most intimate of smiles was shared, and she then turned to visit other stalls. I watched as she walked through the open corridor of vegetable stalls. She moved in a sensuous, ripe-mango way that reminded me of a languid cat. This remarkable woman radiated a perfumed aura of deep contentment and joy. At every stall she paused, as if to breathe in the aroma, texture, and color of the moment. She gave her full attention to every stall holder, whether young or old, male or female. Every person with whom she came in contact seemed to glow in her presence.

Following her movements, I became aware of things that I wouldn't normally have perceived. *I began to see in a different way.* I noticed how the water droplets on the lettuce shimmered in the morning sun. I was conscious of the subtlest combination of scents in the marketplace, such as the aroma of espresso from a small café, combined with the smell of oregano and cumin from the spice stall. I could feel the textures of the world around me much more intimately—the coldness of the cobblestones beneath my feet, for instance, of which I had been oblivious.

All my senses were heightened in her wake. She left a residual energy field that allowed others to experience the world through her eyes. With every breath, she seemed to plunge herself into life as if it was her last day on earth and she was savoring every moment of it. In a short time, this mysterious woman opened a door for me into a dimension of life that was rich and profound: the secret realm of the senses.

Becoming a Sensuous Woman

Your senses are your doors and windows to the world. They are your way of experiencing the life around you. The more conscious you are of your senses, the more sensuous you become. When you look at the truly confident and glowing women around you, most likely they are acutely attuned to their senses. I do not mean in a superficial, hedonistic way, but in a serious, fine-tuned way that allows them to sense all sorts of feelings, facts, and awareness that others may miss.

Our senses are complex receiving stations for all life around us, and the more sensitively we attune to them, the more attuned to our environment we become. The sensuous woman deeply experiences and projects a total awareness of all of her senses. She responds and appreciates the sounds, sights, tastes, aromas, and textures of her environment.

Most people equate sensuality with sexuality; and indeed, it is the woman who is in touch with her senses who can experience most fully her sexuality. The more you can experience another person through your senses, the more total is your union with that being. However, as you expand your senses, not only your sexuality but all areas of your life will be enhanced.

Our senses are gateways to the world, but cultural and religious denial of our senses has created an uncertain attitude toward cultivating them. Many people in today's world are cut off from their senses, and therefore distanced from experiencing their life as fully as they can. As babies, we are sensuous creatures. When our mother touched our toes, our entire body responded in rapture. Our entire body—not just our toes—experienced that sense of touch. But as we entered society and school, we began learning *about* our body, instead of learning *with* our body. We've thus become distant from our ability to fully sense our multidimensional, mysterious, and abundant world.

Separation from our senses restricts us and keeps us from being radiant women. It restrains our freedom of choice, distorting how we both perceive and conceive the world. In addition, it keeps us from experiencing the present moment, with all the joy and wonder that is available in it. There is a deep peace that comes when you perceive your world fully and completely. It is a peace that comes from being present and not thinking about the past or worrying about the future; just experiencing the sights, the sounds, the smells, the tastes and the feeling of each moment. At any given moment, we are saturated in an ocean of sensory experiences.

Lying on a Soft, Green Grassy Hill

Take the time to become deeply relaxed, and then imagine that you are lying on a soft, green grassy hill on a warm, early summer afternoon, staring up at the clouds. *Feel* the warmth of the ground beneath you and be aware of the different areas of your body that touch the earth. Feel the slight breeze as it lightly dances across your body. *Smell* the warm summer air. It smells a little of the earth and of fresh-mown grass. *Listen* to the drone of insects . . . and the faraway sound of birdsong as it wafts through the air. *Taste* the fresh sweetness of a blade of grass. *Look* at the clouds as they billow and change into endless fantasies, silhouetted against an azure sky. As you recline, in your imagination, on the grassy hill, let all your sensory perceptions penetrate and fill you. Feel calm, serene, at peace . . . and totally in touch with the universe.

Canoeing by Moonlight

Relax, close your eyes, and imagine that you are in a canoe in the middle of a lake, under a full moon.

Feel the slight chill in the air. *Smell* the damp, pungent odor of the lake. *Listen* to the rhythmic cadence of the paddle as it glides through the water. *Taste* the moistness of mist as it gently rises from the surface of the lake. *Look* at the dancing, softly muted reflection of the moon on the lake . . . and the dramatic outline of the trees against the far shore. Take a minute to be completely and totally aware of the richness of sensory experiences on this full-moon boat ride. Make it as real in your imagination as you can. See if you can be aware of all of your senses at once, rather than isolating one at a time.

Visualizations like those suggested here can help you to perceive the world through your senses more deeply. Scenes from your own past that are pleasurable memories are also good for sensory visualizations. Remembered pleasures prime your spirit. You may find after doing these exercises that your sense-awareness will have a keener edge, and your capacity for pleasure will deepen.

The Sensuous Experience of "Right Now"

This sensuality exercise is one you can do anywhere and at any time. It will expand your ability to experience fully, and respond appropriately, to your inner and outer environment.

Take a breath and allow your senses to open. What are you seeing right now? What do you hear? Listen to the sounds close to you, including those inside your body, then expand your awareness to hear the sounds in the distance. What can you smell right now? Allow your sense of smell to expand. Notice the subtle scents in your environment. Are you aware of any particular tastes? What is your body feeling right now, externally and internally? Feel the temperature of the air against your skin. Be aware of the surface of your skin, and how your clothes feel against it. Now be aware of all your senses at once ... experience the sights, sounds, smells, tastes, and feelings that are within you and around you. Allow your sense perceptions to expand outward farther and farther, until you can imagine the rarefied air of distant mountains and the chill of deep seas. As your sense perceptions expand, so do your sensuality, your femininity, and your connection to all of life.

To Become More Sensuous . . . Slow Down!

To delve into the secrets and mysteries of a sensuous woman, you must slow down. This is not always easy in a world that requires us to constantly strive and hurry. In the forties and fifties manufacturers announced many time-saving devices for women such as the automatic dishwasher and the washing machine. There was even chauvinistic concern about what women were going to do with so much time on their hands. Now, in an era when we have thousands of time-saving machines, we have less time than ever. We are hurrying faster than ever before.

Each day, take time to slow down, even if it is only for a few minutes. Breathe slowly. Move slowly. Eat slowly. Ancient mystics knew that when you go slow you can enter into other dimensions. This is one of the many purposes of meditation: it allows you to go slow enough to transport yourself into different realms. One such place is the realm of the senses. When you enter this sacred space, a deep sensuality can begin to germinate within you.

There are a multitude of dimensions that coexist within our normal reality. The dimension that we call "reality" is a creation of the collective unconscious that is formed by agreement. An example of this can be found in the field of art. For example, the reason why one painting is considered great and another is considered poor, is because people agree that one painting is good art and another is bad art.

If you go fast, you are a part of the ordinary reality shared by most people. However, when you slow down and begin to *look* slower and *hear* slower, you will notice an expansion of your ability to experience the physical (and nonphysical) worlds through your senses. In other words, you become more sensual. Georgia O'Keeffe is an example of an artist who knew how to slow down and delve into the mysteries and sensuality of flowers.

It may sound strange, but the most sensuous that I ever felt was during the two years that I lived in a Zen Buddhist monastery. I would sit in a lotus position, sometimes meditating for sixteen hours a day. We were instructed to face a wall when we meditated, so as not to be distracted. We were also told to keep our eyes open, so we wouldn't be distracted by mental images. Hour after hour, I would stare at the wall. This sounds like torture (and sometimes it was), but most of the time it was truly amazing.

When you slow down and are silent, remarkable things occur. For example, once as I was meditating, I watched the shadow of a plant move slowly across the wall in front of me. I felt deep rapture as I became conscious of the sonorous rhythms and movements of the universe, reflected in the journey of the leaf's shadow. My whole body quietly vibrated with sensuous ecstasy. As I entered into a sacred solitude, the barrier between me and the world, created by my frenetic mental activity, dissolved. I then could experience the joyous sensations of the physical world through my senses.

We are usually so busy that we don't experience the pulsating, changing rhythm of life all around us. It is very difficult to become sensuous when you are going fast and spinning ahead of yourself. Taking time for yourself to be still will allow you to indulge your senses. Slow down and merge yourself into every aspect of your inner and outer environment. Create moments of sacred solitude where you can rest, relax, renew, and plunge into your senses: you will expand your ability to become a truly fulfilled woman.

Pleasuring Your Senses

After you begin to fully experience the beauty of the world around you, the next step is to pleasure your senses. Just as a plant that receives a perfect amount of sun, water, and nutrients will flourish, you soul will thrive when your senses are fed. Feed your sense of sight by looking at beauty. Look at the way a vine hugs your old garden wall, the way the steam from your tea forms swirling mists on a cold morning, see beauty out of the window as you sit at your desk by looking up at the clouds as they twist and turn. As you see beauty, so you become beauty.

Pleasure your sense of hearing with melodic sounds: your lover breathing softly beside you; your favorite jazz CD; the children's laughter as they play across the street. There are always beautiful sounds around us, we just need to be still to hear them.

I love pleasuring my sense of taste. I love the sublime flavors, colors, and textures of great food. It gives me enormous joy. Curiously, when I am pleasuring my sense of taste, I don't overeat. It's when I'm under stress, and not really tasting and smelling my food, that I do eat too much.

Pleasure your sense of touch with wonderful fabrics. I have some fabulous linen towels that I got in Finland. Every time I use them, I luxuriate in the delight of their rough texture. Sleep between smooth, cool cotton sheets; rest against velvet throw pillows. Go out into nature and place both hands on the bark of an old oak tree; hold a smooth stone in your hand, turn it over, and stroke its contours. Sensuously brush your hair or indulge in self-massage, or have a lover or a professional masseur touch your body.

I revel in my sense of smell. Next to my bed, in my bathroom and on my desk I have bottles of essential oils that I occasionally inhale. The aroma is intoxicating. And before going to bed, I spray my sheets with a natural scent of lavender or frankincense. Drinking in the smell of sun-dried laundry fresh off the line, a freshly peeled orange, the air just before a storm, or rose-scented candles, are all ways to pleasure your sense of smell.

Radiating Sensual Poise

There is nothing so alluring or so appealing as a woman who enjoys herself and her life through her senses. Sensuality is your connection with this ancient and primordial power of womanhood. It unites you with the living spirit in all things. Here are some things that you can do to deepen your sensuality.

Create a sensuous self-image: You are constantly creating a mental picture of yourself in your subconscious mind. These mental images influence the way you look, feel, and act. They create your self-identity. These images are a result of the beliefs you have about yourself. To radiate sensual poise, and to experience pleasure in all aspects of your life, it's valuable to impress a picture on your creative subconscious mind of yourself feeling and being absolutely sensuous. As you do this, you'll find that you feel more and more sensuous. Imagine a womanly energy filling your entire body, then visualize yourself doing something sensuous, such as eating a ripe peach or floating in a tropical ocean lagoon.

Move your body in a way that makes you feel sensuous: The way you walk says a lot about you. It can say that you are rushed, depressed, frantic, or tired. It can also say that you are a luscious woman who is radiating majesty and strength. As an exercise, try walking *as if* you were completely sensuous. Move in a way that communicates a voluptuous energy, and you will begin to feel juicy and ripe.

Use your clothing and adornments to feel sensual: Your clothing and accessories can also contribute to (or detract from) your feeling sensuous. Wear things that make you savor all your senses. These will be different for each woman. For one it might be a softly flowing silk skirt with an angora sweater, for another it might be a wraparound dress that clings seductively to her breasts. For another, it might be a rainbow-colored scarf that excites her senses.

Becoming a Woman of Mystery and Allure

There are times in life when I want to be a wholesome, natural woman, and there are times when I desire to be alluring and mysterious. During those times, I want to glow with a Mona Lisa smile, as though I have a delicious secret. There is great value in exploring all aspects of yourself, and it can be especially delightful to explore the part of you that is alluring and enigmatic.

Every woman has inner mysteries. You radiate mystique when you become a sacred vessel for your inner mysteries to glimmer through. This is not something that you do; it is an awareness that you can cultivate within yourself. Here are some ways to activate the alluring and mysterious woman within you.

See the world through your sacred sanctuary: There is a sacred sanctuary within you where you can connect to your feminine and Goddess forces. It is a place in your imagination where you are so deeply grounded and connected to the original source that nothing can uproot you. It is where you can claim the mystery of your erotic and sensuous nature. It might appear as an inner garden filled with statues of ancient Goddesses, or it might be a pillared temple where priestesses in diaphanous robes waft from one space to another. No matter where you are, you can visualize your inner sanctuary and even imagine yourself within it. You can do this waiting for a bus, standing in line at the bank, and sitting at your desk. Wrap your inner divine place around you and it will envelop you in a mysterious aura of serenity.

Leave your lingerie at home: Not wearing underwear doesn't work as well if you are wearing trousers, but it is glorious if you have a skirt or dress on and you can feel air circulate between your legs. You have a secret that no one knows. Imagine the energy of your womb radiating into the center of the earth and back up into your body, creating a holy channel between the earth and your body. This works even if you have to wear a conservative business suit: no one but you will know that beneath the conventional surface is a full-on delectable woman, who is charging her inner batteries from the energy of the earth.

Create your personalized perfume with your own feminine juices: This is a technique that goes back to ancient times. Take a small amount of the feminine juices from your vagina and mix it with your perfume or some essential oil and dab it behind your ears and between your breasts. There is a life-force potency in these fluids, and even though no one can consciously smell them, a subtle aroma will surround you with an enthralling womanly energy.

Taking Pleasure in Every Moment

We live in the wine country of the Central Coast of California. Our land is surrounded by vineyard-covered rolling hills. In the distance, the Pacific Ocean mists can be seen tumbling over the Santa Lucia Mountains. One sultry summer evening, I walked up our dusty road to the grassy hill that forms the highest point of our land. As I stood knee-high in wild oats, I absent-mindedly watched the clouds flit and dance over the distant mountain tops. Delicate, moist, and almost pink, the taste of the clouds seemed to swirl through my being. The sunset in the west and a full amber moon rose majestically in the east. My arms reached out to embrace her glow. I imagined I felt her surface against my breasts as I hugged her deliciously close to me.

I didn't always believe in enjoying myself. I thought pleasure was something you could have after you had worked hard, or something that had to be deserved. I sometimes thought that pleasure was reserved for wealthy people who had time and money to spare. I didn't realize that pleasure is necessary for life.

I was nineteen when I was struck by the realization that pleasure could be as necessary to one's well-being as air, water, and food. I had been going to Michigan State University and working hard to keep my grades up, hold down a job, and maintain a relationship. I raced from one class to another, then ran to my job, then hurried off to see my boyfriend. At that time in my life, I believed that my worth was dependent upon how hard I worked and how much I achieved.

In a short period of time, the pressures of my life intensified, and I fell apart. I was sexually propositioned by a professor I respected; I lost my job as a reporter for the campus newspaper because I'd written about the shoddy construction of an apartment complex (the corporation that owned the complex threatened to withdraw advertising if I wasn't fired). The worst thing that happened, however, was finding out that my boyfriend and my best friend were having an affair. I felt devastated, betrayed, and deceived, and I foolishly took an overdose of sleeping pills that landed me in the hospital overnight.

After I got out of the hospital, a friend said, "Denise, you need to get out of Michigan. Drop out of school and get out of here. This is a negative environment for you." She packed my bags and put me on a plane to visit my sister in Hawaii. I arrived in Honolulu shell-shocked.

My sister took me for walks on the beach and into the tropical rainforests where we swam in waterfall-fed pools. I felt guilty about doing these things. I felt that I didn't deserve to enjoy myself because I wasn't working or being productive. I hadn't earned it. My entire sense of self-esteem rested on my productivity. I felt that if I wasn't working I didn't deserve joy or fun. As weeks passed, I slowly began to realize that my value as a human being wasn't entirely dependent upon what I did. I was valuable just being who I was.

I gradually developed the ability to sit and enjoy life without having to *do* anything. I didn't have to earn it. I learned that watching the ocean waves ebbing and flowing was a valuable activity. I learned to dance outside while warm, tropical rain cascaded over my body, and even to laugh with abandon. A whole new way of being in the world began to open up for me.

My journey into pleasure, however, wasn't always easy. One day I got a phone call telling me that my grandmother had died. After I got off the phone, a friend offered me a slice of homemade bread. I'll never forget the taste and smell of it. It was warm, rich, and chewy, and the aroma was comforting. I enjoyed it so much. Suddenly, I stopped chewing. A wave of guilt washed over me, and the bread turned to sand in my mouth. I was filled with shame. I felt guilty for enjoying myself when my grandmother had just died.

Feeling terrible, I walked outside and collapsed on the grassy lawn. A small daisy got my attention. A slight breeze caused its petals to shimmer slightly as they caught the light of the sun. It was beautiful. On the ground next to it lay some scattered, wilted daisies that had been run over by a lawnmower. I looked back at the single daisy, so vigorous and shining. It wasn't hesitant to be beautiful, even though its neighbors had been cut down. It didn't hang its head in shame. It was beautiful *because that was its nature.*

In that moment I realized that denying myself pleasure didn't help anyone. I recognized that it was okay and even beneficial to experience joy whenever possible, *because that is our nature.* Just as young children can be filled with joy and delight because that is their nature, as grown women it is still our innate nature to be happy. We don't have to *earn* our pleasure.

If I feel unhappy and miserable, it doesn't improve anyone else's physical condition, put food on their table, bring my grandmother back, or change her suffering. It is especially vital, even in the worst of circumstances, to feel pleasure, because pleasure is contagious. It creates an energy that spreads in all directions like the ripples created by a single stone dropped in a still pool. If I can find even the smallest bit of joy in the most terrible, dark times, it may make a difference to others.

I now believe that pleasure is a necessity, not a luxury. Not only does it help heal and balance you, but it helps others around you. Your spirit needs pleasure just as you need food, water, and air. When you are enjoying yourself, your immune system is strengthened, your spirit is renewed, your creativity soars, and your life force expands. When this happens, your relationships flourish, your career advances, and you are able to be even more productive. (This last benefit is mentioned for people like me who sometimes equate productivity with value.)

Is your metaphorical "glass of water" half full or half empty? Pleasure is a point of view. You *can* make lemonade from lemons! Some people feel that everything has to be perfect to be pleasurable; a sunset view has to be unobstructed, wine has to be served in crystal, and a home has to be completely neat and tidy if anyone is to be invited in.

The problem with this point of view is that it limits the amount of pleasure that you can experience. Life is messy, not perfect. Sometimes there is a telephone pole in front of the sunset, wine comes in paper cups, and people arrive at your door when your house is in disarray. When this happens, you can either complain, be disappointed or resentful . . . or you can have a great time. It all depends on your point of view. *Being perfect is the death of pleasure.*

I know about trying to have everything perfect, because I'm a recovering perfectionist. (I have periodic relapses—old patterns die hard.) The problem with being a perfectionist is that it offers very narrow opportunities for enjoying yourself. When you let go of being perfect—and embrace the idea that no matter what is going on you can enjoy yourself—your life sings with enjoyment. Imagine how much joy you could sow into the world with this attitude. I'm always impressed with the Dalai Lama, who carries the weight of the suffering of his people on his shoulders, yet always seems to be enjoying himself.

When I lived in the Zen monastery, we were told teaching stories. Here is one of the stories that I love:

> A monk was chased to the edge of a very steep cliff by a hungry and ferocious tiger. He quickly glanced down the cliff . . . it was a hundred feet down to the canyon floor but there was a lone sapling growing out of the side of the cliff. He scrambled over the edge and hung on to the tree. The tiger hung his head over the cliff, roaring fiercely at his prey. Slowly the roots of the sapling began to be pulled out of the earth. The monk looked at the canyon below and the tiger above and sighed. Then, seeing a small, white flower that was growing through a crack in the cliff wall, he smiled and said, "Ah, what beauty!"

There will be times in your life when you will be confronted with a difficult situation that you can't change, no matter how hard you try. However, you can always change your point of view. In any given situation you have a choice. You can focus on what is beautiful and wonderful or you can concentrate on what is terrible and disturbing. You always have the choice to center on pleasure. To change the quality of your life, change your focus.

As a suggestion, when you are in a troubling predicament, ask yourself "What is good about this situation?" over and over again, until you discover what is good or valuable about the situation. Your subconscious mind is like a computer: it can only respond to the questions it is asked. If you ask the right question, sooner or later your mind will come up with a great answer. If you ask a self-defeating question like, "Why am I always in these situations?" or "What's wrong with me?" your subconscious will come up with a self-defeating answer like, "You're in this condition because you have no self-confidence." Answers like this do not empower you, nor do they propel you toward pleasure.

What about really tragic times? Is it possible to experience pleasure then?
Absolutely! It can be especially healing during difficult times. My father
had just died and my family had gathered for a memorial service at his
home. The house was filled with large formal arrangements of funeral
flowers. Everyone was sad and solemn. Then, spontaneously, my sister
took all the flower arrangements and layered them against a wall, making
a huge stage backdrop. A madcap idea seemed to grab our souls at the
same time. We all raced though the house, yanking sheets off beds and
wrapping them around ourselves, creating makeshift costumes. Standing
in front of our newly created flower "stage," we began to do impromptu
skits. Everyone roared with laughter. My father's wife, who was deeply
bereft, laughed so hard that tears rolled down her face. It was an incredible family event that we have relived again and again. I feel that my
father's spirit was comforted to see his family experiencing such joy.

The potential for pleasure is always around you even in difficult times.
Step forward into it. The possibility for pleasure is here, even when you are
feeling tired, stuck, or angry. Have you ever tried allowing yourself to feel
the joy of all your emotions . . . not just the ones that you label positive?
Pretend you're an actress, and revel in a juicy role. Let your character
experience a whole range of emotions. Cherish them, even when you are
in the midst of a drama. Take the time to stop for a minute or two and step
out of the drama in order to savor and experience the full range of your
feelings. Such a pause can be completely divine. Then you can jump right
back into the drama, if you want. Why not enjoy every aspect of your life,
instead of just a rare few moments?

The Spiritual Practice of Pleasure

Almost every spiritual tradition has practices that facilitate growth, such as
meditation, yoga, chanting, or praying. However, of all the spiritual practices in which I have participated, the most powerful for me is the practice
of experiencing pleasure.

Many of us have been raised with the belief that in order to grow as a
person, we need to suffer. When I was growing up, my grandmother used
to say to me, "Denise, suffering builds character." I believed her, and it did
make the suffering that I experienced in my childhood more tolerable
when I thought that it was building my character. I also know that many
times great individuals have risen up out of the ashes of their suffering,
overcoming great odds, to become remarkable human beings.

Often growth comes from overcoming suffering; however, it doesn't
have to be this way. *You don't need to suffer to grow.* Pain can encourage

spurts of growth, but you can grow even more amidst joy. My greatest spiritual transformations have come through ecstasy, love, and pleasure. When I allow myself to feel washed with waves of sweet pleasure and happiness, it's easier to become my glorious self.

To use pleasure as a spiritual practice, take ten minutes in the morning to experience as much pleasure as you can. Sit in a meditative pose, take a walk, or luxuriate in the bath: really enjoy the simple moments in life. So often when we are walking or bathing, we are thinking about something else. Surrender to the experience. Allow it to lap over you like great cosmic licks of love. It's important to remember that true pleasure is different from addiction. Addictive behavior usually entails overindulgence to numb pain and to separate yourself from your experience, whereas this spiritual practice allows you be aware of what you are experiencing.

I had driven four hours in heat and traffic to get to San Francisco to give a talk. I was tired, hungry, and cranky. They told me there was a parking lot, but when I got there, there wasn't, and I drove around for twenty-five minutes trying to find a place to park. I was mad because this meant I was going to be late. I hate traffic, I hated being in the noisy, crowded city. I didn't want to go into my lecture grumpy, so I had a talk with myself.

"Denise, what if this was your only opportunity to make a difference in the world? What if this was the only talk you would ever give in your lifetime? What if something magical and wonderful was to be started this night? What if your words tonight would forever change the life of someone in the audience? So, Denise, if any of this was true, wouldn't you enjoy yourself immensely this evening? Wouldn't you be totally exhilarated to be here?"

"Yes!" I answered. I could feel a sense of wonderment and joy spreading through my body as I strolled into the hall to the several hundred people. Instead of being tired and crabby during my talk, I really enjoyed myself. At the end, I got a standing ovation. Afterwards, the manager came up to me with tears in his eyes, and said, "I have been working here for over ten years. We have an event here almost every night and there has never been a talk that matched yours. Thank you!" Taking a few minutes in my car to talk myself into pleasure made a difference to me and to many others.

In every moment there is a way that you can experience extreme pleasure. Right now, as you read this book, where is your pleasure? Is it in the weight of the book in your hand? Is it in the textures and colors that surround you or the music that plays in the distance or in the fact that you have eyes to see with and ears to hear with? Find ten ways that you can feel pleasure right now. Pleasure can be elusive. Sometimes you have to look for it and grab it to your breast. What could you do right now that would be totally pleasurable? Could you make a face at yourself in the mirror? Stretch out tall as if you could touch the ceiling? Could you laugh out loud hysterically as if you heard the funniest joke? Could you turn on music and dance wildly for one minute? Or maybe remember the best erotic experience you ever had? Or take a one-minute catnap? There are thousands of ways you can capture pleasure and create an outrageous experience in this moment. Go ahead. What's keeping you? Grab it.

The more pleasure you have, the more will come into your life. And the more you share, the more comes back to you.

Pleasure Exercise

- What gives you the greatest pleasure now?
- What gave you the greatest pleasure as a child? (This is often a helpful clue to things that would give you pleasure now.)
- What helps you enter into a state of pleasure?
- What pleasure do you bring into the world?

Creating a "Joy Journal"

One of the most meaningful activities in my life is my Joy Journal. I used to write a journal every day, but whenever I reviewed it, I would usually throw it away. It was just a reminder of all the rotten experiences in my life. I decided there needed to be a better way to keep a journal. So, I conceived the idea of a Joy Journal. This is a journal where every day I write down all the wonderful, special things that occurred that day and then I illustrate or decorate the page. It's really fun!

I have decorative stamps, so I can put hearts and stars all over the pages. I also use watercolors, colored pencils, felt pens, crayons, stickers, clippings, recycled cards, and photographs (you can also take a Polaroid photograph each day and stick it into your Joy Journal)—a whole basket of cool stuff. Making an illustration of your entry deepens the experience of that day. Rather than just written words, the end result is that when I review my life by scanning through my Joy Journal *I am creating a positive and wonderful past* for myself. Instead of thinking what a miserable past I had, I am anchoring and remembering all the great things that have happened in my life and the all the things for which I am infinitely grateful. (You don't have to do your journal every day. Don't feel guilty for not doing it every day . . . just praise yourself whenever you do it.)

Here is an entry:

Sunday, May 6: David and I went to the store to buy Adirondack lawn chairs. The people at the store were great and helped us load the chairs into the truck. We drove to the top of our hill and placed the chairs facing west to watch the sunset. We drank ice-cold beer and ate corn chips. Ah! So beautiful. Golden light everywhere on tall grasses and distant hills.

I drew a picture of the lawn chairs on top of the hill with a big smiling sun setting on the mountains to the east. Every time I see this picture, the memory fills me. (See Chapter 13, "Boundless Creativity," for additional information on keeping a journal.)

The PQ Test: Measure Your Pleasure

Another thing I designed for myself is a personal PQ (pleasure quotient) test. At the end of each day I review my day. I write down the ten major activities of the day and assign a number to each activity from 1 to 100. A "1" means it was the most miserable, horrific, rotten experience imaginable; "100" means that it was awesome, outstanding, and absolutely amazing. I add up all the scores and divide by 10 to see what my PQ is for the day. Sometimes I even graph these on graph paper to track how well I'm doing at increasing my pleasure.

Here's an example from Joan, a woman who attended one of my seminars:

1. Shower with lemon grass soap and cold, refreshing rinse	35
2. Breakfast: toast and coffee on deck in sun	87
3. Phone call with Sara, put legs up and opened window	63
4. Meeting at work with sales team. Balloon Motivation Game	92
5. Working lunch at MacBeth's. Great waiter	89
6. Picked up dry-cleaning—two pieces missing	12
7. Jennifer's after-school soccer game. She kicked butt!	100
8. Macaroni and Cheese dinner and mashed potatoes (ugh—fattening!)	5
9. Answering e-mails	8
10. Read bedtime story to kids	87
Total PQ for the day	51.8%

Be honest with yourself. Don't rate something 90 if it was really a 10 just to get a high PQ.

If you notice that your PQ is consistently low, you need to devise ways to increase your joy in the activities of your day. For example, if your morning drive to work usually rates about 10, maybe playing classical music (instead of the radio news) could jack the score up to 25. Perhaps spraying the interior of your car with an essential oil mixture so it smells wonderful could take it up to 50. Leaving a few minutes earlier to take a more scenic route might take it to 70. Whenever you find a low pleasure quotient for any regular activity in your life, say to yourself, "What can I do to make this an even more enjoyable experience?" and then use your creativity to find ways to increase your pleasure in that activity. May you have a once-in-a-lifetime experience more than once in your lifetime!

Feminine Radiance

Radiance: you've experienced it, or at least observed it. The first time most women experience radiance is when they fall in love, especially when their love is innocent and pure. There is a kind of surrendering that occurs when a young woman surrenders to another being and enters a transcendent state. Later in life, radiance can come from lovemaking or a rite of passage such as marriage, from pregnancy and childbirth, from overcoming physical limitations, or from achieving a lifelong goal. It can also come from a deep cherishing of the sacred self, the blessing of a guru, or from meditation.

Although you can recognize radiance when you see it or experience it, what exactly is it and how can you have more of it in your life? Although there seem to be different kinds of feminine radiance, their source is the same place . . . a kind of surrendering. This is not yielding to an outside force, rather it is a sweet, tender acceptance of your inner spirit: a surrender to your sacred self. There is a deep inner glow that comes when you loosen your attachment to your identity and your ego and enter into an expansive, eternal place beyond ordinary reality. Therein dwells the light that is your spiritual heritage and the source of your radiance.

Feminine radiance occurs when you lose yourself in the moment, allowing yourself to be reabsorbed in the outer universe at the same time as you dissolve into your inner universe. It is an exquisite 'now-ness' where you are suffused into a divine love: love of self, love of others and love of the Creator.

The core of feminine energy is love. When you come from this essence, you become absolutely radiant. Some women are born with physical attractiveness, yet there is nothing so beautiful as a woman who has a divine inner glow. Eventually, physical beauty fades, but radiance deepens with age. A radiant woman shines: not only do her eyes shine but her heart shines. She gives and receives love powerfully, passionately and tenderly. Regardless of her age, the physical condition of her body, or the style of her clothing, there is a perceptible light that seems to flow from the radiant woman, touching all with whom she comes in contact. She is a gracious sacred vessel for the love and light of the universe to flow through.

When you activate and embrace your radiance you become a blessing. Your presence in the world becomes a blessing. You bless others in ways that you may never be aware of, just by being who you are. In your essence, you are light and love. When you open your heart and surrender, bliss and joy shine from every pore in your being.

Uncovering Your Radiance

Basically, radiance is a state of being rather than something you do, but there are some practices that can help to uncover your natural glow.

1. **Being present**: The mind is like a butterfly that flits from one flower to the next. Seldom do we find ourselves nestled in the exquisite and eternal ocean of here and now. When you are, you can connect with your true self that is beyond the chattering of your mind. When you take the effort to focus your drifting consciousness to become fully awake to the present moment, you will discover the glorious light that dwells within you.

2. **Sweet surrender**: To some people the word "surrender" has negative connotations. They equate surrendering with resignation, defeat, or failing to fulfill your potential. True spiritual surrender does not mean that you are passive. It doesn't mean that you have to put up with negativity or that you can't take positive action to make changes in your life. Sweet surrender is the inner wisdom to accept unconditionally the circumstances of your life in the understanding that there is a reason for everything (even if you do not know what that reason is). Surrender is an act of power and an act of faith that means relinquishing negative judgments about your life. It allows you to move out of reaction, opposition, and resistance, and to observe your circumstances from a neutral place. There is a place inside you that is divine and holy. When you release struggle and strife, and surrender to that sacred space, radiance fills you.

3. **Self-acceptance**: Who you are is enough. What you are is enough. There isn't something that you have to achieve to be enough. You already are. You are enough right here and right now, no matter what

form your life takes. This doesn't mean that you won't continue to grow. You are always growing because that is the nature of life: everything is always changing and growing, and in this moment you are enough just as you are. No matter what judgments you have made about yourself, you *are* absolutely remarkable. Your judgments about yourself are not who you are: they are only a small grain of sand on the shore of the infinite, ever-present spirit that dwells within you.

4. **Allowing love to flow through you**: There is a vast wellspring of love within you. It is never-ending and will last for ever. Sometimes we believe that there is a limit to love, so we only mete it out a bit at a time. Sometimes we put conditions on it. We say, "That person deserves a little bit of my love and that person deserves a lot." The universe is filled with love, but we measure the amount and kind of love we give as if it was scarce and had to be conserved. There is no limit to love. The more you give, the more you have: this is a universal law.

The truth is that you are not separate from the world around you, and the only person or thing that you ever really love is your greater self, in other forms. Love deeply and fully; instead of being the giver or receiver of love, *become* love itself. Say over and over, "I love *who* I am; I love *what* I am; I love what I'm doing; I am love," until the truth of it bores its way into your deep subconscious mind. Radiance will then fill your life.

In today's world, we eat but don't taste, look but don't see, listen but don't hear. You are here on the planet to be happy. It is all that is required of you. And when you are happy, you become a healing force that powerfully and magnificently heals the planet. If you want to help the world, be happy. Pleasure your senses. Be juicy, sensual, and glorious. Taste, touch, smell, hear, and explore your universe. Accept yourself exactly as you are and radiance will flow through you to the world.

SACRED SEXUALITY

I WAS a sexual late bloomer. Actually, I probably would have bloomed early, but the repressive atmosphere of the Midwest in the early sixties meant that "good girls" didn't have sex. The emotional scars of some of my childhood experiences probably also contributed to my reticence about exploring my sexuality. However, I wasn't completely inexperienced; in high school I'd had a few kisses, which for the most part were unsatisfactory. My first kiss occurred when I was sixteen. I frantically wiped my mouth and exclaimed, in a less-than-lady like manner, "Ugh. It's like kissing a wet fish!" I didn't realize that kisses were "wet." Somehow I thought they would be dry, like grandma kisses.

High school was a strange environment with mixed messages for a girl exploring herself as a sexual being. You were judged to be "cold" if you didn't "put out," but if you did "put out" then you were called "a slut." I decided being "cold" sounded better.

When I graduated from high school, I moved from a small farming town in Ohio to a large urban area in Michigan, where I went to college. The flower-child, make-love-not-war movement was starting to take root. It seemed like everyone was wearing bell bottoms, making love, getting stoned, and protesting the Vietnam War. The feminist movement was growing. Women were supposed to throw off the shackles of male oppression and take charge of their lives, unfettered by domination of the opposite sex. It was so exciting, and amidst all the so-called free love, I felt like an old maid because I was still a virgin at the age of nineteen. It seemed like everyone but me was having sex. One morning I decided to take action. I woke up with the determination that I wouldn't stay a virgin one more day.

I grabbed my books and rushed off to my first class, which had about 200 students in it. My resolve to lose my virginity was uppermost in my mind as I looked around the class to pick out a likely candidate. One good-looking young man seemed to tower over the others as he put his books on his desk. *He's the one!* I thought. After class I sauntered over to him and managed to get asked out for a date that night.

I was really nervous while I waited for him to pick me up. The other girls in my dormitory, who had previously been appalled at my lack of sexual experience, waited excitedly with me. He picked me up and my friends waved me off with surreptitious winks. We drove to a local drive-in cinema. Shortly after the film started, I explained my mission to him. He was at first amazed, then completely elated with my suggestion as we drove back to his apartment. "Really?! I mean really?! You want to lose your virginity, tonight? I mean, really? Oh, wow!"

My resolve wavered for a moment amidst his boyish exuberance, but I convinced myself that I was ready to be "liberated." As we thrashed about in bed, I remember thinking, *This is all there is? What's the big deal? This is completely overrated.* My first foray into sexuality was uninspiring, and it was a number of years before I truly began to understand the power, mystery, and majesty of a woman's sexual energy . . . and to comprehend what I had lost that night.

It is not an accident that candles, flowers, incense, music, and wine, which all connote romantic love in today's world, were also the substance of sacred rites and religious ceremonies in ancient times. I believe that there is a forgotten but powerful cellular memory of sex as being something beautiful, mystical, and sacred. In ancient cultures with mystical traditions, and especially during the time of the Great Goddess, sexuality was considered to be an expression of life. It was natural, wholesome, and sacred. It was a means to experience a transcendental experience of connection to the Creator. It wasn't cloaked in repression, shame, and guilt as it often still is in Western cultures. Lovemaking was viewed as a path to mystical experience. It was a way to become closer to the Divine, and therefore a form of sacrament. It possessed the power to rejuvenate the body, and to bring spiritual illumination and transformation.

The womb (I use the word "womb" to include your vulva, vagina, cervix, and womb) was the sacred vessel for the spirit of the earth. The penis was the pinnacle of the heavens. When heaven and earth came together, they created a power that was holy. The renowned archaeologist, Marija Gimbutas, writes about the "fusion of the phallus with the divine body of the Goddess." In sacred sex, every man is a god and every woman a Goddess. Currently, however, we live in a culture that doesn't teach us that lovemaking can be sacred. Although great progress was made during the sexual revolution of the sixties, even today many women believe that sex is shameful, embarrassing, or guilt-provoking. People are less inhibited and more accepting of sex than before the sixties, yet sexuality isn't considered a hallowed part of life the way it once was. Sex is titillating, exciting, and is being used to sell anything from cars to beer, but it is not sacred. Today's sexual atmosphere contributes to an environment that promotes inhibition and even contributes to sexual abuse. It's difficult to experience ecstatic sex if you carry emotional sexual wounds and negative sexual beliefs.

Healing Sexual Wounds

Emotional wounds caused by negative sexual experiences and traumatic events suffered in childhood can cut deep into the female psyche. Healing is not always easy; some scars never seem to heal. Have you ever been making love and then with a slight look, a small gesture, or a certain touch everything suddenly stops, just as if you've been splashed with cold water? If so, you are not alone. Usually, this happens when a core wound has been subconsciously reactivated. You might not even remember what the incident was, because it lies buried deep in your subconscious, but somehow you know it is there by the reactions of your body.

I used to feel as if I was going to throw up any time my breasts were touched in a particular way. I couldn't remember all the events from my childhood, but nevertheless my body remembered. I would immediately, sometimes violently, wrest my body out of my lover's arms. My journey to releasing the trauma caused by childhood sexual abuse began a number of years ago during a ceremonial sweat lodge. It was powerful, moving, and healing. (A sweat lodge is a sacred Native American tradition in which hot rocks are taken into a small igloo-like structure originally made with branches covered with animal skins, now usually covered with canvas and blankets.)

We sat naked, huddled in the darkness, staring at the glowing red rocks in the center of the sweat lodge. The heat that radiated off the rocks was intense. Prayers for purification were said in a ceremonial manner: "Creator, Great Mystery, purify me. Make me whole." The sweat produced by sitting close to hot rocks is thought to cleanse and purify the spirit as well as the body. A gourd was filled with water and poured on the glowing red rocks. Intense, searing steam surged from them. I couldn't breathe. The blistering steam seemed to cut into my skin, my eyes, and my lungs. Wave after wave of nausea rolled through my body. Suddenly, I saw an image of *him* touching me. I felt the same disgust as I had as a child when I was repeatedly violated. Hidden memories boiled up to the surface of my mind from some darkly shadowed depth inside me.

The memories were gut-wrenching and painful, but I also felt as if something that had festered for a long, long time was finally being lanced. The sweltering sauna-like heat seemed to dislodge old wounds from my soul.

I stepped out of the sweat lodge into a starlit evening feeling dizzy but somehow lighter. I walked "sky-clad" to a grassy hill, lay face down on the earth and prayed, "Grandmother Earth, take away the pain. Make me whole! Help me heal!" Soft, gentle, loving energy seemed to rise up from the earth, and embrace me. I felt cradled by the Earth Mother, and I wept.

I am not completely healed from my childhood sexual abuse; maybe I never will be. There are still painful memories that haunt me, but the ceremonial experience I had in the sweat lodge so many years ago began a powerful process toward wholeness.

A sweat lodge is just one kind of ceremony that can facilitate sexual healing. There are many other ceremonies that can help. However, the most valuable rituals are those that are direct from the heart with a powerful goal of transformation. Even a simple ceremony, in the right spirit, can make a big difference. For example, standing under a waterfall, or even under a cold shower, holding the intention strongly that you are being washed clean can have a powerful effect.

Womb Purification Ritual

In some African and Egyptian cultures, there is a ritual for purifying the womb that is especially powerful for releasing sexual trauma.

Place a fireproof pot or cauldron on a fireproof surface on the floor. On it, place dried herbs such as sage or cedar (which were traditionally used by Native Americans for purification rituals), light them, and then gently blow out the flame so they continue to smoulder and create a thick smoke. (This is called smudging.) Or, take a small charcoal briquette—they are sold in most places that sell incense—light it, and place it in the fireproof pot. Then, place frankincense and myrrh, which are also traditionally used for purification, on the burning coal. This should also create a volume of smoke.

Now, spreading your legs, stand over the pot of smoke and let the smoke cascade over your womb. (The smoke won't actually go inside you.) Visualize the smoke cleansing and purifying any negativity or trauma from that area of your body while offering this prayer:

Goddess, Great Mother, I ask for your assistance and guidance for the purification of my womb. I open my womb for healing. As the sacred smoke washes over my womb, I release energy blockages, past pain, and wounds from this part of my body and call in sweet, pure life force. Today is the rebirth of my womb, and I give thanks for all that is given. May my womb be filled with love.

Complete the ritual by anointing your vulva with a natural oil (olive, almond, or refined sesame oil) scented with a couple of drops of rose or lavender essential oil, as you visualize the entire area filled with light and love.

Women's Circles for Sexual Healing

Joining a support group for any kind of sexual healing can be enormously valuable. Rather than suppressing sexual wounds, this kind of group can help you begin to release them. To heal our wounds, we need to be willing to go deep into the memories that our wombs retain. We need to be able to call up the pain and say, if this is what it takes, then so be it. To find a support group for healing sexual abuse in your area, try calling a support hotline (see Resources). A great place to start is by reading Ellen Bass and Laura Davis's book, *The Courage to Heal: A Guide for Women Survivors of Child Sexual Abuse* and *The Courage to Heal Workbook*. There are also many great support groups and books that can help facilitate healing from an abusive relationship or from rape. It is only after you address and begin to heal sexual wounds that you can truly embrace and celebrate your sexuality.

Your Sexual Mission Statement

Creating a mission statement is an excellent idea for any area of your life that needs clarity and focus. It can be especially valuable for gaining clarity about your sexuality. The first step is to take time to examine your beliefs about sex. The barriers to your sexuality arise from negative experiences you have had in the past, and from the beliefs that you have taken on from your family, culture, and religion. Your sexual morals can be beliefs that you have accepted from others without examining them to see if they are appropriate for you. To create your sexual mission statement ask yourself these questions:

- What do I believe about sexuality?
- Do I believe that sex should only happen within marriage?
- What do I feel about homosexuality and bisexuality?
- Do I believe that sex is natural, or do I feel that it is embarrassing?
- How do I feel about masturbation?

There are no right and wrong answers, just your truth. Notice the emotions and feelings that occur as you examine your beliefs.

When I examined my opinions about sex, I noticed that I had a conscious doctrine that I wanted to believe, but I also had deeper, subconscious beliefs. For example, I consciously asserted that sex was natural, healthy, and wholesome. Yet subconsciously I felt that it was embarrassing and shameful. Problems arise when your conscious and subconscious minds are not in accordance. The soul loves the truth, so when examining your beliefs, look for what you actually believe, rather than what you think you should believe. Here is my current sexual mission statement:

- To know that my past does not determine my sexual future.
- To accept my sexual feelings with love.
- To move toward a deeper understanding of the spiritual aspects of sex.
- To remember that my body deserves to be honored and revered.
- To be willing to open myself to more intimacy.

The Womb: A Place of Power

Goddess-oriented and earth-based religions honored sexuality as a natural part of the great cycle of life. They also worshipped all parts of a woman's sexual organs. There are cave paintings dating back to 35,000 B.C.E. that depict the Goddess baring her wondrous vulva. In prehistoric caves of southern Europe are descriptive carvings of the vulva, thought to be objects of worship. But the arrival of patriarchy turned what should have been revered as one of the most precious parts of our body into something that was shameful or ignored.

The womb is the portal of human life. When the spirit of the womb is respected, honored, and revered, your skin will glow, your eyes will sparkle, and you will radiate an inner sense of serenity and magic. When this spirit is denied, unheard, condemned, and abused, the womb can become a receptacle of disease and a storehouse for negative emotions. When the womb is dishonored, she reacts in negative ways. There are many reasons why a woman might have fibroids, PMS, cervical cancer, painful menstrual cycles, cramping, discharge, an unnecessary hysterectomy, a tilted uterus, or some kinds of infertility. However, I believe there is often a connection between a woman's relationship with her sexuality and the physical and emotional health of her female organs. To honor and cherish your sexual organs, it is valuable first to discover these parts of your body.

I found the sixties exhilarating. Although it was a time of change and upheaval for me, it was also an exciting time. I was passionate about an ending to the war in Vietnam, and I also belonged to a women's circle. It was the generation of burn-your-bra, consciousness-raising, and the resurgence of feminism. We would seethe at the injustice that women had suffered through the ages, read feminist manifestos, and generally support each other in our journey to understand what it meant to be a woman.

It was a common practice in women's circles at that time to try and understand our bodies and begin to move beyond shame and guilt about them. It may sound strange, incredible, or even horrifying now, but it was fashionable then in women's groups to obtain a speculum and, using a mirror, for each woman to examine her own genitals. We looked at our vulvas and inside our vaginas. For most of us, it was the first time we had ever seen them. The responses ranged from "Wow! I had no idea what it looked like!" or "Oh, it's beautiful!" to "Ugh! I kinda wish I'd never looked!" No matter what the response, the exercise and the subsequent discussion seemed to bond us together even more deeply as women. Looking back, I'm amazed at the courage we had to share such an intimate thing together. It was the first time I had ever really seen what my genitals looked like. How odd that, as women, there is such an essential part of our anatomy that we have rarely seen, and that we are ashamed to look at. It is a part of us that deserves to be acknowledged and honored.

Depending on your background, this exercise might sound fascinating, absurd, humiliating, disgusting, weird, or even hilarious, but at the time, we all considered it an important step in the advancement of women. The sixties allowed us to own our bodies and to celebrate all parts of them. I found that participating in a women's circle was incredibly empowering.

Discovering Your Vulva

This exercise, which you can do in the privacy of your own home, is still a valuable thing to do. Begin by taking time to create a sanctuary in a quiet place. Play soothing music, arrange flowers, light a scented candle. Find somewhere comfortable to recline. Spread your thighs and place a hand mirror between your legs. Relax, and when you are ready, look into the mirror while carefully and gently exploring your anatomy. Notice what feelings and emotions arise as you do this. You might feel shocked, sad, scared, uncomfortable, or surprised. You also might feel loving and caring. It's important to be aware of your reactions. When you're complete, you might want to thank this part of your body and imagine sending love into it with the words, "I love you unconditionally. You are a special part of me."

The Voice of Your Womb

It's time to reclaim your womb. You can do this even if you have had a hysterectomy. A powerful life-force energy is stored in that area, even if you are missing the physical tissue of your womb. Your womb is not only the potential birthplace of a child; it is also the energetic birthplace of your creativity and of your self. To heal is to give birth to yourself.

One of the most powerful exercises that a woman can do is to have a dialogue with her womb. This will often allow you to tap into information about your self, of which you were previously unaware. Eighteen years ago, when I was teaching a course that I called the "Mysteries of Womanhood," one of the most potent exercises that each woman did was to engage in an internal dialogue with her womb. This exercise brought about immense healing for many of the participants.

Talking to Your Womb

To hear the voice of your womb, first relax in a safe place. Play some soothing music. Close your eyes and imagine that you are talking to the spirit of your womb. A simple way to do this is to imagine that you are very small and can enter your womb. Pretend that she has a personality and a voice. Silently ask her questions and listen to her responses. This inner dialogue will often allow you to gain a deep understanding of the issues and emotions that are lodged in your womb. Here are some sample questions:

- How do you feel? Is there anything you want to share with me?
- How do you feel about being touched?
- How do you feel about sex?
- Do you prefer the touch of a man or a woman?
- How do you feel about your sexual orientation?
- How do you feel about my current relationship and/or my past relationships?
- Do you have anything to tell me regarding diet, exercise, or your needs?

Visualize walking around inside your womb. What sensations do you experience? What emotions? Do you see any areas that seem especially dark? Imagine that you have a magic wand, and use it to focus healing light and energy on any area that seems stagnant or dark. You can call upon the Goddess of your womb to help you make your womb into a sanctuary. Make it as absolutely beautiful and fabulous as you can. You could imagine it as a sumptuous chamber with soft sensuous pillows, elegant flowers, and light streaming into it through stained-glass windows. Make it a place where you would feel safe and beautiful. The energy that you create during this meditation will continue to radiate into your womb long after you have completed it.

Cherishing Your Breasts

Your womb and breasts are inextricably related. They are the parts of your body that designate you as female. In the distant past, a woman's breasts were revered. In Egypt, it was believed that the Milky Way was the abundant outflowing of the breasts of the moon Goddess. Some traditions speak of the breasts of the Goddess as nursing the world. The famous statue of a multi-breasted Artemis at Ephesus suggests that her bounty is flowing for all beings. Our breasts provide nurturing energy for our children, for our lovers, and for ourselves. (Even if your breasts have been removed or altered, there is still an energy field in their place.)

In our present culture, we no longer honor our breasts as sacred. We use demeaning words for them such as "hooters," "knockers," "melons," and "boobs." In Western culture, one in six women develop breast cancer. It's also not uncommon for women to have tumors and cysts in their breasts.

In our culture, women judge their breasts as too small, too big, or too saggy and rush to have surgery done on them. We have forgotten that they deserve to be loved. When you cherish your breasts, you will be the recipient of their innate nurturing energy. The energy field around the breast area is an outer representation of an inner ability to comfort ourselves and others. As you pleasure and honor your breasts, there is an etheric energy that flows from that area into your entire body. This energy can instil a deeper sense of being nourished within you.

Maintaining the Physical Health of Your Breasts

- Make sure that you have regular checkups and examine your breasts regularly yourself, especially after the age of forty.
- In a shower, alternate between hot and cold water to stimulate and energize your breasts.
- Reduce the amount of deodorant you use, and unless it's a special occasion, do not use antiperspirant. The lymph glands under your arms that dispel waste products are connected to your breasts. When you clog your natural flow of perspiration, you clog your body's way of eliminating toxins. This can contribute to a buildup of stagnant energy and toxins in your breasts.
- Eliminate underwired bras; or only wear them for special occasions. They slow the flow of lymphatic fluids away from the breasts. Especially do not sleep in an underwired bra. Research has shown a correlation between sleeping in an underwired bra and a heightened occurrence of breast cancer.
- Cut back on caffeine, which can contribute to fibrous breasts, breast pain and cysts.

Cherishing and Honoring Your Breasts

- Rub your hands together to warm them, then gently cradle your breasts in your hands and allow the warmth to penetrate deep into the tissues. Visualize love and energy flowing from your hands into your breasts.
- After a warm bath or shower take almond, sesame, or olive oil (you can add lavender essential oil to it) and massage your breasts. Stroke them as gently and lovingly as a lover might.

Having "It": Developing Sexual Radiance

There are some women who seem to radiate their own light; there is something about them that is almost magnetic. They walk into a room and everyone, male or female, feels their presence. Call it sexual radiance or sex appeal—whatever it is, they have it. It's powerful and it doesn't seem dependent on physical looks.

I know a woman who has pocked skin, drooping shoulders, and who, as a result of a childhood injury, walks with a slight limp. Her hair is thin and droopy and she has a double chin, yet when she walks into a room, something happens. It seems like the light gets brighter. Conversation steps up an octave. And people are drawn to her almost like moths to a light. She isn't especially witty or bright, and she definitely isn't beautiful by anyone's standards but she has "it." I used to watch her at parties and gatherings and was continually astounded at the effect she had on people.

One summer afternoon, we sat lazily curled up in big rattan chairs on the veranda of her home, sipping iced tea in the sun. I asked her if she knew why she had such a mesmerizing effect on people. She was quiet for a minute, closing her eyes and turning her face toward the sun. In a soft, slow voice she said, "I have a sense of my own style and my own presence. Even though I am insecure in many ways, I also know that I am a remarkable woman. Every woman has something about her that is amazing, but very few truly believe it. Even though I don't fit the normal view of beauty, I know I am desirable, radiant, and sensual. People are drawn to a woman who is comfortable with who she is." She said this with a total lack of self-consciousness, and I never forgot her words. To be a sexually radiant woman is to have a sense of your own style, to know who you are, and especially to believe that you are gorgeous no matter what form your body takes.

A fabulous way to wake up your sensuous self is to read erotic literature written by women. There are also some juicy, inspiring compilations by women's writing groups who get together to write erotica for pleasure (see Resources)—you might even want to consider doing something similar yourself. It's fun!

I like to take erotica on planes to make my journey more pleasurable. Flying usually makes me tired, dehydrated, and exhausted. However, when I have some erotic literature to read the time flies, and I am more sparkly at the end of my trip. Usually I try to be very discreet about my books on planes, but on one flight an elderly woman in her eighties walked down the aisle, looked down at my book and said, "You're reading erotica. I love to read those kinds of books!" Before I had time to blush, the businesswoman across the aisle from me said, "Oh, I do too! If you finish it could I possibly read your book?" It made me realize that I am not the only woman who enjoys erotic literature!

There are also some luscious films and videos you could watch (www.goodvibes.com is a good source). They are much more sensuous and erotic than hard-core, badly lit, badly acted porno films. It can be deeply sensuous to curl up in your favorite overstuffed chair in front of the fire on a rainy afternoon with a seductive erotic movie. What bliss!

Perhaps one of the best ways to wake up your sensuous self is with a vibrator. I'm sure that women in ancient times discovered just the right place to position themselves in a mountain stream so its flowing waters could create wonderful orgasms. How they would have envied the vibrators of today. You deserve pleasure, and it's all right to explore and pleasure yourself with a vibrator. It cannot replace a lover, but it can give you joy and allow you to relax. The more you learn about your body and your orgasms, the more empowered you are as a woman. When you discover what is pleasing to your body, you can then communicate this to a lover.

Marrying Yourself

Amber, one of my very dear friends, is a gorgeous, luscious woman who had been in many relationships yet always seemed to be searching for Mr. Right. One day she decided that instead of looking for the right man, she would become the right woman, so she decided to marry herself.

When she first told me she had done this, I really wanted to laugh. It seemed so bizarre. Lots of quips were on the tip of my tongue, like "Who carried who over the threshold?" Before I could say something truly stupid, I looked into her face. I could see her deep sincerity, and that what she had experienced was moving and profound.

It's very difficult to experience love from another if we don't love ourselves. Amber embarked on a journey to love herself, and its culmination was a wedding for herself on a Florida beach one warm spring evening. She spent the entire day by the sea writing about her life and what she wanted to create for herself in the future.

She told me, "During the day, I became clear on my personal values. I realized that courage and love were very important to me and that my biggest value was 'honor.' The moment I realized that I wanted to honor myself and my soul, there was a shift for me. I decided that instead of waiting for a hero, I would be the hero until that special man showed up in my life. My hours on the beach were such a sweet time for me.

"That night in my beach cottage I lit a heart candle, arranged some flowers, and cooked myself an amazing dinner. I sat on the windowsill, feeling the warmth of the ocean breeze and listening to some awesome music. I wanted my commitment to myself to be as deep as if I were committing to another person, so I looked up at the stars and then read out the vows that I had worked on all day. I said, 'I will always cherish you, Amber' and, 'I vow to love and honor and cherish your dreams.' I then put a ring on as a symbol of my commitment to myself.

"Right after that, a wonderful man came into my life. I know that if I hadn't married myself, none of these remarkable things would have happened. Marrying myself was really and truly the first conscious decision that I made to absolutely commit to myself and to my life. It was my first step in falling in love with myself."

A Self-Marriage Ceremony

- Take a day for yourself in a beautiful place. You might want to book a room in the desert, by the sea, in the mountains, or somewhere with a beautiful garden. (Some women also enjoy inviting friends to their wedding, so decide if you'd prefer company or solitude.)
- Find somewhere that feels safe and serene, ideally outdoors, and take some time to evaluate your life. Use a journal to help you put your life in perspective. What have you stood for in the past? What have been the presiding values in your life? What kind of person do you want to be in the future? What values do you wish to live by? What vows do you want to make to yourself?
- Create a beautiful space for yourself either in nature or in your room. Adorn your body in a special way for your wedding. Make your vows to yourself and seal them with a ring, necklace, or gift.
- Every year on the same day, renew your vows to honor, cherish and love yourself.

Erotic Massage

When I was in my twenties I taught erotic massage classes. (Erotic massage is focused on sensual and even sexual enjoyment, whereas ordinary massage is more therapeutic in nature.) They were fun, outrageous, and also deeply spiritual. I never planned on their being spiritual, but inevitably that's what everyone said afterwards.

I've always loved creating atmospheric environments, so when I taught erotic massage I designed the environment to be as opulent and sensuous as possible. For example, for one seminar I decorated the room to look like a scene out of *A Thousand and One Nights*, with thick Persian carpets, brass incense burners with plumes of frankincense smoke billowing throughout the room, and flickering candles, in a room draped with fabric to look like a Bedouin tent.

Another time, I decorated the room to look like an Indian palace, with brilliant, richly colored silk saris and mandalas decorating the walls, sitar music playing, and a crackling fire in the fireplace. A young man dressed as Krishna played a flute during the class, and my girlfriends dressed in saris to be the attendant *gopi* girls. (*Gopis* were shepherdesses who danced with joy and rapture in the presence of Krishna, Their dance was called "The Cosmic Dance of the Universe" because it symbolized the marriage of heaven and earth.) The *gopi* girls in my seminar joyously danced throughout the room, dropping grapes in people's mouths, and stroking them with peacock feathers.

It was in these courses that I began to learn the healing power of sexual energy. I remember one young woman attended who had been crippled since she was a small child. Everyone was nude in my courses, so there was an atmosphere of openness. This courageous woman said that no one except her doctors had ever seen her without her clothes on. During the course, she went though layers of fear, shame, and eventually tentative openness and joy as she allowed her body to be massaged. By the end of the course, her withered, crippled body had begun to relax and straighten up. It seemed nothing short of a miracle as she slowly stood up and shakily walked across the room. We all wept for joy. It is no wonder that erotic massage was considered holy by ancient cultures.

I also saw the potential healing power of sexual energy in those courses, for when it is no longer confined to just your genitals, it becomes a powerful, rejuvenating, life-force energy for your entire body. Erotic massage can be a complete erotic experience without genital orgasm. It is a way for the entire body to experience sensual enjoyment, so that *all* parts of it can respond. Too often, sexual sensations are confined to just one part of the body, instead of being a holistic experience.

Erogenous is from the Greek, and literally means "generating love"; erotic massage can expand the sexual experience so love can be generated. This type of massage is a phenomenal way to establish an intimate communication that can go much deeper than words. Touch can convey emotions and feelings. Your deepest thoughts can be conveyed nonverbally through the pressure and rhythm that you use. (Although it is valuable to take a course in massage, you can definitely make it up as you go along.)

Erotic massage can be likened to a dance or a piece of music. A good dancer involves their entire body and soul in their dance, and so it should be in your massage. If your thoughts are elsewhere, that gets communicated through your hands, and if you are feeling accepting and caring toward your lover, that also gets communicated. Music can be a wonderful addition to erotic massage. Find something soothing that you both enjoy, then let it act as a guide for the tempo and rhythm of your massage. Allow the intensity of your passion and love to flow through your hands.

Because bodies and preferences are so different, the best way to find out how to pleasure your partner is by communication. And the best way to communicate in this delicate area of human relationships is with great diplomacy. For example, if your breast is being massaged too deeply, instead of saying, "You're not doing that right," say, "That feels good . . . I'm wondering how it would feel if it was even lighter. Ahhh, that's great!" It's important to communicate what you enjoy, and to comment on your partner's technique in a way that's very loving.

When giving erotic massage, it's valuable to have one person be the giver and one the receiver. This way, if you are giving the massage, you can keep your focus on creating joy for your partner. And if you are receiving, you can completely let go and surrender to the experience. Use erotic massage as an opportunity to learn to receive. Surprisingly, it can be very difficult to open ourselves to do this. (This is true in life, as well as in lovemaking.)

Accept the sensations and the enjoyment that you are feeling during the massage as a gift of love from the person from who is massaging you. Surrender yourself to the experience. As you are able to receive and accept this gift, this receptive attitude will begin to spill over into the rest of your life, and you will find that you are able to receive the bounty of life more fully.

Sacred Sex

In the last few decades, sexual taboos and inhibitions have begun to be broken, but unless there is a correct understanding of the use of the power of sexuality, sexual liberation will only contribute to a feeling of emptiness, lack of purpose or fulfilment. We are constantly assaulted by sexual images. As a result, when we begin to make love, we often focus on the outer form rather than the inner experience. Lovemaking only becomes truly meaningful when you allow yourself to be fully present in the moment.

When you are making love, get out of your head and into your heart. Ask yourself, "What is real and authentic right now?" "What am I experiencing physically and emotionally right now?" Take time to breathe, tune in to your feelings, and acknowledge them. Stay conscious of the present moment. This state of being enables an inspiring, intimate, and real experience. When you are in the deliciousness of the present, you can experience the core essence of your partner. When you release mental images, thoughts, and projections that keep you from being in the present moment, you can begin to understand fully and deeply the great beauty of yourself and your partner.

Lovemaking becomes sacred when you view it as a sacrament to the Creator and when you treat yourself and your lover as holy. It can be a transcendent experience, in which you cherish and celebrate each other. You might want to create an altar beforehand. Place it in the bedroom and put special objects, such as a candle or fresh flowers, on it. Dedicate your lovemaking to a particular purpose—to health and vitality, perhaps, or to personal or world peace. An energy is created when you make love, and when you have dedicated it, the energy pours out from the lovemaking to that particular focus or goal. When you intend your lovemaking to be holy and sacred, it becomes so.

Erotic Visualization

All mystical traditions make use of visualization for spiritual transformation. Doing an erotic visualization with your lover is a wonderful sacred-sex technique. Sit comfortably opposite your partner and visualize yourselves as aspects of the Divine. Breathe in a very deep, relaxed manner, and see yourself as an erotic Goddess of love and your partner as a God of love. In other words, see each other as exalted. Then make love as if you really were the God and Goddess of love. Alternatively, imagine you and your lover enveloped in a golden sphere of light as you make love. This will keep the energy circulating and increasing, rather than diminishing.

Sacred Breath, the Sexual Rejuvenator

Channelling sexual energy upwards through the body's energy centers or chakras is a great way to prepare for lovemaking. This can be done by using the breath. As you inhale, visualize energy moving from the base of your spine up to the top of your head. As you exhale, imagine it moving down again.

Eastern mystical teaching stresses the importance of the breath as a way to align and channel creative sexual energy. In the initial stage of lovemaking, your breath should be slow and deep, a breath that extends your lower abdomen when you inhale and contracts it when you exhale. This is a very natural way to breathe; it is the way we breathe when we are asleep. However, most people, when they're awake, breathe into their upper chest instead. Both Tantric and Taoist texts emphasize that love-breathing should be deep, from the diaphragm. One Tantric breathing technique is for a couple to sit or lie down close together, facing each other, and for one of them to breathe out at the same time as the other breathes in, each person breathing in the other's breath. The breath should be natural, never forced. Another technique is to synchronize your breathing, inhaling and exhaling at the same time. This is a powerful way of attuning with each other.

As the couple faces each other doing either of these techniques, there will be a powerful alignment of their chakras. To increase this alignment, touch each other's heart chakra (the energy center at the middle of the chest), and imagine you're breathing into your partner's heart center. It is valuable to maintain eye contact while doing this.

To open the first (base, sexual) chakra before lovemaking, practice the Breath of Fire. This is a very rapid breath that is done while standing. (This should not be practiced by anyone who is pregnant, ill, or has high blood pressure.) Stand up straight and allow your body to be very relaxed. Then let your pelvis thrust forward and back as you breathe rapidly. This opens the first chakra so that energy can move up from the earth through the body and out of the top of the head. It increases the amount of healing energy that can stream through you during lovemaking.

Outrageous Orgasm

I'm going to tell you a wonderful secret. There is a way to have an orgasm that rocks your soul and makes you feel like you have dissolved into bliss. It's a *full body* orgasm. During an orgasm, most women have a localized sensation in their clitoris and maybe in their nipples. However, when you were a baby, as I mentioned before, your entire body responded in ecstasy to the slightest touch. When we were young, we instinctively responded to stimulation with our entire body, but as we became adults, we shut down different parts of our bodies, and our sexual experience became centered primarily in our genitals. We can create awesome orgasms with our imagination and a great vibrator, but for this kind of orgasm you need to have a partner whom you cherish and with whom you feel safe. (I'm going to talk about "him," but it could also be a woman.) The following instructions are written from the perspective of your being the receiver, but you can also use them to be the giver. In erotic massage, it is best if one person is the giver and the other is the receiver. This way you have the experience of fully receiving the massage, without the distraction of having to give back, or vice versa. (The next time you do erotic massage, you can switch roles and become the giver instead of the receiver.)

- Create a sensuous, sacred space for your lovemaking. The room should be warm and cozy. Drape the lamps with scarves. Light some aromatherapy candles. Place fresh flowers in vases and fruit in bowls. Chill some champagne or juice.
- Sit cross-legged so you can look into each other's eyes. Look deep into the eyes of your lover and synchronize your breath so you are both breathing at the same time.
- As you breathe together, focus on letting go and surrendering. Open yourself more and more to the essence of your beloved. If you feel any fear, just notice it and continue to open and reveal your soul. Go beyond the surface and the personality, and connect to the essence of the one opposite you.
- Keep gazing at each other until you feel a deep sense of connection and harmony. Focus on being present, rather than on the orgasm you expect to have.
- Imagine that your breath is going down into your pelvis and activating the life force that dwells there.
- Visualize yourself as a Goddess and your partner as a God. Hold, caress, kiss, and hug each other. Be conscious and present with every movement. Allow yourself to fully experience whatever is authentic and true. Feel the energy building with every breath you take. Know that this energy is burning away any impurities in your soul and is healing and regenerating both of you. Then recline comfortably to receive the massage.
- Your lover warms oil in his hands and begins a relaxing back massage. The back often holds a lot of stress, so this is a good place to begin. As the muscles in your back and shoulders unwind, your whole body will begin to let go. When you are finished with the back, end with very soft, light, feathering movements. If your partner is ticklish, try moving your hands more slowly. The deep massage relaxes the body and the feathering excites the body.
- He continues to alternate deep massage with a light, feathering touch over your entire body, but without touching any of your sexual organs. The alternating deep and light massage is very arousing. The intensity of feeling slowly builds until he finally touches your sexual organs.
- As you lie on your back, comfortably supported by pillows, your lover kneels beside you. He places one hand on your heart chakra and one lightly touching your vulva, but without moving his hands. Look into each other's eyes and feel yourself opening and letting go. Let everything else disappear. Let the past and the future disappear. Only now. Only this. Only here. Breathe together deeply and fully. Surrender to love . . . surrender to the moment.

- As you continue to look into your lover's eyes, he begins to massage and caress your vulva to the point just before orgasm, then stops, allowing the sensations to subside. Every time he does this, it heightens the ultimate orgasm. This is exquisite agony. Not only does it prolong pleasure, but also it intensifies the orgasm.
- The ecstasy of an outrageous orgasm comes from surrendering. When you finally orgasm, hold the intention of surrendering. You are not giving up your identity when you surrender. In fact you are letting go of your limited identity and embracing your greater identity that is a part of all things. It doesn't matter if you surrender to God/Goddess, your lover, your higher self, or to love. It is the act of surrendering that is transforming.

Following the Path of Passion

There are many reasons why one in three marriages ends in divorce. One of them is because one partner has sex outside the marriage and the other partner feels betrayed. This can occur even when the relationship is good but the sex has become routine and mundane. It is human nature to desire variety. It is often the forbidden fruits that seem to taste the sweetest. When two people are in a committed relationship, their connection should expand their capacity for sexual enjoyment rather than restricting it.

To keep the intensity of pleasure in a relationship, add the element of mystery. Surprise your partner. Do something daringly different. Act out a sexual fantasy. Drape a sheet around yourself and greet your lover with grapes and an erotic dance. Ancient Chinese, Japanese, and Hindu traditions all make use of play-acting as an enhancement of sexual ecstasy. Be unexpected and provocative . . . and have fun. Take separate cars to a hotel and hire a room for the night like two clandestine lovers. Experiment with different lovemaking techniques and positions. Become a woman of mystery and keep your lover guessing, and you will have their attention for a long time.

When passion fills every pore of your being, your body, mind, and spirit glow. Passion isn't confined and limited to sex. It means celebrating all your relationships, living life fully, enjoying all your experiences, and delving into your senses with gusto. When you begin to allow passion to paint your soul, your lovemaking will be outrageous, no matter what form it takes. Let passion be your path. Let it be a burning love for everything and everyone. Let your fire and your longing to be a vehicle for Spirit to move through consume you, and your lovemaking will be awesome.

A recent *Newsweek* article declared that more and more women are continuing to be interested in sex not only into their forties and fifties but well into their sixties and seventies. I thought it was a timely article because lots of older women were always interested; they just didn't tell anyone because they were brainwashed into thinking they couldn't have sex after menopause. We now know that this is ridiculous . . . older women are more interested in sex than ever before! They don't have to worry about getting pregnant so they are free to enjoy themselves fully and deeply without fear (however, condoms are still a necessary precaution).

The Reluctant Partner

My husband is a rock of stability and support. We have been married for almost thirty years and he has seen me through many phases of my spiritual journey. He has been supportive, but he has been an observer rather than a participant. He is what is called a "man's man." He worked as a builder for years, and likes watching football and baseball on television while eating chips and drinking wine or beer. His yells are momentous if his team wins. He hates shopping, sharing feelings, and New Age music. And he loves me totally and forever, which means more to me than the fact that we don't always share the same beliefs.

Many years ago, when I wanted to start practicing sacred sex, he thought it was one of the dumbest suggestions that I had ever made. He liked the sex part, but he wasn't so sure about the sacred part, especially when it meant that we had to sit opposite each other and look into each other's eyes. I would arrange the room with flowers, candles, and incense, and bathe both of us lusciously by candlelight. When we sat on the bed gazing into each other's eyes, he would last about two minutes before he would start giggling. Sometimes he would laugh until tears rolled out of his eyes and say, "Can we have sex now?"

In the end, we came up with something of a compromise: sometimes our lovemaking is mystical . . . and sometimes it is not mystical at all. I wanted to tell you about my experience because sometimes sacred sex sounds so incredible, but the reality doesn't always match the ideal. Sacred sex isn't something you do, it is the way you approach your lovemaking and the feeling that you have inside yourself. It is a place that dwells inside you. So, create sacred sex in your own way. Enjoy yourself, no matter what form your lovemaking takes, whether it is slow and meditative, or raunchy and rollicking, and remember, it's sacred if you say it is.

THE ART OF
ADORNMENT

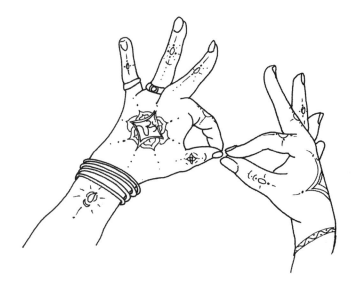

I collapsed into an old, overstuffed chair. It was a blisteringly hot day, and I squirmed with discomfort as my bare legs stuck to the plastic cloth that covered the chair. It had been tossed there as a protection from construction debris and paint. We were remodeling our home, and every available place to sit was covered with plastic, paint, and plaster.

My hair was covered with sweat, dust, and paint. I looked at my hands. They were splattered with plaster and dirt. My body was covered with so much grime that it was hard to tell where my shorts ended and my legs began. I definitely didn't feel like a Glorious Woman; I felt like the chewed-off end of an old rope.

I really needed to change the way I felt, so I drew a luxurious bath, perfumed the water with rosemary oil, and lowered myself into its soothing warmth. My body hummed with pleasure. Taking a moment to determine exactly how I wanted to feel, I decided on "fresh" and "vital."

The first step I took toward freshness was to thoroughly cleanse myself. I took a bristled brush and scrubbed every inch of my body. After a cold, refreshing shower, I rubbed myself dry, invigorated by the roughness of a sauna towel. Afterwards I adorned my body with oil scented with grape-fruit and mandarin, lavishing deep strokes of it all over my body. The smell was revitalizing.

Choosing clothes that made me feel vibrant, I threw on a crisp white linen shirt over linen trousers. As I put my clothes on I affirmed, "I am surrounding myself in a mantle of fresh and invigorating energy." I only occasionally wear jewelry, but I chose a sparkling green necklace and matching earrings, saying to myself, "My energy is as sparkling as this jewelry." I colored my lips with bright pink lipstick and my cheeks with shell-pink blush. And then I danced through the mist of a citrus perfume that I sprayed into the air. The final touch was a flower behind my ear. I felt fresh, blessed, completely delicious, and divine.

In ancient times, the mystery school initiate, priestess, or shaman all practiced the high art of adornment. Before a ceremony or celebration, they would pay careful attention to decorating their body. These ancient women understood that changing a woman's appearance could have a remarkable effect on the way she felt and the energy that she radiated. Changing her outer form could initiate an inner trans-formation.

When a woman wanted to step into the realm of the divine, her body was first carefully and ceremoniously cleansed and purified. It was massaged with scented oils, special clothing suitable to the event was carefully chosen, and makeup—such as red berries for the lips and charcoal for the eyes—was used to highlight her face. Her hair was oiled, scented, and arranged with flowers, herbs, or jewels. Adorning her body helped a woman to become a sacred vessel for spiritual energies to flow through.

In today's world, we may have a intuitive memory of these ancient rites, but we have lost the purpose and the power of adornment. When we style our hair, put on jewelry, choose our clothing, or make up our faces, we are reenacting the outer vestiges of this lost art, but we are unaware of any possible inner significance. Nevertheless, you can reignite this forgotten art, and learn how to change your appearance so it has a remarkable effect on the way you feel and the energy that you radiate.

A woman who is an alchemist of adornment understands how to

combine her clothes, makeup and body ornamentation to change the way she feels. She knows how to create delicious moods for herself the same way a gourmet chef can create splendid tastes through the combination of ingredients. By embellishing her body in particular ways, she can create and experience even the subtlest nuances of emotional expressions. For instance, she can change her emotional state from "whimsical" into "earthy" and then into "stately," simply by changing the way she bedecks her body. There are three things she needs to achieve her magic. First, she needs to become clear about exactly how she desires to feel; second, she needs to choose actions, accessories, and adornments that will support her intention; and third, she needs to affirm her intention with every item that she places on her body.

Anointing Yourself with Fragrant Oils

The process of alchemical transformation begins with the cleansing and anointing of your body. The word "anoint" means to apply oil or ointment, but it also means to administer oil during sacred ceremonies as a sign of sanctification or consecration. Applying lotion or oil after bathing is often routine and rushed, but it can also be a sensuous, holy process. You can literally sanctify and consecrate your body while you ceremoniously apply fragrant oils to your body.

Anything you put on your skin will be absorbed into your body, so I prefer to use pure oils, lotions, and essential oils rather than creams with preservatives and chemicals added to them. After a bath, try using olive, almond, refined sesame, hazelnut, or macadamia oil as a base and then add a few drops of essential oil to scent it. There is much more life-force energy in these combinations than in synthetically perfumed lotions that have a petrochemical base.

If you use fragrance with your anointing oils, the scent should be in alignment with the intention. For example, if I am working on a writing project, I use oils that contribute to my feeling like a writer. So after I bathe, I moisturize my skin with a small amount of almond oil, to which I have added a few drops of the essential oils of juniper and fir. While I do this, I say to myself, "My spirit, mind, and emotions are clear and focused." I find that the stimulating effect of these two essential oils contributes to my mental clarity while I sit at my computer. I feel I am enveloped with the mantle of the sacred writer who calls upon her muses, rather than being a hack slugging out copy.

Here are some suggestions for choosing essential oils (it's best to use just one or two at a time):

basil—uplifting; good for thought processes.
bergamot—uplifting yet calming.
cedarwood—reduces stress.
eucalyptus—cleansing, invigorating.
fir needle—refreshing, cleansing.
frankincense—relaxes fear, opens intuition.
geranium—emotional harmonizing.
juniper—stimulating, purifying.
lavender—calming, soothing.
lemon—uplifting; metal alertness.
myrrh—inspiring, strengthening.
neroli—calming, stress-reducing.
orange—uplifting, joyous
patchouli—sensuous, inspiring.
pine—cleansing, purifying, stimulating.
peppermint—toning, invigorating.
rose—emotionally soothing, opens the heart.
rosemary—mental clarity, stimulating.
sage—purification.
sandalwood—spirituality; self-expression; sensuous.
ylang-ylang—sensuality; self-assurance.

Here are some mantras to use while anointing yourself:

- "With this oil, I bless myself and my body. Every part of my being is radiant and whole."
- "I am a glorious, divine woman. My body and my spirit are holy and sacred. I cherish myself and my life."
- "With this oil, I offer prayers of gratitude for my life. My spirit is strong and beautiful and I am blessed."

Clothes with Attitude

The clothes you wear say a lot about you. They can say anything from, "I'm sweet and feminine" to, "Don't mess with me. I'll bite your head off," or, "I love nature and being close to the earth." Even if you are not consciously trying to convey a message about yourself, your personal clothing style always presents a message about you. Your personal style can even have a negative effect on you. It may communicate to your subconscious mind, and to the world at large, a message that is not in alignment with who you desire to be. For example, your practical shoes and clothes may say, "I'm a no-nonsense person," when in fact you yearn to be wild, whimsical, and capricious. Wearing a hot pink top and zebra-striped shoes instead can immediately catapult you out of your "practical" identity.

This personal style can also be used to communicate and affirm the woman you're striving to become. When your clothes make you look downtrodden and depressed, you will encounter circumstances in your life that will make you feel even more despondent. When they make you look vibrant and energized, you will draw experiences into your life that will contribute to your experiencing even more vitality. If you want to be more assertive at work, the strong, tailored lines of a "power" business suit will contribute to this feeling. If you yearn to become more feminine, gracious and flowing, choose clothes that make you feel fluid and graceful.

To use a clothing style that will help you change your life, it's valuable to ask yourself a few questions first: Who you are dressing for? Are you dressing for yourself, or are you dressing to meet the expectations of others? Are you dressing the way that you think someone of your position/age/socioeconomic level/status should dress rather than in a way that suits your soul? If you are thinking, *I'm too fat/old/young/wild/conservative/professional/motherly* to wear an outfit you love, then maybe it's time to challenge your limiting definition of yourself.

To expand your parameters as a woman, dare to wear clothes that allow you to step out of your comfort zone. Experimenting with your clothing style will help you to experience other ways of being in the world. Nothing terrible will happen to you. In fact, you might uncover some incredible qualities within yourself. Wear something completely different and unlike you. Do you always wear floral print dresses and pearls? Then try a black leather jacket and tight jeans. Or vice versa. If you always wear soft, flowing clothes, try going for rugged outdoor wear. You may discover an earth Goddess hiding inside you. When you change your outward appearance, almost by magic, inner changes will begin to occur.

There was a time in my life when I was afraid of getting close to people. I equated closeness and intimate relationships with being hurt, so I kept my distance. I was also hiding from myself. Sometimes I would tell myself everything was fine, but deep inside I would be feeling hurt or afraid. My real feelings were buried so deep, I was not even aware I was feeling them.

The clothes that I wore during that time in my life covered most of my body. Subconsciously, I thought if I covered my body, I would be hidden from other people. I wore oversized blouses over full-length trousers and often threw a large scarf around my neck, which created yet another layer between me and the world.

I knew that changing my clothing style would have an effect on my life, and I was ready for a change. But my clothes were a part of my identity, and changing my style was one of the most difficult things I ever did. I decided to wear clothes that *revealed* me, instead of hiding me. One hot summer day I went out in public wearing a form-fitting sleeveless top and shorts. I felt so exposed. I kept thinking people were looking at me and judging me. (In fact, I don't think they actually even noticed me.) At that time in my life, I severely judged my body's shape and size, so I believed that others would have the same judgments about me.

Even though it was painful, I allowed myself to experience the uneasiness and embarrassment. I used my feelings as tools to dig deep inside and discover old memories and negative decisions about myself that had been locked away for a long time. As I began to uncover and release these negative beliefs about myself, my discomfort subsided, and now I love being able to wear revealing clothes as well as concealing ones.

Sometimes it's valuable to get a friend to help you reassess your clothing style. A fashion-savvy friend of mine recently said, "You're in the middle of a transition in your life, Denise. Let's go through your wardrobe and see if your clothes match who you are becoming." We sat in the middle of my bedroom and she said, "What kind of person would you like to evolve into?" I thought about her question and told her that I wanted to exude a healthy and vibrant energy. I then tried on every item of clothing and for each one she asked, "Do you feel healthy and vibrant in that outfit?" Almost every item of clothing evoked, "No!" By the end of the afternoon, I had a huge pile of clothes to give away, and a very, very small pile of clothes that matched my intention for the future. I felt great! Although I have a lot less clothing now, everything that remains in my closet makes me feel vibrant and propels me towards my intention for the future.

I heard of some very interesting research in the Netherlands with cancer patients and the healing power of clothing style. A doctor believed that when someone got cancer it became a part of their identity—in other words, their identity became someone with cancer. So the doctor had the innovative idea that changing the identity of a patient could have a positive effect on their health. He had his patients wear styles that were completely different than what they usually wore, with amazing results: almost everyone improved and some terminally ill patients even had spontaneous remissions.

I also heard of another research project which looked at men in their eighties. A group of these elderly gentlemen were divided into two sections. One group of men lived life as usual, while the others wore the kind of clothes they had worn in their twenties and listened to the music of their youth. The test results were remarkable. The men wearing the clothes of their youth had lower blood pressure, stronger immune systems, and were generally in much better health than the other group. I believe that the shift of identity from an old man to a young man (encouraged by changing their clothing style) had a marked effect on their health. I'm not aware of any research done on groups of "hip" elderly people who naturally dress in current fashions and listen to popular music, but it seems that this could also be a way to remain young and full of life.

Sacred Shawl: Your Vestment of Power

On several occasions, I have been given shawls by my aunts on the Cherokee side of my family. This is an ancient tradition that is found in many cultures. Traditionally, a young woman is wrapped in a shawl, robe, or special scarf that symbolizes her connection to the tribe and to the long lineage of the grandmothers and great-grandmothers of her people. The shawl was a woman's mantle of power and was given to her with ceremony and ritual.

When I was given my first shawl, I was instructed in every part of the symbolism of the shawl, from the fringe to the stitching, as well as how to wear it. I was told that the zigzag stitching on the edge represented the life of the woman who had made the shawl. The stitching on my shawl indicated that the relative who had made it had a very balanced life because the stitches were close together. I was told that I should stand tall whenever I wore it, and always look straight ahead, never down or up, for a woman wearing her shawl accepts her life with strength and grace, and avoids being pulled into the high or low extremes of life.

Since the earliest times, the working of cloth was not only for creating clothing to protect against the elements; it was also done to create hallowed objects that were used as a form of protection and honor for the wearer. A prayer shawl was commonly woven to help a woman to invoke magic. When she wore it, she could step into her power, help other women with their fertility, and divine the future.

As a Glorious Woman, you may want to consider having a special wrap, shawl, robe, or blanket that is your "mantle of power." You may want to make it yourself or choose it especially to be your sacred vestment. If you make it for yourself, you may want to ceremoniously cleanse and purify the cloth before you begin to sew. You could also consider saying prayers while you make it; even sewing special crystals, stones, or gems into it; or embroidering it with symbols or meaningful words. Whenever you wear your sacred shawl, imagine that your spirit guardians, ancestors, angelic helpers, and guides are wrapping you in a strong, protective, safe energy to help you through your journey in life. If there are times when you need special strength, you can use a scarf for the same purpose. It may look like an ordinary scarf to others, but you will know that it wraps you in a protective energy field. You may want to spray your scarf periodically with a mixture of essential oils, spring water, or flower essences to continue to renew its potency.

Or, you could make a quilt. With each stitch or piece of patchwork, weave your intention and your prayers into the cloth so that at nighttime you are covered in its wonderful energy.

Awakening Your Personal Style

You are unique: There is no other woman like you. You are beautiful. Let your personal style express who you are and what you stand for. Be bold and passionate, and most of all, be honest. Take time to look deep within your soul to discover what styles, textures, fabrics, and colors reflect your spirit. With the dedication of a samurai, get rid of any clothes that aren't congruent with who you really are. Love and appreciate any clothes in which you feel strong and confident.

The colors of life: Choose colors that not only make your skin tone look great but also feed your soul. Color is energy, and every nuance of feeling and every aspect of nature has its own color signature. Discover which colors enhance your energy: close your eyes and imagine that your body is filled with color. Go through all the colors of the rainbow and all their variations, so that for green you'd look at light spring green, deep forest green, moss, khaki, and so on. Notice how you feel as you imagine your body filled with each color. You will find that there are some colors that make you feel strong and some that may make you feel weak. Choose colors for your wardrobe that make you feel healthy and vibrant.

Expand your senses: When choosing your style, take into consideration the way different fabrics feel, sound, and even smell. For example, cashmere feels very different from starched cotton; when you move, taffeta has a very different sound from silk, and wool has a different smell from linen. These may be subtle differences, yet the look, feel, sound, and smell of your clothes creates your most immediate environment and can have a profound effect on the way you feel about yourself. Choose a style and fabrics that allow your senses to be nourished and pleasured.

Activate your intuition: Ask yourself, "If I knew the perfect style for me, what would it be?" And listen to what your inner voice says, even if it seems wild and outrageous. Another exercise to help you find your style is to use your imagination to "try on" different styles and then notice how you feel in them. Scan through fashion magazines and imagine yourself dressed in the different styles, noticing which outfits make you feel great. There is a place within you that absolutely knows exactly what your style is and how to manifest it. It just takes a little practice and the willingness to still your mind and open your heart.

Accept yourself: When you don't know who you are, it can be difficult to immediately determine your style. Know that you are an emerging Glorious Woman, and the more you discover and learn about yourself, the more easily you'll be able to determine your style.

Magical Makeup

I don't very often wear makeup, but when I do, I create a ceremony around it. With each application, I feel that I am blessing myself and giving my radiance the opportunity to shine. I love the voluptuous feeling of the blush-brush against my cheeks, and the luscious sensation of the lipstick as it glides across my lips. When a woman is sexually aroused, her lips and cheeks redden as the blood supply increases to those areas. When we redden our lips and cheeks, we are creating the illusion of being in a turned-on state. When I apply makeup I feel that I am honoring and blessing my sensuality.

The most important makeup that you wear is that around your eyes. The first eye makeup was made in the Middle East, the cradle of civilization, in the form of kohl. It was worn not only to beautify the eyes but also for spiritual purposes. The black paste was thought to protect the woman who wore it and also to increase her ability to see into spiritual realms. To reestablish this dimension of eye makeup, every time you shade or darken the outline your eyes or use mascara, hold the intention that you are able to see more clearly, physically, and spiritually.

A Makeup Ceremony

Put some foundation in your palms, and imagine that your hands are energizing it. As you smooth it over your face, say, "I am a radiant, beautiful woman." As you put makeup around your eyes, affirm, "I see the truth in all situations." As you put lipstick on, think to yourself, "I speak my truth."

Mehndi

Many women think it fashionable to decorate their hands (and feet) with henna or felt markers. This time-honored practice is known by the Indian term *mehndi*. The intricate and beautiful patterns can deepen your connection to the feminine spirit within you, and the designs help to activate your energy. Putting symbols, such as the sign of infinity or the symbol for "om" on the top or bottom of your feet can be grounding and empowering. Although no one else may be able to see them, *you* will know they are there. You can either obtain a *mehndi* kit, have yourself decorated professionally, or create your own designs that are meaningful for you.

Tattoos

Tattooing has a long and interesting history. In numerous shamanic traditions throughout the world, tattoos were thought to be magical and protective. The people of the Chukchi region of northern Siberia tattooed pictures of their allies and guardian spirits on their bodies for protection. An ancient practice that has survived into present times is that of sailors getting tattooed to protect themselves from drowning. The Maori people of New Zealand (like other Polynesians) also have a long tradition of tattooing. They tattoo their faces with spirals, and believe that the elaborate designs will guarantee a safe passage into the next world.

In many ancient traditions, tattoos were considered a form of protection. If you choose to adorn your body with tattoos, think carefully about the symbolism and placement of each tattoo. Ideally your tattoos should have a sacred meaning, and should be positioned with care, for they will have an influence on your energy fields for a very long time.

The Healing Powers of Jewelry

Traditionally, jewelry has been worn by women not only for the sake of beauty, but also for sacred purposes. It was used to invite Goddess energy into a woman as well as to protect and to promote healing. Various stones and symbols were used. To this day in India, as part of the ceremony for a newborn child, bracelets of silver, copper, or gold are placed on her legs and hands to ward off negative energy. In today's Western culture, we still retain the practice of wearing jewelry for beautification, but we have, for the most part, forgotten that it can be used for mystical purposes.

To use your jewelry to enhance your energy, first focus on your intention for yourself. Then carefully chose jewelry to magnify it. Each type of stone or metal elicits a particular and unique kind of energy. Some activate healing, others promote soothing and relaxing energy, while others were used to evoke vitality. For example, silver is connected to the moon and has a receptive energy, while gold is connected to the sun and has a more expansive energy. (See Chapter 3 for a list of the magical qualities of minerals.)

Your necklaces and rings can provide a continuing source of spiritual renewal, strength, and protection. For this to happen, they should be cleansed and blessed, especially when you first obtain them. To cleanse your jewelry, place it in sunlight for 3–5 hours or smudge it with the smoke of sage or frankincense. Then hold it between your hands and dedicate it. For example, you could dedicate a necklace to love: imagine love flowing through your hands into the necklace. When you put it on, bless your throat and heart chakra, saying, "May I speak my truth and may my heart be open." When you slide your wedding ring back on to your finger after taking it off to do the dishes, give yourself blessings for a strong and loving marriage union. When you put on a toe ring, bless your feet, saying: "My feet are my solid foundation. I step forward with grace and ease."

Navel Jewels

For thousands of years, women in the Middle East have worn navel jewels. The navel area was considered sacred because it was the prenatal point of contact between a mother and child, and the channel through which a child received life-giving fluids. Many early Goddess shrines were viewed as cosmic navels, centers from which life force flowed into the world. Belly dancers often set jewels in their navels and called attention to the area with tattoos or paint. It is not uncommon today for young women to pierce their navel and then place a ring with jewelry in it. If you do this, remember the powerful, sacred feminine roots of this ancient practice. Your navel jewel becomes the point where energy flows from you into the world and where you can receive energy into yourself.

Bindis

A bindi is a decorative mark or ornament that is placed on the third eye area of the forehead (between and slightly above the eyes). It is thought that ornamenting this point can help one to open to spiritual realms. Bindis are fashionable now, particularly among young girls, but if you wear one with the intention of opening to your intuition and your spiritual awareness, it can happen.

Talismans

Every ancient culture has used magical talismans. Often in the form of small charms, they were thought to attract favorable influences to the wearer. In the Middle Ages, they were worn to attract the positive astrological influence of a particular planet. For example, to attract love, the talisman of Venus was worn. A Glorious Woman's jewelry can also serve as a kind of magical talisman. A sacred symbol, such as the Star of David, can be worn on a necklace for protection. A Christian cross, an image of Kuan Yin, or the Sanskrit symbol for "om" are all talismans that can strengthen and even help protect the wearer. Or an image of a heart could serve you as a talisman of love.

Talismans can be worn where they can be seen or they can be used in a traditional manner and hidden beneath your clothing. If you choose to conceal your talisman, it can be worn around your neck beneath your shirt, or tucked into your bra or even into a pocket, especially if it is the type of talisman that consists of a small pouch with special objects in it.

To create your own talisman, you must first decide what purpose it will serve. Do you want it to enhance your career, love life, or health? Once you have determined your goal, choose items that support it. For example, if you desire protection and grounding, obtain a small obsidian or haematite bead, a piece of amber, and a few grains of red earth. Then make or purchase a small pouch. This can be made of anything, but silk, wool, or leather are often used. Once the pouch is filled with your objects, it should be consecrated to charge it with magical powers. Light some sage or incense and hold the pouch in the smoke as you pray for protection and to be grounded.

Mystical Amulets of the Goddess

Although in our culture the Goddess has been lost for over a thousand years, remnants of her are still being found throughout the world. One of the most potent reminders of her bounty is the small carved talismans and amulets that honored her. These ancient relics were carved from wood, bone, or stone, or modeled from clay or metal. They had carefully carved images of the Goddess and her sacred symbols. They were worn or carried on the body as a way to connect magically with the mysterious and wondrous powers of the primordial female deity.

Some of the common images on these charms were voluptuous representations of the Goddess, bodies with full breasts and broad hips. Some amulets were just breasts, which were worn as a pendant. These have been found in Palestine, France, Switzerland, Italy, and Czechoslovakia dating back as far as 26,000 B.C.E.

Often Goddess amulets were highly sexual and sensual, representing fertility, reproduction, and the earthy aspects of the Goddess. Some Goddess images were birdlike, with extended wings perhaps symbolizing her flight to other worlds. The Goddesses on the amulets sometimes had the head of a snake or were entwined with serpents, which represented the transformational qualities of the Goddess, just as a snake is transformed by shedding its skin.

Another very common and universal form of Goddess amulets were spirals, of every shape and size. The sacred spiral represented the spiraling nature of the universe. People in ancient times intuitively understood what modern science has discovered: the moon spirals around our planet, our planet spirals on its axis and around the sun, and our solar system spirals through the galaxy and the galaxy spirals throughout the universe. The sacred spiral was the symbol of the divine feminine forces of nature. Most mind–body–spirit stores carry necklaces and jewelry that are reproductions of these ancient amulets.

In an almost mystical way, wearing replicas of ancient Goddess images seems to activate a powerful connection to Goddess states for many women. Simply by wearing such an image or keeping it on or near your body, it becomes a remarkably powerful talisman. Or, you can mold your own Goddess amulets out of clay for yourself or others: these will be even more powerful because of the love that you have poured into them.

Adorning Your Hair

As modern women, we arrange, cut, dye, spray, curl, and straighten our hair, but we rarely adorn it. Our hair is so much a part of our womanly nature that in many male-dominated, conservative cultures in the past, women have been required to bind or cover their hair.

I believe hair is part of your power as a woman, and it doesn't matter if it is closely cropped or halfway down your back. It is the conduit for the energy that surges from your crown chakra at the very top of your head. Having your hair exposed allows this energy to flow up into the heavens and allows heavenly energy to surge down through you. Even if you are bald or have lost your hair to chemotherapy, take a few minutes to expose your head to the skies and allow the freedom of the wind and the sun to caress the top of your head, and life force to flow through you.

To increase this powerful energy, you can place adornments in your hair. My Cherokee grandmother used to wear a single turkey feather in her hair. (I have this feather—it is one of my most precious possessions.)

A feather-shaft is hollow and forms a channel for energy to enter and leave through the top of the head. Many native cultures use feathers as adornments. They believe that the feather carries the spirit of the bird, which can help you connect to the heavens.

Combs, headbands, and even hats can all be used as hair adornments if you place them in or on your hair with intention. For example, if your overall aim is to be more successful in your career, then as you fasten a comb say, "As this comb arranges my hair, so my life is being arranged for success."

There are times when you may want to cover your head. In many cultures, the head is covered during times of mourning. This is because it is during these times that a woman wants to pull her energy within. When she covers the top of her head, it keeps her energy from flowing freely. There are also many religious orders in which the hair is covered. This allows initiates to focus their attention and energy inward. If you have been putting out more energy than you are receiving, you may want to either cover your head with a hat or scarf, or place a comb near the top of your head to help contain your flow of energy.

Adorning Yourself with Flowers

To instantly refresh your energy, place a flower behind your ear or in your hair; create a lei of flowers to wear around your neck; or make a wreath to crown your head. Flowers carry the subtle yet powerful power of the earth. Every flower has a unique, etheric quality that you can use to enhance your energy field. Your energy will feel fresher and more glorious.

The Finishing Touch: Sparkling the Aura

After you have adorned yourself, layer after layer, from your sacred bath, via anointing yourself with oil, applying makeup, putting on clothes and jewelry, and adorning your hair, there are a couple of things that you can do to complete your transformation. Choose one of the following:

- Rub a few drops of essential oil on your hands and then pass them all over your body, just a few inches from the surface, to cleanse and uplift your auric field (this is the invisible yet very real energy field that surrounds your body). Visualize your energy becoming sparkling and bright.
- Fill a spray bottle (the kind that is used to mist plants will do) with spring water, essential oils, and flower essences, and spray it over your head and body or create a cloud of mist that you walk into. For

example, if you have been feeling lackluster, you might set the intention of feeling alive and passionately interested in life, and therefore mix in five drops of rosemary oil, five drops of wild-rose flower essence, plus a few drops of brandy to keep the mixture from clogging the mister nozzle. As you envelop yourself in this mist, say, "I am filled with vitality and zest!"

- Take a drop of frankincense oil, anoint your third eye with it, and then dab it behind your ears to "sparkle" your aura.

- Use your favorite perfume to bless your body and clothes while you focus on your overall intention. Lightly spray yourself or take a small amount and anoint yourself behind the ears, between your breasts, and lightly on top of your head. (Note: Some people have allergies to perfume, so it's considerate to be sparing with strong perfumes. If possible, choose perfumes that have natural ingredients rather than chemical or synthetic ones.)

You have a calling in life. We all do. You can use the way you adorn yourself to propel you forward toward your destiny. Within you is a place that absolutely knows your soul's needs and has a vision for your future. You have an inner spirit that is alive with vibrant life force. Let your body be a blank canvas for this vitality to express itself. Adorn yourself with fabulous physical manifestations of the inner qualities of your soul. To stay vibrant and radiant, keep moving, changing, and evolving your adornments, because you will continue to change and grow into an even more Glorious Woman.

LIQUID PLEASURES

WATER is a strong ally for any woman. It has the ability to connect you intimately with your feminine nature and thus can be a great source of power. In its purest essence, water is potent and sacred. It has the capacity to purify, replenish, rejuvenate, and even heal you. When you understand the secrets of water, you can begin to comprehend one of the mysteries of being a woman.

In ancient times, water was considered to be feminine. Many cultures believed that water had a living spirit with which women could commune. Drinking water (preferably from a pure spring) is, of course, essential to humans. Communities therefore grew up around water; and often a spring would form the center of a settlement. Women would gather on the riverbank or lakeshore to do their washing and at the well to draw water for their families and animals. And it was here that women would discuss the weather, their crops, and the business of the town. Stories were shared, along with strategies for meeting life's challenges. The water-source formed the center of a web of bonds between people. Water was the catalyst for the building of community and the bridging of cultures.

In those past times, women were the traditional guardians of water-sources. The early Egyptians, Persians, Indians, and Greeks, for example, all had female deities associated with wells, springs, and streams. In many ancient cultures, water was considered to be a living, healing energy and reverence was given to the spirit of water for the life she sustained.

Today we have lost this mystical understanding of the power of water. In our culture, water no longer seems alive. It is an inanimate fluid that we drink when we are thirsty and use for cleaning our car, clothes, dishes, or body. But it is not the precious and cherished vehicle for life force that it was once recognized to be. However, if we reignite our spiritual connection to water, its energy can bless every aspect of our life.

Your Intimate Connection to Water

Our connection to water is primal. It forms a kind of backdrop against which we live out the course of our lives. Water is a metaphor for the eternal journey of the soul, since it is continually giving birth to itself through evaporation, precipitation, flow, and return.

The longing to yield ourselves to the comfort of water in its various forms goes back to the beginnings of our individual lives and the beginning of life on earth. From immersion into a baptismal pool, to relaxing in a warm bath, to swimming naked on a moonlit night in a tropical lagoon, the pleasures and meanings associated with water are profound. There is something very powerful, almost orgasmic, about waiting with outstretched arms to welcome a summer shower. We begin life in water in the womb, and throughout life we are universally drawn to its soothing, cleansing, healing, joy-giving qualities.

This deep attraction is not hard to understand, given the fact that our bodies are more than 70 percent water. Your life on the planet began as a fertilized egg, which was more than 95 percent water. In your beginnings, you were almost all water! And the water that flows within you didn't start its journey with your birth, and doesn't stop with your death. That very same water within your body has gently flowed down the Ganges River, it has been a gentle mist high in the Rocky Mountains, and a cloud over the Amazon rainforest. In fact, the water that is now in your body has been inside countless plants, animals, and people.

Water is highly absorbent; every drop of water in your body contains a psychic imprint of the deep seas, Arctic snows, and tropical rainforests where it has traveled. You are truly a part of all things. Additionally, I believe that there is a genetic imprinting that connects the water in your body to all waters and creates a yearning within you to meld with water.

When you put one drop of water near a larger pool of water, the single drop is drawn toward the larger pool and merges with it. In a similar way, the water in your body is drawn to the sacred waters of life. You indeed have an intimate connection to water.

Not only does water hydrate our cells and cleanse our bodies, it also has profound spiritual qualities. Literally, water reflects consciousness, and our life has a connection to the consciousness of the water within and around us. And now modern research supports what ancient mystics have always known: water contains secrets of life.

Scientists have been studying the wondrous and mysterious properties of water and have documented findings that confirm that thoughts, emotions, and music affect the molecular structure of water. This is very important information to be aware of because the human body is composed of billions of cells that each hold water. The quality and the energy of the water in these cells make an enormous difference in your overall well-being.

Water is a very yielding substance: it changes its physical form from ice to fluid to steam. It is also a very absorbent substance: it alters its molecular shape quite readily and obviously when there are contaminants in it; and *the vibrations of the environment and your intention can change the molecular shape of water.*

Masaru Emoto, an eminent Japanese researcher, has documented the molecular changes in water created by environmental energy, thoughts, and emotions. He freezes droplets of water from different places and photographs them using a special microscope. (When you freeze water, it forms a crystalline shape similar to the structure of a snowflake. Every drop of water freezes in some kind of structural pattern.) Emoto discovered that freezing water drops from a particular source created particular patterns. For example, water from natural springs or pure mountain streams demonstrates perfectly formed geometric patterns, whereas water from a polluted river looks half-formed, distorted; or sometimes when pollution is very high, shows no observable crystalline shape at all.

Although each ice crystal photograph is different (no two snowflakes have ever been the same), similar crystal shapes occur within a similar water source. For example, 100 separate photographs taken of water from a particular Japanese river reveal a common structural tendency.

Emoto was so fascinated by his results that he decided to experiment with other variables. He took some distilled water and placed half of it between loudspeakers relaying classical music. The other half of the water was not in the vicinity of the music. The difference in the molecular shape of the water was remarkable. The Beethoven *Pastorale* water created exquisite, evenly patterned snowflake-like structures when frozen, while the other half of the distilled water showed almost no crystalline structure. The music had literally changed the molecular structure of the water. His research extended into other kinds of music, including heavy metal, which showed fragmented, distorted shapes.

The most stunning aspect of Emoto's research occurred when he and his colleagues decided to take distilled water and project thoughts and emotions into the water. They would type a word on to a piece of paper and then tape it to a glass bottle overnight. The water was then frozen and photographed. The results were phenomenal. Positive words such as "thank you," "angel," and "love" revealed splendid symmetrical crystalline formations. Negative phrases like "you fool," "you make me sick," and "demon" yielded erratic, chaotic patterns. The researchers also prayed over the water and found astonishing crystalline structures were formed as a result. They additionally found that placing nature photographs underneath or near the glass-enclosed water made a remarkable difference to the structure of it! (Some of his results can be seen at wellnessgoods.com/art_wat_messages.html)

These scientists have demonstrated that our thoughts and emotions can affect the vibrational energy and structure of water. They have shown that water is highly responsive to its environment.

This research is extraordinarily valuable because it shows that, purely by using a focused intention, you can empower and bless the water that you use internally and externally. For example, hold a glass of water in your hands and intend or imagine life force flowing into it. You will actually change its molecular composition in a positive way. Or, take a pitcher of water and place it on a picture of a beautiful flower or a photograph of any lovely natural scene and leave it overnight. You are charging the water with vitality, in much the same way that a priest would bless it, and thus creating holy water. Drink it the next morning or pour it into your bath so that it can refresh and nourish your entire body.

Water for Purification

Throughout history, water has represented purification and cleansing. One well-known example of this is India's holy river, the Ganges, which is revered by millions of Hindu pilgrims who bathe in its waters every day to spiritually cleanse and purify themselves.

It was not uncommon for water to be used in ancient initiation and purification ceremonies especially for women. For example, the coastal Nootka Indians of northwest Canada used the sea for initiation rites for girls emerging into womanhood. A young woman would be put into the ocean and have to swim a long distance back to the shore. As she swam in the deep, cold sea, her courage and the deep feminine force and mystery of the sea transformed her into a woman.

Legends about great, purifying floods are found in many cultures of the world. The biblical story of Noah and his ark is perhaps the best known of these, but the ancient Sumerians and Greeks told similar stories, as did the Native Americans. The kind of momentous cleansing and subsequent rebirth of the earth that is represented by these flood stories is reflected on an individual level through the sacrament of baptism. Although baptism is often considered to be a Christian ritual, many other religions and cultures have also used water for rites of purification.

Maintaining Your Energy Throughout the Day

Male and female energy are different. It is essential for a woman to continually purify and renew her energy. If she takes a break to replenish herself after each time that she projects her energy outwards, she will find that she can maintain her energy all day long.

This need for continual replenishment during the day perhaps goes back to the time when women were gatherers and needed to preserve their energy throughout the day in order to care for the children, and gather and prepare food. They needed to sustain themselves for these ongoing tasks, which made demands on them throughout the day. On the other hand, men would have periodic bursts of activity, when they went out hunting. When they returned from the hunt, they could then take a long rest to restore their energy.

One of the best ways to keep renewing yourself is to purify yourself with water, either by washing, drinking, or misting yourself with scented water. This last is one of the easiest ways to refresh yourself. Mist your face occasionally with the intention that you are cleansing yourself. You might want to add two or three drops of essential oil to the water: pine, peppermint, lemon, grapefruit, sage, and juniper are all good oils to use. I often carry a small mister in my bag. It is especially great to use when stuck in traffic. (As an added bonus, it also helps hydrate your skin.)

Salt Bathing for Purification

Have you ever come home from a shopping trip or a gathering of people and felt dirty, even though you didn't work up a sweat? Your auric field has probably picked up negative or stagnant energy from other people. Our aura absorbs the energy of people and situations and it can also absorb the negative emotions of others. You can work hard outdoors and yet not feel dirty, because your aura has soaked up the energy of the plants, so you feel clean. However, you can spend all day in a fluorescent-lit office filled with cantankerous people and come home feeling grimy. This occurs because your aura has assimilated the energy of the office.

One of the fastest ways to cleanse yourself using water is to combine it with the purifying effects of salt. Salt has been used to release stagnant energies from homes and people for thousands of years. To cleanse yourself of negativity, or when your aura feels grungy, put up to a pound of salt in a warm bath and soak in it for at least twenty minutes. Or, you can add one pound of Epsom salts and soak for seven minutes. Rinse yourself with cold water and your aura will shine.

Salt can also be used in the shower. Take a small handful of salt, mix it with a little water, and briskly rub your skin until it glows. Do not, however, rub so hard that you hurt yourself. In order to purify yourself, do this with the intention that you are releasing anything that you don't need in your life. Complete your shower with a cold rinse and you will step out of it sparkling!

Sacred Symbolism for Water Purification

Sacred symbolism is a way to use everyday tasks to purify yourself and also provide meaning in your life. For example, as you shower and the water cascades over your body, say to yourself, "I'm releasing all that is not needed in my life. I'm giving it back to the Great Mother for renewal." While standing in the shower, imagine all your unwanted stress coming to the surface of your skin. Scrub it away with a bar of soap and let it wash down the drain. Ultimately the water that flows off your body will return to the sea where it, and all the residual energy it carries, will be purified.

When you wash your hands, say to yourself, "I am washing my hands of situations, emotions, and thoughts that do not strengthen and empower me." When you take a bath, affirm, "I am soaking in the liquid nectar of the Goddess. All that is not needed in my life swirls away from me down the drain." You are participating in ancient rituals for purification.

Water for Rejuvenation and Rebirth

Big Island, Hawaii; many years ago: I'm in a beautiful fern-filled grotto. At the far end of the grotto, nasturtiums cascade over the bank next to a tropical waterfall. Sparkling water tumbles and splashes down the rocks into a clear, deep pool. I am in my early twenties and I'm standing next to the man I'm about to marry. I listen to the judge talk about the joys and responsibilities of being married. It's an intimate group that has gathered for our wedding: the judge, his wife, a couple of friends, David, and me. The judge stops talking. He looks closely at me and then looks deep into David's eyes and says softly, "Walk over to the waterfall." We are surprised, but we walk around the pool and stand next to the waterfall. The rippling water sounds like the ebullient laughter of children.

The judge, who's also a proponent of natural living, calls to us across the pool, "Stand naked under the waterfall."

What? Take my clothes off? Take off everything? Stand naked under the waterfall? Arrrggghh!

His words put me into a kind of shock, then, suddenly, a calm filled me. A muted memory nudged at the edge of my mind; of sacred waters in an ancient time. In the depths of my being, I knew what I was being asked to do was profound and holy. The request to stand nude with my beloved under the flowing waters no longer seemed strange or wrong. In fact, it felt very right.

David and I dropped our clothes on the moss and climbed over the rocks until we stood on a rock ledge with the bracing water showering over our bodies. The judge then dived into the pool, swam over to the waterfall, and climbed up on the rocks to stand with us while water cascaded over all of us. He held our hands and said, "Water is the source of life. It is purifying and renewing. You are now reborn into a new life. I pronounce you husband and wife."

As I stood naked under the waterfall, I felt something primal and sacred occurring. The gracious waters seemed to be washing away some of the darkness of shame and suffering from my past and childhood. In its place was something clean, bright, and new. My wedding was not just a commitment to another human being, it was a profound spiritual renewal and a new beginning.

Healing Baths

In every ancient culture with esoteric traditions, women have used baths for healing and renewal. The sacred bath was steeped in ceremony: rare oils were added to the water, flowers were floated on the surface, and flickering candlelight lit the bathing chamber. The bath was the place where a woman took refuge from her busy day to renew her spirit and soothe her soul. In the same way a baby is soothed in its mother's arms, the feminine energy of warm water is healing and renewing.

Perhaps part of the magic of baths is the subliminal reminder of being gently immersed in our mother's amniotic fluid. When you soak in a bath, a residual memory of the safety of the womb is activated. Its gentle, caressing rhythms allow you to truly relax and feel safe. Dr.

Frédéric LeBoyer pioneered the technique of gently floating newborn babies in warm water just after delivery. Almost universally, babies who were upset or frightened became calm and relaxed when immersed in the water.

To increase the life-force energy in your bath, stimulate the water by swirling it with your hand or your foot. Research shows that swirled water is fresher and cleaner because swirling revitalizes the electrical charge of the water molecules. This is why running streams are much cleaner and healthier than still and stagnant water. Although the water in your bathtub is not necessarily inert, the simple act of swirling it changes its molecular structure and additionally invokes the feeling of naturally flowing water.

To stimulate your immune system, rinse off in cold water after either your shower or bath. Switching between hot and cold water stimulates the circulation and is thought to also stimulate the immune system. Native Americans step out of the intense heat of the sweat lodge and splash in the icy water of a nearby stream, believing that this strengthens the body and purifies the spirit. Many past and present-day health practitioners advocate not only taking cold rinses, but actually dipping or swimming in cold water as a way to stimulate the immune system.

Listening to Water

Many people attribute the restorative properties of sitting by the sea or by a mountain stream to the negatively charged ions created by the moving water. Numerous studies have shown the health benefits of a negative-ion environment, from lessening depression to accelerating the healing process for burn patients. However there is also a deeper reason why these places are so healing. The murmuring sound of the sea and the babbling rhythm of a mountain stream are reminders of the greater rhythm of life. The human body is filled with rhythms from the cadence of our breath, to the beat of our heart, to our hormonal cycles. When we are in a naturally rhythmic, watery environment, our body synchronizes and harmonizes itself with the rhythm of nature.

Neurological research has found that listening to the rhythms of water can boost the immune system. Studies report a positive response in the neuroendocrine hormones and the sympathetic nervous system when subjects listened to a recording of water. Not everyone has the opportunity to spend time near the sea or mountain streams, but you can activate some of the positive effects of these places by playing one of the readily available CDs of the sound of naturally moving water. (Make sure that it is a natural recording and not a synthesized version created in a sound studio.) Another way to gain these positive effects is to make or obtain a fountain for your home. I feel that the sound is even more important than the way the fountain looks, so spend time arranging the water flow and the rocks to get a sound that is soothing.

Drinking Water: Elixir of Life

Most women understand the importance of drinking water, but few understand how essential hydration is to their physical, emotional, and spiritual well-being. Your body is comprised mostly of water, and therefore water consumption is imperative. Your cells swell with each glass of water you drink. Imagine pomegranate seeds left in the sun to dry; they will shrivel up as their water content evaporates. This also happens to your cells. A minimum of eight glasses of water a day is recommended to keep healthy and fit. A study done at the Fred Hutchinson Cancer Research Center in Seattle found that women who drank more than five glasses of water a day were less likely to develop colon cancer. Other studies have found there is less risk of bladder cancer, kidney problems, or kidney stones when the body is properly hydrated.

Water also has beauty benefits: it strengthens and tightens the skin, giving the face a healthy glow. How do you know if you are drinking enough water? Your urine should be almost clear, with a faint yellow tint, and your skin moist. Pinch your hand; if the skin puckers or keeps the pinched shape after you release your fingers, you are dehydrated.

Consider the Source

It's imperative that you drink the highest quality water you can. There are several things to take in consideration. Tap water is not usually the best source: in the United States, two billion pounds of pesticides are used every year, and most of them end up in the water table. That's eight pounds a year for every American. Also, according to the Environmental Working Group (EWG) in Washington D.C., manufacturers dumped more than one billion pounds of toxic chemicals into rivers, lakes, and other bodies of water between 1990 and 1994. In addition, about 450 million pounds are dumped via sewage. About 1,000 new chemicals are created and introduced into the environment and our water each year. Yet the Federal Safe Drinking Water Act only addresses 100 contaminants.

America isn't alone. All major industrialized countries suffer from water pollution. However, some European countries do a better job of protecting their population from atrazine, a commonly used pesticide. It's banned in many countries, including Sweden, Germany, and Italy. In Switzerland, where atrazine is manufactured, the drinking water standard for the substance is thirty times stricter than in the US.

Water from the country may be as dangerous as urban water. According to the EWG and Physicians for Social Responsibility: "Every spring, farmers across the Corn Belt apply 150 million pounds of five herbicides—atrazine, cyanazine, simazine, alacholor, and metolachlor to their corn and soybean fields. Every spring, rains wash a substantial portion of these chemicals into the drinking water of 11.7 million people in the Midwest." They state that none of these herbicides are removed by the conventional drinking-water treatment technologies that are used by more than 90 percent of all water companies in the United States. To date, we don't know the effect of ingesting one, let alone a combination of these chemicals.

In July 1999, a *USA Today* article cited a government report that concluded that much of the United States' groundwater and many of its streams are contaminated with unhealthy levels of pesticides and fertilizers. Many of the streams that were most heavily polluted with insecticides were in metropolitan areas such as those of Dallas–Fort Worth, Las Vegas, Tallahassee, and Washington D.C. Chlorine, which is in 96 percent of agricultural chemicals and (as a purifier) in most tap water, combines easily with other substances in water to produce organochlorines, which have the potential of being carcinogenic.

Here are some points to consider when choosing which water to drink:

Tap water: As discussed above, most tap water has a number of contaminants and pollutants, so it's a good idea to invest in a water purification system. Reverse osmosis is preferable to charcoal filters. Do research to get the best quality system you can afford, and change the filters promptly, otherwise bacterial growth can create worse-quality water than before.

Bottled water: Bottled water is regulated, but not rigorously. It's only required to be as safe as tap water. In fact, your bottled water may be nothing more than tap water. Industry information states that approximately 25 percent of bottled water actually comes from a municipal water system. In 1999 when the Natural Resources Defense Council randomly analyzed samples of bottled water, it found that approximately a third of the 103 brands tested contained higher levels of contaminants than were allowable under government or industry guidelines.

Bottled at source: If you choose to drink bottled water instead of purified water, drink still (uncarbonated) spring water in a glass bottle that states that it is bottled at the source. Spring water that comes in plastic bottles will often absorb some of the plastic (especially if the bottle becomes warm), so every time you drink this water you are getting a dose of petrochemicals. The reason that spring water should be bottled at its source is because otherwise the water is transported in large tankers to a bottling factory and can sometimes become polluted by trace chemical residues inside the tanker.

Carbonated water: Avoid carbonated water because it contains carbon dioxide. Used to make the water bubble, it is also a waste product of the human body. Whenever you exhale, you release carbon dioxide into the air. So when you drink carbonated water, you are taking in a product which your body is trying to rid itself of.

The pH of the water: It's imperative for health that the water in the human body has a balanced pH. When your body becomes either too acid or too alkaline, it can become weakened. If your body is too acid (and therefore has a low pH), over time this contributes to cardiovascular weakness, an acceleration of free-radical damage, and brittle bones.

If the body is too alkaline, which is much less common than acidosis, you may have digestive problems, poor elimination, and immune system problems. A study done at the University of California on almost 10,000 post-menopausal women showed that those who had higher acidic levels were at greater risk for low bone-density than those with normal pH levels. I suggest that you invest in pH test strips available inexpensively at your chemist, and test your water. It should be in a normal range, between 6.2 and 7.2.

Eat living water: Eat organic fresh fruits and vegetables with a high water content. The water within these is shimmering with vigor. A freshly picked organic cucumber yields remarkable health benefits from the living water inside it. Whenever you can eat living water, it stimulates and strengthens your entire energy field.

Energized water: Energize your drinking water in natural sunlight or moonlight, with your prayers, or by swirling it. Energized water is rejuvenating and affirms your connection to this great originator of life.

Earth is a water planet, being in this way unlike any other in our solar system, and our life comes from and is fed by water. We are replenished physically by it, and at the same time we are also nourished spiritually. As you acknowledge and honor the spirit of water, you will find that the spirit of water will purify and bless you.

12
WOMANLY
ENCHANTMENTS

Y OUR innermost dreams can come true—not passing fancies, but your true heart's desire. Instead of wishing, waiting, and hoping without success, there are timeless feminine enchantments that you can use.

A note here about the word "spell." Some people get squeamish about this word. They have images of a witch with big wart on her nose, stirring a cauldron filled with dead frogs and other nasty things. In fact, spells have always been a form of female magic. Currently, in New Age vernacular, this ancient art form is called "manifestation." Spells have always been an expression of a woman's ability to give form to the formless. When a woman in ancient Mesopotamia tied two fresh twigs together and placed them on her home altar, asking for a husband for her daughter, this was a form of spell. (If you have trouble with the word "spell," then substitute "manifestation.")

To become an enchantress, it is valuable to understand that there is a tightly woven web of energy that connects all matter. We are able to influence this web of creation through our personal vibration, thoughts, and prayers. This is the underlying understanding that allows rituals for sacred living and enchantments to work. When you combine imagination with a strong intention, you can manifest reality. This has been a womanly art for thousands of years. In fact, many present-day philosophies such as "mind over matter," visualization techniques, affirmations, and positive thinking all have their roots in this ancient feminine art form.

Spells work. They really do! I don't understand exactly how they work, but over and over again I have seen remarkable results produced when a woman weaves her own magic through the time-honored methods of enchantment. Intention is the power behind enchantment. It is what gives it the energy to manifest. The more specific and clear you are about what you desire, the easier it is to manifest it. It's important to examine your subconscious intention (which may not be the same as what you consciously want), and to take the time to be aware of what you really desire. Discover the true outcome you want, and believe that you can achieve it. You need to really believe that you can manifest your dream. If you create an enchantment but don't really believe it will happen, chances are that it won't.

Carmel, a woman who attended one of my intensive seminars, did an enchantment for a new job. Within a week, she was offered a job with another company. She was ecstatic! However, a while after she started the job, she wasn't happy. She couldn't figure out what went wrong. When I spoke to her, I realized that what she actually wanted in her life was freedom, and she had thought a new job would give this to her . . . but it didn't. She attained what she consciously wanted, but not what her deepest desire really was. I suggested that she perform another spell, but instead focus on freedom. Not long after she did a freedom spell, she was offered a position in which she was able to travel and was also able to determine her own working hours.

A Little-Known Secret about Manifestation

There is a little-known secret of manifestation: in order to be an expert at enchantments, you must be willing *not* to have the object of your desire. When you master this, you will have the ability to manifest your dreams.

"How can that be?!" you may ask. "How can someone want something and also not want it?"

The secret is that you must not be attached to the results that you desire. You must offer your desire from the pureness of your heart and trust that who you are, what you do, and where you are, is enough in that moment . . . and then accept all that life brings you. You must trust the process and know that everything has its own time and reason. When you do this, your dreams almost magically begin to come true.

Enchantments are a bit like planting seeds; sometimes you must give them time to germinate and grow. You wouldn't plant a seed one day and then go out and start shouting at the earth the next morning, "Come up, damn you!" and rant and rave because you didn't have fruit the next day. Plant your wish, give it a focused intention, and then completely let it go. Know it will move to fulfillment in its own time.

The more willing you are to unconditionally accept and love what you are, what you have, and where you are in life, the easier it is to create more. Life gives us what we focus on. If you focus on what you lack in your life, you will create more lack. If you come from the attitude that what you have is great, it would be fun to have more, and you aren't attached to getting it, you can create miracles.

We lived in Seattle for twenty years. The Northwest is a splendid place with snow-capped mountains, lush green forest, and rugged ocean shorelines. There is nowhere that is more beautiful, when the sun shines. However, when it's gray and overcast (which is most of the time), it is dreary, grim, and depressing. I desperately wanted to move somewhere that was warm and sunny. I did all the enchantments I could think of. I meditated on our new home. I visualized us already living there. I prayed to the Creator. I made an altar dedicated to our new home. I made a collage of pictures from magazines of houses that looked like the home of our dreams and meditated on it. Our real estate agent in California even asked her women's group to visualize us finding our new home. Nothing worked.

We looked for a new home for *four years*. We flew to California from Washington State (a distance of 1,000 miles) *fourteen times* to look at property. I forgot what I knew so well—that I needed to be willing *not* to move. But for those four years, I couldn't accept that. I knew I had to get out of the rain, into the sun. I just *had* to.

One day I surrendered. I just let go and completely released my yearning to move to a sunny climate. I had done everything that I knew how to do to and nothing seemed to work. I called our real estate agent and said, "Stop looking for a house for us. If we haven't found anything yet, maybe we're not meant to move." I felt lightness fill me as soon as I said the words. I surrendered and accepted where I was and who I was. Instead of feeling that I wouldn't be okay until I had a new home, I began to love and appreciate my beautiful space in Seattle.

Then magic happened! A couple of days later our agent called and said,

"Guess what: I've found the perfect place for you!" Thirty days later, I was living in my new home—and it was absolutely the home of my dreams. Enchantments work, you just need to let go of your attachment—your *need* to have what you want them to bring you and allow them to unfold in their own way and time.

Your Dreams Can Come True!

Most of us are programmed as children to believe that dreams only come true in fairy tales. We are told from our earliest years that we shouldn't ask for too much because it is selfish, or because we will be disappointed when it doesn't happen. And then as we grow into adulthood, there is an unwritten rule that we shouldn't talk about our wants and desires openly. We also subconsciously believe that there is only so much success to go around, and if one person gets some, then there is less for us. Hence, when someone wins the lottery, instead of saying, "How very wonderful for that person. I'm so glad they won," most people grumble because they believe that there is a limited amount of good fortune in the world; and one person's success is another's failure.

We accept a life where dreams don't come true because we believe "that's life." We feel that we are mature and level-headed when we experience disappointment and lack of fulfillment, because that is the "real" world. And then we surround ourselves with people who share the same beliefs. Ultimately, our reality is created by what the people around us agree to at the time.

Many women feel deep inside that they don't really deserve to have their dreams fulfilled, so they unconsciously sabotage any notion of success because they feel unworthy. It is now time to stop the tyranny of self-sabotage. If you keep doing the same things in life, you will get the same results.

Right now, this moment as you hold this book in your hands, is a new chance. It can be a new beginning, a time to embark on a new way of thinking. Today you can begin taking control of your life and directing its course, rather than always being influenced by the mass consensus.

Most women accept, without hesitation, the limitations formed by their early childhood conditioning, their family, society, and the media. They allow the beliefs and assumptions of others to dictate the course of their lives. Enchantments involve making a choice about the direction of your life, and true choice comes from a deep place within you of wisdom, intuition, and trust.

To step beyond the boundaries of what is normal and acceptable, and the people who tell you it can't be done, takes courage and initiative. Listening to your inner voice can allow you to be authentic and to tune into your true heart's desire. You are ready. Let this be the day you begin.

You are always manifesting, whether you are aware of it or not. You create your reality out of your beliefs and ideas about the world around you. A woman who believes that men are arrogant will be surrounded by arrogant men. She will also draw to her other women who have similar beliefs, thus validating a "victim consciousness" that supports her inner convictions. A woman who asserts that men are supportive and loving will be surrounded by men who are.

The challenge is to choose the circumstances of your life instead of manifesting your reality by default. Be pulled into the future by your vision of what you desire, rather than being pushed by the pain of your negative beliefs. Focus on what you do want in life, rather than what you don't want. Whenever you do an enchantment, always concentrate on the positive. A friend told me that she was going to do an enchantment to get all the people in her office to stop smoking. I suggested that she affirm what she wanted rather than what she didn't want. So she affirmed, "I breathe only clean air." Shortly afterwards, she was promoted to an office where no one smoked.

Manifestation Is a Sacred Art

Both my parents were scientists, and when I was young I also wanted to be a scientist. I have an interest in science as well as spirituality, so it is always exciting for me when they overlap. Science reveals that absolutely everything in the universe is created out of atoms, and between these atoms is a vastness of space. In fact, it's been estimated that only .0001 percent of the universe is solid, and the rest is empty space. Unmeasurable, yet nevertheless very real, an innate intelligence exists within this vast space that arranges and rearranges atoms into various forms of animate and inanimate life. This is not dissimilar to water, which with the same chemical composition can become rain, snow, fog, or ice.

Einstein called this vast intelligence "the unified field"; religion calls it God. Native Americans call it the "Great Mystery." In other words, there is a life force within everything. And you can influence this energy through your thoughts and words. In the Bible it says, "In the beginning was the word." This is true. In this day of new beginnings, your word can become law in your universe.

Your intention can issue out from you in the form of an enchantment, like a great wave. The stronger and clearer this wave signal is, the more quickly and powerfully you will manifest the form you are calling up. Manifestation is ultimately a sacred act, for when you are manifesting, it is an act of creation.

An Attitude of Gratitude

Women who are masters of the use of enchantments to create their heart's desire also understand the power of gratitude. They are enormously grateful women. When you focus on gratitude, joy, love, and appreciation, you will bring more of them into your life, and into the world. When you focus on a feeling of lack or on what you fear may come, you are sending a strong message to the Universe to send you whatever you fear. When you are truly grateful for what you have, who you are, and where you are, miracles abound. Give thanks daily, hourly, as often as possible. Appreciate all that is wondrous and special in your life; and everything will grow in abundance, bounty, and glory.

Simple Spells

Upon rising: "I open my arms in gratitude and love for the glory of this new day. I call upon the Goddess to guide me this day, that her joy may fill me and flow through me. So be it." (Face toward the rising sun and open your arms as you say these words.)

Upon bathing: "My body is purified by these healing waters. I am renewed by the nourishing Spirit of Water. I am in the flow this day and always!" (Whether you are taking a bath or shower, the water should be running when you say these words.)

When putting your clothes on: "I am hereby enveloping myself in a mantle of beauty and grace. Blessed be!"

When taking your clothes off: "I'm shedding all that I don't need from my day and from my life. So be it!" (Visualize what you desire to release as you undress and say these words.)

When cooking: "I call upon universal life force to fill this food with vitality and love. All who partake of this food will be nourished by this bounty." (Hold your hands, palms down, over the food that you are preparing. Visualize energy and light flowing from the Universe into your hands and then into the food.)

When driving: "I am safe and protected. Angels before me, behind me, on either side of me and above me, keeping me safe and blessed in a golden circle of light." (Imagine your car surrounded by large, protective angels.)

Going to a gathering: "I gain wisdom and joy with each person I meet." (Project your energy into the room or space so you can feel the walls and corners.)

Starting work: "I am creative, dynamic and mindful. My work is enriching to me and to others and I am enriched by those with whom I work. I call upon the muses and the Great Goddess to help me be of service this day."

Special Enchantments

Below are a few samples of spells. Often the most powerful enchantments are the ones that you create for yourself. It is not the form of the ritual that creates magic, it is the purity of your heart and the intensity of your intention—and, of course, your willingness to surrender it all to the Creator.

An Enchantment for Children for Healing the World

Deb is a wonderful American friend of mine who lives in the Middle East. She was there during the attack on the World Trade Center in New York. Afterwards, it was a frightening time for everyone. Deb is the kind of woman who believes that change often begins with children, so a few weeks after the attack she visited a first-grade class (the teacher is a friend of hers). In the class there were Pakistani, Lebanese, American, and Palestinian children, who had been reading about fairies.

Deb put a globe in the center of the room on a beautiful bright cloth. The class sat in a circle around it and Deb gave them each a fistful of "fairy dust" (glitter, to us mortals). Then she told the children to close their eyes and think of a place in the world where they wanted to send a "happy wish." She told them that they could send fairy magic anywhere they wanted . . . it could be where their grandparents lived, or where they lived, or anywhere they wanted to have peace and happiness. Deb said, "Put your wish into the fairy dust."

The children scrunched their eyes and wiggled their fists, and wished really hard. Then she counted to three, and all sprinkled the "fairy dust" on to the globe. They did this with their whole heart and soul. The ones who had magic wands (many did, since they had been learning about fairies) waved them over the globe, and then they all giggled and clapped. I love this enchantment and wanted to include it in the hope that you might share it with your children.

Blessing for the Coming Month

On the first morning of the waxing new moon, arise before dawn. Face east. In front of you there should be a white candle, a bowl of water in a clear glass container, and a white rose, or any white flower.

Light the candle, hold your palms over the water allowing love and energy to fill the water and say aloud: "I call upon my guardians, guides, angels, ancestors, and allies to join with me to bless the coming month. May your healing guidance bring blessings to me and my friends and family during the coming moon cycle. May our hearts be filled with joy and love. I affirm this for the greater good of all. So be it and so it is."

Blow out the candle and slowly drink the water, feeling grace and peace fill you.

Spell for Attracting Love

A night or two before the full moon, place two pink candles close to each other. Make a circle of rose quartz stones in the shape of a heart around the candles. Take rose essential oil and anoint the area between and above your eyes (your third eye) and in the center of your heart chakra.

Light one candle and say aloud: "My love, you are being drawn to me as I to you. May our hearts intertwine and may our love be strong. Whether you be on land, air or sea I call you to me."

Visualize yourself being held in the arms of your lover. Then take the first candle, light the second candle with it, and allow both to burn for at least ninety minutes.

Spell for Abundance

Create an altar with objects that represent your desires. For example, if you desire to pay for your child's college education, procure a diploma or make a tiny facsimile of a diploma and put your child's name on it *as if they had already graduated* and place this on your altar. Or if you want to go on a romantic tropical holiday with your husband, place a seashell on your altar. It's better to put objects that represent what you would spend money on rather than focusing on the money itself. (Remember, miracles work in many ways: perhaps you won't have to pay for the vacation—it might come as a prize or a gift from a friend.) You can also take a magnet and wrap a high denomination bank note around it to draw prosperity to you.

Take three green candles and place them on your altar in a triangle. Say aloud, with passion: "I am a very prosperous woman. Abundance is flowing to me right now. With every breath I take, I am becoming more and more prosperous. I am infinitely grateful for all my present prosperity and I have and I am open for even more!"

Light each candle, saying: "I am grateful for my past. I am grateful for my present. I am grateful for my future."

Pitfalls of Enchantments

Enchantments, whether you call them "creative visualizations," "spells," "affirmations," or "manifestations" all use the same mechanics. And all of these enchantment techniques have similar pitfalls. The downside of all of them is that it's easy to get into an ego trip when you first discover that your thoughts can have an effect on your reality. So often, when a woman begins to step into her power and discovers her ability to manifest, she feels a surge of power and that she can do anything. She may begin to drive everyone around her crazy. I remember once going to much trouble to pick out a very special gift for an acquaintance. As she opened her present, she beamed at everyone around her and announced: "This is exactly what I wanted. I manifested this. This is my creation!" and bounced away without saying thank you. I wanted to yell, "You created it . . . but I bought it!"

After a woman gets comfortable with manifesting, this feeling of omnipotence begins to drop away and can be replaced by a feeling that she is responsible for everyone's ill fortune; or she will feel guilty that she hasn't stopped bad things from happening to others. This is also a type of ego trip. Each person is responsible for creating her own experiences. You are not responsible for the fate of others.

Another pitfall is for a woman to see something negative that happens to her as coming from someone who is "projecting negative energy" toward her. Almost always, when something negative happens to you, it is not a "psychic attack;" rather it occurs because you have some inner conflicts that haven't been resolved. If you feel that there are negative forces around you, chances are there is some limiting belief or unresolved negativity within you and you have projected it on to someone or something else. Look within.

Learning the womanly art of enchantments is sacred and holy. It reminds us that there is an immense creative force in the universe that we are part of. It connects us to our own deep creative nature and allows us to make our innermost dreams come true.

BOUNDLESS CREATIVITY

EVERY woman needs to be creative. Although today's world revolves around goals, accomplishments, and being productive, we each need to have a part of our life that is completely free, a place where we can surrender, trust our instincts, and express our soul.

You were born creative. You have a creative force inside you. We all do. It resides in every cell of your body and in the vast spaces between the atoms of your being. To express your creativity is a holy act, for it forms a bridge between the invisible and the visible, bringing spirit into form.

When you are being truly creative, time stands still and you enter into a dimension that can carry you beyond the ordinariness of life. Ancient mystics knew this; that is why they often used artistic expression to enter into spiritual trance states. For example, shamans in native cultures throughout the world used dance to enter into a mystical state to receive messages from the gods. In the Far East, painting mandalas was a way to transport into spiritual realms. Native Americans used drama to activate healing forces and to connect with Great Spirit.

Your creativity is a channel through which you can travel to sacred spaces within yourself; it is your window to the divine.The hallowed energy within you can also travel outwards through this channel to be expressed in the world. When you are being creative, whether it is by painting, sculpting, writing, dancing, acting, or cooking, there is a powerful life force that is being transformed into a viable form. In the deepest sense of creativity, your life becomes your art. It becomes your personal creation, which is constantly evolving. This occurs when your creative expression is not something you learned, but is an innate natural flow of your energy and vitality.

If you cap this natural stream, your spirit withers as surely as a flower that has been plucked from the vine. Blocking your creative force forms an obstacle between you and the Creator. It also impedes your ability to find solutions to any challenges you are facing, because you then have difficulty hearing the messages from Spirit. The greatest solutions come through spontaneous insight rather than logic and reasoning. If you allow your creativity free rein, you can hear the voice of the Creator and become stronger, healthier, more radiant, and self-assured.

Some of the greatest blocks to creativity are the desires to get the approval of others; to do it perfectly; and to do it as others have never done it before you. Being creative often means defying the norm—defying current opinions and beliefs. It means raising your fist to the heavens and declaring, "This is who I am. This is what I stand for. I don't give a damn about your judgments." It is when you are able and willing to do this that you can truly express yourself.

Creativity also means sometimes getting messy and creating projects that are unruly, untidy, and definitely not perfect. Accept that chaos often precedes creativity, and it's not up to you to constantly judge the value of what you have created or to compare what you've done to the creations of others.

It's not true that "there is nothing new under the sun." You are absolutely unique, and there has never been any being like you, nor will there ever be. You are "new under the sun." No one else in the world has the same unique blend of life experiences, beliefs, and perceptions as you. Hence, the creativity that flows through you is clearly individual. The soul of the world needs your rich variety and depth to remain vital and alive.

When you enter into the realm of creativity, there is an enormous amount of risk. You need to be willing to be open, to be the receptacle for the river of energy to flow through you. You need to trust your process and not judge yourself. And you need to be open to the possibility of being misunderstood, because what you have created may not always fit into the norm. You also have to push up against the self-imposed barrier of wanting to "do it right."

My daughter was a good student, and she went to a highly academic middle school. It was a great school in many respects, but the art produced by the students seemed contrived and cramped compared to the spontaneous, exhilarating art done by students at less academic schools. It occurred to me that the kids at my daughter's school were so programmed to "do it right" academically, that the same qualities that made them "good" students made them restrained, obstructed artists.

Research has been done that compares the age that a child learns to read with his or her ability to be a creative problem-solver. The study found that the earlier a child learned to read (a rational, mental activity), the less creative she was in her later life. I believe that part of the reason for this is that when a child is catapulted into early academic achievement, they step into the realm of doing it "right or wrong" and this diminishes the creative flow. So remember that in the creative process, there is no right or wrong way to do it. Allow artistic expression in whatever form it appears.

In creativity there is no failure. However, if no matter what you try, your mind keeps viewing what you do in terms of good and bad, you need to jump into the creative experience with both feet, and be willing to do it badly. In fact, relish the experience and be willing to be a "failure." If someone asks what you are doing, cheerfully say, "I'm doing an incredibly lousy painting!" Be glorious in your defiance! What you resist, persists, and if you are constantly resisting failure, guess what? You will continue to view yourself as a failure. Embrace your self-judgments, have fun with them, savor them, and they won't run your life.

You wouldn't chastise a toddler if they couldn't walk at the first try. So why beat yourself up for so-called failure for not doing something the way that everyone else does it. Besides, you didn't fail; you just learned something new and different about yourself. All authentic creativity reveals aspects of the self. Your art isn't so much a reflection of outer life but a powerful force that you can use to understand and also shape your own inner life.

Creativity was thought, in many ancient cultures, to be a way to reach the heavens and connect to the gods. In Greek mythology, the Muses were the nine Goddesses of the arts and of creativity. They were the daughters of Zeus, the king of the gods. Among other things, they ruled over poetry, drama, song, and dance. All creative inspiration from the Muses was thought to spring from the Divine Feminine Spirit.

A muse embodied inspiration and motivation. She was thought to breathe life into the ideas of the artist and give birth to his or her creations.

Often worshipped as a Goddess, the muse of ancient times played, to a certain extent, the role of the patron saint. A struggling musician, for instance, would pay homage to his muse, asking for assistance and guidance in his pursuit of a "divinely inspired" song. Or a poet might look to her muse to lighten her verse and to embellish her phrasing. The muse, full of light and energy, both resurrected the genius in despondent artists and increased the already active creativity in others.

The Muse of Art

Not long ago I was given some of the artwork that I had done when I was a child. It was the first time I had seen any of my childhood art in thirty-three years. As I went through a stack of my paintings and drawings, I was amazed. They were good. Really good. I had no idea that I had such skill. I wondered why I had stopped painting.

As I reached back in my memory, I recalled an incident when I was sixteen years old. I loved painting, it was the only time I could truly remove myself from the trauma that was occurring within my family. When I had a brush in my hand and a canvas in front of me, everything else in my life disappeared. In my teens I won some awards at the country fair and had even started to sell some of my paintings. I was thrilled when I received a commission to do a painting of a winter landscape. I was offered $100, which was an enormous amount of money in a rural farming community in 1967. This would be like offering a $1,000 to a sixteen-year-old now.

I worked on the painting in the art room at my school. I was so excited and so proud of it. It was finally complete, and I was ready to present it to the new owner. I went to school to pick it up and was shocked to see that it had been completely changed. Someone had repainted my entire canvas. I had done a realistic painting, and it was now stylized and modern. The art teacher smugly strolled into the room and said, "I knew that you were going to present your painting to Mr. King today, and I didn't want you to be disappointed when he said he didn't like it, so I repainted it for you." I went a bit numb, thanked her for her help, and took the painting to give Mr. King. I don't think he liked it much, but he paid me anyway (I do think that he would have liked my original painting). I never painted again.

As I looked at my childhood paintings, I realized that I had taken the comments of the art teacher to heart and had given up painting because I believed her when she told me that my art wasn't any good. As I looked at the stack of my childhood art, I had an epiphany. I suddenly realized that the art teacher didn't repaint my painting to help me, but because she was jealous that I was selling my paintings. I sobbed as I thought of all the years that I hadn't painted because I believed her. In that moment, a dam broke inside me and I grabbed some paper and pens and began drawing. I began pouring out my heart on to the paper. My painting surged with colors, shades, and movement. No longer leashed by the inner voice that said I wasn't an artist, I let my spirit fly. It didn't matter what the end result was: I knew I was free to paint again.

My husband is an excellent artist. Many years ago he was a builder, but he didn't enjoy his work. I asked him what he wanted to do with his life. He said, "I want to be an artist." I believed in my husband and wanted to support his vision for the future, so I told him to follow his dream. For several years, for hours every day, he sketched, drew, painted, read art books, and took art classes. His spirit flourished, and he began to paint wonderful landscapes and portraits.

During those years, people would ask me, "What does your husband do?" I would reply, "He is an artist." Their next question inevitably was, "Has he sold anything?" When I replied that he hadn't, they would smirk or raise their eyebrows, insinuating that he was not a real artist. *You do not need to sell your art to be an artist.* Being an artist is not reliant on whether people purchase your work. It is what is in your soul. David has now become a remarkable plein-air artist, and his art has appeared in prestigious galleries, but that doesn't make him more (or less) of an artist. He was an artist even before he drew his first sketch. The spirit of the artist always lived within him.

Before you pick up a paintbrush or purchase a sketchbook, allow the spirit of art to fill you. Be the artist. Feel the artist within you. Carry yourself as if you were an artist. Allow the spirit of art to move you, as if the paint were jumping out of the tube and flying on to your canvas. Use color and movement to express yourself. Paint your feelings. Paint your dreams. Paint wildly and lusciously. Express yourself, all of yourself. Remember that chaos precedes order. So be willing to make a mess.

For goodness' sake, don't judge the finished product. Tell your inner art critic to hush. In many native cultures, once art is complete, it is destroyed or blown to the four corners of the world, as in the case of Hopi and Tibetan sand paintings. These native people recognize that it is within the creative process, rather than the finished product, that spirit flows and comes alive.

To start, I suggest getting *big* pieces of paper and painting as you feel. If you feel timid, paint the timidity. If you feel agitated, paint that. Your painting can carry you into places in your soul you have never touched.

Writing Your Spirit

Since I've written a number of books, people often ask me, "How do you start? Where do you get your inspiration?" I want to make up something grand and say that I meditate at 4 A.M. Then I call upon the Muse of Writing, who comes and speaks directly to my soul, giving me great insights for the day. But most often writing for me consists of waves of patterns of avoidance, guilt, judgment, obsessive-compulsive behavior, and overeating. (I once gained 15 pounds writing a book.) In order to write, I have to suppress my inner critic, saying to her, "Shut up! I'm stronger than you"; remember to take time for myself each day; and try not to be distracted by those really "important" tasks like organizing the silverware drawer for the third time in a month.

However, in the midst of the nail-biting and teeth-gnashing of writing, there are times when I feel as if wisdom is flowing through me. During those times, hours sail by. I'm on fire with something I want to say, and I can't get the words out fast enough. When I'm complete, I feel cleansed to my bones.

When the fever of writing fills you, every word becomes an elegant way to discern, express, and integrate your life experiences. It doesn't matter whether you write about experiences from your own life or about those experiences that exist in your inner life. It doesn't matter if you are writing for yourself, or writing for publication. The process and the benefits are the same: writing allows energy and life force to flow through you, which can strengthen and heal you.

Just Begin!

Many years ago, I received a phone call that had a dramatic impact on my life. A publisher called and asked me to write a book about dreams. I said, "Yes, no problem. I can do that." I hung up the phone . . . and freaked out. I wasn't a writer. How could I possibly write a book? I had never written a book. At the time, I taught people how to work with their dreams, but how could I possibly write a book about it?

I sat for hours in front of a blank computer screen. I'd write a little bit, then tell myself it was no good and delete it. This went on for weeks. I was under such stress that decided I needed to see a therapist. She was intelligent, wise, and compassionate. When I explained my problem, she said, "That's easy. Just begin—and be willing to do it badly." I was shocked. I cried out, "What? You have a Ph.D. from Harvard, and you're telling me to *just* write the book, even if it's bad?"

She said, "Yup, that's my advice to you. And when you get it done, tell yourself it's good enough." I was disturbed by her advice, but I went home and began to write—this time without my inner critic judging and evaluating every word. It was amazing. The words just flew out of my soul. The advice the therapist gave me was some of the best I've ever received. My first book is not a masterpiece, but it is still selling years later, and I continue to get letters every week from people who have enjoyed it . . . all because I was willing to just begin.

Let Go of Your Inner Critic

I used to go through a period with every book when I hated whatever I had written. When my first book was published, I was so convinced it was terrible that I cringed every time anyone asked me to sign it. Book signings were an ordeal for me because I was sure that once they got home and read my book, the book buyers would feel that they had wasted their money. After I wrote *Sacred Space*, I even tried to convince Linda Gray, who was the editor-in-chief at Ballantine Books, not to publish it. I said, "Are you sure you want to? It's not really a very good book." They took it anyway, and I was amazed when it became a best-seller. Even though I'd had a number of books published by then, I was convinced everything I had written was terrible and I'd never be a "real writer." As I'm looking at the sentence I've just written, I'm realizing how incredible this sounds. How can someone who is a published writer feel this way? When you have low self-esteem, you will believe the most ridiculous things about yourself.

Since I really wanted to be a "real writer," I decided to buy some books on writing. This was a big mistake. One book said you can tell you are a true writer because you write for joy and pleasure. I didn't usually write for the joy of it. I wrote because I had some information that I thought might be valuable for others. Writing was really hard for me and definitely not fun. The more I read about becoming a writer, the more I was convinced that I'd never become a real one. I was so depressed. In the meantime I kept producing books. My editor suggested that I throw the writing books away. It was good advice.

As my self-confidence has grown over the years, I rarely go through such tortuous depths with everything I write. However, on those rare occasions when I do hate what I have written, I have found it enormously helpful to gently accept whatever I'm feeling. When I do this, something wonderful and spontaneous always occurs. The more I can accept myself and my work, the more I write something that completely delights me. And now there are times when I do write just for the joy of it. Perhaps I have become a real writer after all.

Inner Listening: Waiting for Writing to Be Born

To find your own voice in what you write, you must learn how to be quiet and really listen to your inner voice. Breathe, relax, and embrace silence. Gather it into your soul and gently notice the messages that float to the surface of your subconscious mind. Out of nothingness is born the world; out of your emptiness comes your greatest inspiration.

I've always met my deadlines, but with this book I missed two. This was a completely new experience for me. Although I was initially upset with myself for not finishing on time, I came to realize that creation comes when you let go of struggle and enter into a place of trust. I stopped exerting so much effort and began to listen to my inner self. By listening and waiting, slowly the book took shape.

The Muse of the Journal: The Courage to Tell Your Story

My first journals were definitely not satisfying. I would write down everything bad that happened to me in a day. Sometimes I'd get so furious I would end by ripping the page to shreds or scribbling all over it. All my friends were writing journals. They all had these enigmatic smiles as they scribbled away, like they had a secret friend and confidante. I felt left out. My journal wasn't a friend or a confidante. It was a confessor that I neither liked nor trusted. My journal was one more reason to feel guilty. If I didn't write in it every day I was plagued with self-recrimination. After a while, I would throw it away, and then a few weeks later get a new one and start up again. It was a vicious circle—I had a love/hate relationship with my journal

Finally, I had a few realizations about journaling and entered a period of my life where my journal became a remarkable vehicle for healing. Here are the realizations I had:

1. **Decide who you are writing for**: Are you writing just for yourself? Is your journal a personal memoir of your life to pass down to your children? Being clear on who your audience is will help you decide what to share in your journal.
2. **Determine why you are journaling**: What results do you desire? Is your intention to vent? Is it to chronicle your life? Is it to give your current perspective for future reference? Is it to activate your creative juices? Knowing why you are journaling will give you clarity regarding how to do it.

3. **It shouldn't be a chore**: Don't make your journal one more thing on your daily "to do" list. It should be a joy and an inspiration. Don't beat yourself up if you don't do it for a while.
4. **Choose a special book and pen**: To journal is an exceptional experience and the form should match your intention.
5. **Accept the process**: If you don't like what you write, accept it and keep writing. Fill your journal with the light as well as the dark side of yourself. Let every page be a chapter from your soul.

My journal has now become my dear friend and healer. She listens to the songs of my heart and the dark valleys of my life. She is a sacred receptacle, containing my dreams, my fears, my love, and my celebrations. She helps me diffuse the darkest of times and celebrate the most joyous of times.

I have two journals. One is what I call my "Glorious Woman Journal" where I write everything. If I'm mad, glad, exhilarated, hurt, raging—it all goes in this journal. It's not always in good English. It has incomplete sentences. It goes on paper the way it comes out of my heart. My second journal is my Joy Journal (see Chapter 8). It is filled with the special, magical, cherished moments in my life.

The Glorious Art of Letter Writing

A wonderful and organic way to express yourself creatively is through the art of letter writing. I'm not talking about a hasty e-mail reply, but rather a glorious, handwritten (or typed) letter on lovely paper (perhaps hand-decorated or lavished with wonderful scent) or in a beautiful card. Creating a letter like this can be a holy experience for both sender and receiver.

Choose someone you love or cherish to receive this letter. Find words to celebrate, share, and express yourself in a way that is real and honest. Share your glory or share your pain. It doesn't matter as long as it is authentic. Select paper or a card that is a reflection of your sentiments. Draw, paint, or decorate your letter. If you spray it with essential oil, choose an aroma that reflects the sentiments expressed in your letter.

After you address your letter, place it close to your heart and energize it. Feel a flow of love surging from you into the letter. You have now created a letter that contains life force. An added bonus can be the use of sealing wax to symbolically seal the energy and love into the letter.

A letter that has been created in this way is hallowed. Not only is it a treasure to receive, but the energy associated with it will radiate into the world, and every postal worker who touches it will be blessed by its energy. It will leave a beautiful energy pathway from your home to the home of its recipient.

The Muse of Poetry

Hey, you can write poetry. Really! Every woman has poetry in her soul. It's just a matter of uncovering it. The experience of writing poetry can be intimate and expressive. It can take you directly to the core of a situation or experience, for you don't have to write in full sentences, with all the rules of grammar. Poetry can help you put the mystery of life into words succinctly and directly. Each word elicits a feeling, and you can string these feelings together the way a composer links various notes to create melody. You can use poetry to create a rhythmic symphony of emotions and feelings.

How do you start? As an exercise, think of something beautiful or unusual that you saw or experienced in this last week. Write down the main words that convey the feelings it evoked within you. For example, a couple of days ago a rattlesnake came in our front door. This event roused a myriad of emotions within me, including awe, delight, honor, fear, and deep sadness.

Now list the visual images associated with the experience. These are my images associated with the rattlesnake: undulating, diamond-back pattern, slithering across terra cotta tile; gently trying to capture him with no success; striking fury as his body lashed out again and again; he slips into a crack; worry about him silently emerging and striking one of our guests; when he finally comes out, my husband swiftly kills him before he can slip back in; my deep grieving; his memorial and burial by the front door; thanking the snake for the gift of its spirit.

Now use some of the images to convey the emotion or emotions you felt. Here is the poem I created:

> There have been tremors
> in the fault line of my soul lately.
>
> Brother rattlesnake
> appeared at my front door yesterday.
> Curious at first ... then furious
> Thrashing, striking, a rim of fire.
>
> "Don't despair," I said,
> "you'll be okay."
>
> Again and again, lightning and fury:
> such a valiant soul in such a small body.
>
> Nooooo!
> I can't stop the blow.

Fire extinguished,
brother's body lies limp at my feet.

Shaken, wet with tears,
I hold his pliant form to my heart
and offer it up to the heavens.

For the gift of your spirit, I am honored.
For your death, I grieve.

Tremors stop, the ground is cold.
I'm so sorry.

To write poetry, as in any creative writing, just begin. Don't judge yourself, and keep going. To step into the realm of the poet read poetry—all kinds of poetry, from Rumi to e.e. cummings to haiku. Imagine seeing the world through the eyes of each poet. Begin to think and feel like a poet. For example, as you greet the morning, imagine that you are seeing the new day through the eyes of a poet.

The Muse of Music

If you have never done anything musical before, start with drumming. Drumming is the most primal of sounds. It takes us back to the womb where the first sound we heard was the rhythmic beating of our mother's heart.

I'm a drum-maker. My husband and I have been making drums for many years. We also drum together. We drum to connect with the cycles of life, to celebrate our lives, to release pent-up emotions, and especially to grow closer to the Creator. I also teach drumming and lead drumming circles. The drum is one of my allies. It carries me to the center of my soul.

Many women in today's world are discovering the power of the drum and are using it to connect with the primordial feminine within themselves. The feminine use of the drum is not new: from Egypt to Rome, thousands of artifacts and statues have been unearthed that depict Goddesses holding drums. Drumming was considered a way of communing with the Great Goddess. The hypnotic rhythm was used to transcend ordinary consciousness and attune with the Goddess. Additionally, drumming was done by women to invoke the life force within nature to bless the crops and to induce fertility. They also used it during birthing rites to facilitate labor.

Drumming can help you find your own rhythm and connect to the greater rhythms and cycles of the world. It's great if you have your own drum, but you don't need a drum to start—two sticks will do. You can even turn over a cooking pot and drum on it. Begin with the two-beat, the heartbeat. Keep drumming until you are filled with the spirit of the rhythm. Don't consciously decide on a beat, just let it happen. It will almost seem as if the drum is playing itself. When this occurs, you know that you have stepped into your creativity. As you drum, you may notice emotions or memories coming to the surface. This is a healing process, so just keep drumming and let them wash over you. If you feel that nothing is happening, just keep drumming. Whenever you drum, whether you are aware of it or not, something powerful is happening.

There is a vibration or rhythm associated with every gland and organ in your body, as well as with every chakra. When you drum, every part of your body absorbs the rhythm that it needs to stay in balance and harmony. Forget about trying to sound good. Just keep drumming.

Jamming with the Gals

Activate your musical creativity by by getting together with some women friends and having a jam session. Get someone to start a rhythmic beat with a drum or by striking spoons together, by hitting sticks on cans or kitchen pots. Follow this "mother" rhythm until the rhythm begins to evolve on its own. Use your voice as you drum. Chant. Howl. Have fun. This is magic. There will be a point when everyone becomes fluid with the rhythm of the moment. You will leave feeling refreshed and cleansed by this rousing, feminine power of rhythm.

Women's ceremonial drumming circles are currently mushrooming throughout the world. Women are gathering their forces, drumming together, and allowing the echo of the drumbeat to project that holy energy outward into the world. Although the form varies, when women come together to drum, they invoke a primordial archetype of feminine energy. The unity of the drumbeats creates a primal core—raw and wild as the Earth Mother herself—which can flow outward into the universe. The drumbeat carries each woman across the boundaries of time and space into long-forgotten memories of the Goddess era, and ancient rites. When "jamming with the gals," drum your passion, drum your power, and please, my dear sisters, drum for peace. The world needs the divine feminine power that can be projected through the power of your drum circle.

When your drum circle is complete, celebrate with a meal. Share your community and your food, knowing that you have reenacted an ancient archetypal journey to the center of the soul.

Finding your Voice

Your voice can be a channel for your creativity. It is also the way that you communicate with the world. Sometimes, however, because of fear or restriction, we lose this creative channel for communicating our truth. One of the ways to regain your "voice" in life is to explore your own primal sounds. To do this, go somewhere where you can make noise without being disturbed: either in nature, a soundproof room, or perhaps while driving.

Just open your mouth and let noise come out. It doesn't have to be pretty or articulate. Just allow sounds to surge up from your belly and out through your mouth. Try going up and down the scale. You'll notice that there are some sounds that make you feel giddy and silly, and some which make you feel courageous and brave. If you sound squeaky at first, it may be because you are restricted. Sometimes such a restriction dates from childhood when we were not allowed to speak our truth.

An additional aspect to this exercise is to make strange, unintelligible sounds, to scream like a banshee, roar like a lion, or howl at the moon. Go inside yourself to find what is real and authentic for you in the moment and then express this feeling with sound. Not only will this exercise help you find your voice in life so that you can speak your truth more and more, you will also find that your ability to sing beautifully and creatively is increased.

The Muse of the Meal

Preparing food can also be a fabulous way for the Glorious Woman to invoke her creativity. There can be true alchemy involved in mixing ingredients together, not only to create excellent flavors, but also to create the right feeling and sensations. *The chef's emotions can be felt in the food.* Two dishes absolutely identical in ingredients and presentation can have completely different tastes as a result of the chef's mood. If you cook to feed the soul as well as the body, magic happens. When positive energy goes into food, its flavors become remarkable. Cooking is a labor of love that is both felt and tasted. Your dishes reveal your spirit.

In the summer I teach intensive residential courses. I have been asked many times by my students what makes the food so extraordinary. I tell them it is the love with which it is cooked. I choose cooks who have a deep understanding of the creative alchemy of cooking and how to energize food. Their love infuses the food with good feelings, and the effect can be tasted.

The Muse of Storytelling

The art of storytelling is ancient. When women are together, we tell our stories to each other. The most sacred stories are about our lives, for story is the holy wafer that creates communion between women. Our stories allow each of us to find common ground, for when we share our challenges and our triumphs, we hear, "Yes, I know what you mean. I've experienced that, too." Our struggles can be lessened by hearing the story of another's difficulties. And our triumphs can be magnified through the power of our personal stories, for in each telling they become richer and fuller.

Our personal stories weave the past, the present, and the future into a tapestry that reminds us that we do not live alone, that we are a part of a long lineage of women who have gone before us and who will continue beyond us. It's important that we recognize that in the retelling of our life experiences, we have become part of a long and continuing chain of oral tradition. Please tell your stories. Let them be heard. Share them with your daughters, your friends—and the world. They are your personal myths, mighty and potent. In ways beyond your conscious knowing, your stories bring benefit to the world; they can inspire, heal, teach, and give strength to others.

In addition to the personal story, there is the entertaining story. The accomplished storyteller puts herself in a near trance state, where she can sense the audience; she then embellishes and emphasizes accordingly. You can practice this art by either creating fables and legends to tell your children at bedtime or by telling your friends an elaborate tale about your weekend. The subject matter is less important than the way in which you choose to portray it. Emphasis, tone of voice, speed, and so on, can all greatly affect the reception of a story. Two people can tell exactly the same story, but its meaning will be understood completely differently.

The Muse of the Dance

As a small child, as soon as I heard the sound of rain pounding on the roof, I would run outside and begin to dance until I was soaked. I swirled and twirled and leapt in great bounds throughout the garden. I would then stretch my arms up into the sky, feeling as if some force from the earth radiated up my body to the heavens. In those moments of ecstatic dance, I could almost taste the richness of the earth as the wet smell of the soil permeated the air. I felt so light and free.

I now believe that these impromptu childhood dances were a reenactment of a genetic memory of times long ago. My dances transported me to a time when women used the power of the dance to journey to the sacred feminine and to uncover secret truths about the universe.

Spontaneous dancing is one of the purest forms of elemental expression. This kind of dance can open an innermost core that cannot be expressed in words. It can awaken an innate wisdom and creativity within you that is awesome and powerful. It has been said that extemporaneous dance is prayer in movement. When you enter into the sacred realm of dance, an alchemy occurs: the disparate and separate aspects of yourself unite and become integrated. Your dance can carry you into a state of divine ecstasy with each step bringing you closer to Spirit.

Dancing the Goddess Within

Dance can also connect you to Goddess energy within you. You can dance alone or with a group. Decide which Goddess you want to activate within yourself (see Chapter 2). Turn the lights down low, and put some music on. Start by placing a veil or shawl over your head and place your hands in a prayer position over your heart. Focus on your desire to illuminate the Goddess energy within yourself and concentrate on the particular Goddess you desire. Imagine her body and spirit slipping into and merging with your body.

Slowly allow the veil to drop. Imagine the Goddess dancing through you. During this dance the qualities associated with that Goddess will begin to flow within you. If this exercise is done in a group, take time to share your experiences at the dance's completion.

Belly Dancing

This is a sensual, fabulous activity for women of all ages and walks of life. Contrary to popular belief, belly dance was not originally designed to entertain men but was a traditional dance done by women for women in celebration of womanhood. It was not done to project eroticism, but to celebrate the awe and wonder of birth. It honored the sacred womb, the origin of new life, and it also strengthened a woman's muscles for childbirth. It continues today as an ancient remnant of Mediterranean female religious practices.

I am a complete neophyte belly dancer, but every time I try it, I can feel a warmth that starts in my groin and burns its way through my body. This fire seems to set my soul ablaze. Some of the added benefits of belly dancing are that it has helped many women who have suffered from PMS and menstrual cramps, and is also an excellent way to tone the muscles after childbirth.

Your creativity is a powerful tool to reunite you with your spirit and to connect you to what is authentic and real. It has a purpose; it is part of why you are here on the planet. All creativity generates a life force that is healing and potentially life-transforming. The energy field created by it radiates far beyond the boundary of your body, nourishing your soul and the soul of the earth. This is important and needed.

Don't wait for inspiration, just do it. Creativity is not what you do, it is who you are. Be creative when you are tired, mad, hurt, or bored. Be creative when you are joyous, silly, or madcap. Remember not to judge yourself. Let your creativity express the inexpressible, and most of all, have fun!

14
REINVENT!
REJUVENATE!

REBIRTH!

So you are ready for a change! You want a fresh start. Maybe you've tried before, and your fresh start always seemed to be a false start. Perhaps that was because you were trying to rework your life instead of reinvent it. When you rework your life, you keep trying the same things that haven't worked for you in the past. For example, if you are on your twentieth diet without results, you are just reworking your life using the same old strategy. But when you reinvent your life, you need to be willing to try new approaches, to see your life with fresh eyes.

A new life begins with an honest examination of why your efforts in previous years didn't work. The past doesn't need to be recreated in the future. Your so-called failures have shown you what not to do in the future. This is valuable information. Don't get discouraged, get determined. After you have been honest with yourself about the past, let it go. If you never fail or are scared or embarrassed, it means that you never take chances, and you have to take some risks to reinvent yourself.

Reinventing yourself takes courage. You might have to reach deep within to find your new self, especially if you have spent years of living in your comfort zone, but nevertheless you do have a wellspring of courage inside you. You wouldn't have gotten this far in this book if you weren't ready for some kind of change. If you are really serious about changing your life, I suggest you start immediately. Decide what your goals are, and then do something completely different than you have done before to attain them. If you wait until the right time or until you are not afraid, you may never rebirth yourself. It really works. Experience the fear, and then do it anyway.

I used to believe that everyone else knew more than I did about me. I believed media messages about how I should look, feel, and act. On the surface I decried the media marketers of our culture, but I subconsciously yearned to look like the airbrushed role models on magazine covers. I also tried to fit the conceptions that my friends, family, and society had about me. It was difficult to know who I really was as I tried to balance home, work, relationship, health, family, and friends. Like most people, I had come to rely on outside sources such as television and magazines, which rarely had my interests at heart, to form my values and define who I was. I would get lost in the hype and become severed from my deeper meaning and purpose. Gradually I realized that if I wanted things to be different I needed to take charge of my life—I needed to reinvent the way I perceived myself.

In my journey to reinvent myself, I learned many things. I realized that the first thing needed to create a "new you" was a willingness and a commitment to change. This is imperative. When you make that commitment with your whole being, almost as if by magic, opportunities and situations present themselves to you. The next step is to take time away from your normal routines and habits. You can do this by going on a retreat. Your retreat can be as simple as renting a cabin in the woods for a weekend to examine your life and intiate an action plan for your future. You might also consider signing up for a week at a growth center, creating a retreat in your own home, going on a vision quest, or visiting a spa.

The most simple and economical retreat can be spending a day in solitude in your home. Taking a quiet day at home to be still, nurture yourself, and listen to your inner messages can have enormous benefits.

Ideally, choose a time when you can have the house (or a room) to your-self without interference from others. Make sure that you don't have any distractions—ringing phones or anything that you have to do. You might want to use the questionnaire at the end of this chapter as a starting point for your day of renewal. A journal can also be helpful to chronicle your experiences and thoughts. It's good to prepare your home retreat room by cleaning it and getting rid of any clutter. If you are not able to go some-where different for your personal retreat, it helps to make your space different. Change it so it doesn't feel the same as usual. Some women limit their food intake or fast for their one-day retreat. If you do decide to eat, prepare your food in advance.

Another time-honored method of self-renewal is the vision quest. I led quests for ten years. The experiences I had with the people who came on those retreats were some of the most rewarding of my life. (I wrote a book called *Quest: A Guide for Creating your Own Vision Quest* to help others create those experiences for themselves.) Going on a quest is a powerful way to reinvent yourself and reclaim a sense of wonder and connection to the earth. For centuries, people in ancient cultures embarked on these rites of passage to gain entrance into spiritual realms and attain self-knowledge. Traditionally a quest took place in isolation in nature. Sitting for a long period of time in reflection in the stillness of a natural setting, fears were confronted, old memories came to the surface to be healed, self-understanding deepened, and a sense of purpose emerged. Sometimes unexplained and mysterious events occurred, and a "vision" was received about one's future.

Native American vision quests often required the person to sit in a wild place for three days and nights, calling for a vision that would give guidance about one's life. This tradition was used as a rite of passage into adulthood because it was felt that the visions received by young men and women would help determine the roles they would play as adult members of the tribe. Later in life they would continue to use this ritualized retreat whenever they need to gain help from the Spirit powers.

Western culture has had no equivalent rite of passage that could help a woman answer heartfelt questions such as, "Who am I?" "What is my purpose?" "How can I live a life that matters?" "What can I do to heal my relationships?" and "How can I get closer to Spirit?" However, you can cre-ate a quest for yourself or participate in an organized quest (see Resources). One wonderful way to go on a mini-quest is to go into the country with sev-eral of your friends. Go to a place where you won't be disturbed. Sit where you can't see each other, but close enough that you can hear each other. Take a journal and spend the day in silence, examining your life. At the end of the day, have a meal together and share the insights that you gained during the day. Even one day such as this can make a difference in your life.

Healing Spas

I had wanted to go to a spa since my early twenties. I had heard about spas where women meditated and participated in spiritual practices. These spas seemed to me to be like female mystery schools. I had a deep desire to go because I intuitively felt it would be a spiritually rejuvenating experience. (I knew that most women went to spas to lose weight or get fit, but I believed these women also had a subconscious desire to renew their spirit.)

Although I yearned to go to a spa, I had lots of reasons for not going. For a start, I thought I didn't have enough time. However, when it was really time for a change in my life, I realized that the time I spent on myself was an investment not just in myself, but in my future and in the lives of those I loved. I felt that taking time to nurture myself could create a healing energy within me that could flow into many others.

My second barrier to going to a spa was money. Spas seemed extravagantly expensive. You could buy a used car for what some spas cost. Every time I had the idea of going, I thought of all the other practical things that my family needed, and I could not justify spending that much money on myself. I had no hesitation in spending money on the house or my family—only on myself. Spending that much money on myself was one of the hardest things I had ever done. Although I went through layers of guilt about it, my husband and daughter encouraged me.

When I finally did go, I regretted that I hadn't gone sooner. Going to a spa was one of the best investments I ever made. The time I spent there helped me to reunite with my sacred self. Almost everyone I met was there because they were also ready for a change in life. In other words, they were also reinventing themselves. Even if you only go once in a lifetime, removing yourself from the normal hectic pace of life and totally nurturing yourself in a spa environment can form a positive template for other experiences in the rest of your life.

Taking a Risk

It's difficult to change if you keep on doing the same things that you have always done. My first step in creating the "new me" was to take a few risks and push beyond my comfort zone. The first spa I went to allowed me this opportunity. The setting for the Green Valley Spa in Utah is stunning: it is surrounded by dramatic mountains. I began by taking some remarkable hikes through the high desert lands that allowed me to gently move through my physical limitations. But the most exhilarating experience of my stay there was rock climbing, which enabled me to push beyond my physical comfort zone. I was nervous about signing up for it, so I talked to one of the climbing instructors. I muttered, "I'd like to try rock climbing but I'm afraid that I'm too out of shape, too old, and too fat." (I'd like to tell you that I said something that was less self-deprecating, but this is actually what I said.)

He replied kindly, "You can do this, Denise. We'll help you."

Early one morning we arrived by van at the rock wall. The rising sun made the rocks glow as if lit from within. I looked up the cliff we were going to scale and thought, *There's no way I'll be able to climb that.*

It wasn't that high, but I was still scared. There was a scrawny guy holding the rope for the climbers. If he was responsible for holding me up, I was concerned. I walked up to him and said, "What happens if I fall?"

He smiled. "Don't worry, I'm holding the rope."

"Um, how much do you weigh?" I asked.

"I weigh 140 pounds. Why?"

"Well, I weigh 165 pounds. If I fall, your skinny ass is going to fly up the side of the mountain, while I plummet down to the rocks!"

He laughed and told me not to worry about it. But I *was* worried.

When it was my turn, I was strapped into a harness. I started my climb. I slipped a toe into a crevice and a finger into a crack and pulled myself up. And then did it again . . . and again. Suddenly everything else in life disappeared. Even my fear disappeared. The only thing that existed was deciding where my hand or foot was going to go. With focused effort, inching my way upwards, I slowly ascended the cliff. I was about three feet away from the top, when my arms and legs started to shake with the effort. I hollered down, "I can't make it to the top: my body is shaking too much."

"Yes, you can," they yelled back up at me.

"No, I can't," I cried out, with tears streaming down my cheeks.

"Yes, you can!"

I looked up at the top of the cliff and then down at the instructors. A dormant inner strength emerged and I thought, *Okay, I'm going to give this everything I've got.* With one immense inner effort, I reached up and pulled my body up to the top. I'd done it! An incredible feeling of exhilaration and joy filled me as I rappelled back down the cliff.

After that climb, something subtle but wonderful began to happen. I began to feel more courageous about everything. Pushing beyond my comfort zone in one area affected other areas of my life. I realized that I had the ability to conquer other challenges that came my way. When you are willing to take a risk and try something new, even if you are afraid, it has a positive impact on other areas of your life.

Sacred Mountain

To reinvent yourself, it is valuable to step out of your normal environment. It's easier to move away from old habits and patterns when you are in a healing place in nature. I believe many of the women who consciously go to spas to improve their fitness are also unconsciously drawn there by the revitalizing energy of the land that surrounds them. (I have found that many spas are built in locations where there is healing earth energy. When you are in these locations, the energy affects you so positively that you can perceive yourself in a new way.)

A number of months ago, I spent some time at the base of Kuchumaa Mountain in Mexico. Walter Evans-Wentz, the Oxford graduate who translated *The Tibetan Book of the Dead*, declared this mountain to be one of the most powerful sources of healing energy in the world. To the Kumeyaay Indians of the area, this mountain has been sacred since before recorded history. Indians still come for pilgrimages from faraway places to Kuchumaa Mountain because they have meaningful mystical experiences and visions there.

The Rancho La Puerta Spa lies in the shadow of this great mountain. When I went there, however, it took me a few days to absorb the energy of the mountain and perceive its spirit. I hadn't realized that when you make a commitment to change your life by going to a spa or a retreat, it's important to leave your ordinary habits and patterns behind. When I arrived at the spa, I brought my busy life with me. I arrived with a suitcase full of paperwork to do while I was there. I found myself racing around from one activity to another almost at the same frantic pace that I did at home. In between a multitude of exercise, yoga, and meditation classes I would sit at my laptop computer to keep up with my work.

At one point, as I was hurrying off to a class, I passed a hammock strung between two palm trees. The soft light that filtered through the trees there seemed luminous. I stopped—looked in the direction of my class—and then looked back at the hammock. With a sublime sigh I lowered myself into it and then spent the afternoon watching clouds scud across the sky. As time slowed down, I could feel the ancient presence of the mountain closer and deeper the more still I became. It was a delicious way to spend half a day. In the moment I left my ordinary life behind, I was enveloped in the spirit of the place.

When you are in a special place in nature, one of the ways your soul will speak to you is through your dreams. A number of the women participants I chatted with at Rancho La Puerta said they had never dreamed as much or as vividly as they had there. One night I had a dream in which an owl was sitting on my head and whispering to me in a soft, low voice. When I awoke, I could still feel its talons on my head. The owl is considered one of the wise woman's totems. During my dream, I could feel a transmission of energy and knowledge occur in a very deep way. Later, when I asked the Mexican concierge at Rancho La Puerta what he thought the importance of the mountain was, he said simply, "It makes people dream."

Every day that I was at this spa, I could feel myself slowing down. I stopped running from class to class and spent time walking on the mountain, sitting in the sun, and being still. All the things that had seemed so urgent and so important in my life began to fade away. This slowing down helped me begin to reclaim my ability to sense energy fields. During lunch one day, I looked at my plate of salads and vegetables. The energy flowing out of the food was palpable. I had rarely seen or tasted such amazing life force in food.

I wanted to discover the reason that the food was so alive, so I visited the spa gardens that lie at the base of the mountain. I talked with the head gardener, who said,"The gardeners here have a very special connection with the land. All the work is done lovingly by hand. We don't use tractors, because with tractors we have lost the spirit. The food that we grow for the spa is produced organically. In Mexico, mountains are seen as feminine, and agriculture has always been correlated with feminine energy. In present times, we have lost contact with the feminine spirit of the earth, and gardening bring us back to it.

"Soil not only accumulates water and nutrients, it also accumulates love. All the workers here know this. We believe that it's possible that instead of harvesting food, we are really harvesting love. Over years and years, the soil here has absorbed love, and we believe that love is in the earth. The food grown on this earth dilutes the problems of people who come here because it is filled with love."

Learning to Receive

On my journey to reinvent myself, I gathered many helpful insights. I learned it was important to take risks and step out of my comfort zone. I also discovered the importance of slowing down, leaving my normal life behind, and placing myself somewhere on the planet that had a vital energy. But there was something missing. I could still feel my old self nudging me from within. It was only when I went to a spa in rural Southern California that I discovered the missing ingredient.

The Golden Door Spa is in a protected nature preserve of almost 400 acres once sacred to the local Indians. It houses only thirty-nine guests at a time, in Japanese-style accommodation. Each room looks a bit like a mystical tea house in the forest. There is something monastic and serene there, almost a hushed softness, which encouraged me to stop the bustling of my mind and learn to receive. This was what was missing.

I'm the kind of person who is always giving out energy. Taking the time to relax and receive nurturing energy has not usually been easy for me. I spent the first few days at the spa trying to give back to everyone. I massaged the neck of the woman doing my nails, and the shoulders of the woman who came to my room to massage me. I was so accustomed to giving to everyone that it wasn't easy to let go and just accept support without having to give anything back. But the spirit of the place slowly embraced me, and for the first time in my life, I allowed myself to completely receive. This was a kind of surrendering. I surrendered my need to please others and to always be busy and productive. Letting go and surrendering often precipitates life-transforming experiences. During my time there, I dissolved into a liquid, serene state that I hadn't achieved since my twenties when I lived in a Zen monastery.

The final night of my stay at the Golden Door, we were all invited to walk the labyrinth laid out beneath the oak trees. A labyrinth is an elaborate pathway in the form of a mandala—a symbol of wholeness—which contains a circuitous path that takes you into the center and back again. It is not a maze, which serves to confuse the mind. Walking a labyrinth seeks to quiet the mind and open inner knowing. This journey is cleansing, healing, and centering. Under the stars, illuminated by flickering candles, we walked the labyrinth in silence. Tears flowed, hearts opened, and I felt myself transported back in time to an ancient sacred rite of passage.

To be able to receive is truly a holy gift. As I was able to fully receive treatments without feeling that I needed to give back (tips weren't allowed), I found that I was now able to receive in many other areas of my life. When I got back home, I found that I could receive more love and also accept support and help from friends and family. I could even accept compliments better.

Total Relaxation

To reinvent yourself, sometimes you need to relax completely and totally.

When you do this, the clamoring of your hectic mind ceases so you can hear the wisdom of your inner voice. It is this inner voice that tells you who you are and what your purpose in life is. American spas usually focus on health and fitness, whereas European spas are focused on pampering and relaxation. They are good places to go if you just want to totally unwind. In most European spas, forget calorie-counting and getting up at five A.M. for your early-morning workout. Just surrender to experience pleasure and to allow yourself to feel completely indulged and pampered. There are times when a woman's soul needs this.

I was on a seminar tour of Europe when I decided to go to the famed Brenner's luxury hotel and spa, in the heart of Germany's Black Forest. This renowned spa has served as a center for rejuvenation for over 125 years. Housed in an elegant old-world hotel, the spa is surrounded by thick forests and mountains. Since the time of the Romans, people have journeyed to this picturesque town to partake of the beneficial healing waters. (There are numerous spas in the area.) In fact, some of the original Roman baths are still in existence. The water there is very healing: perhaps its presence accounts for the mystical energy found in the surrounding forests and the strong presence of devas, elementals, and fairies there.

At first I was disappointed that Brenner's didn't have much of an exercise or fitness program. Then I realized that it was great that they didn't because that meant I didn't *have* to do anything. At Brenner's I just relaxed. I soaked for hours in the healing waters, walked through the forest, luxuriated in elegant outdoor lunches in the park-like Bavarian setting, listened to outdoor concerts in the park, and generally felt like royalty. Every woman should feel like a queen once in her life, and an old-world spa is a superb place to do this.

"Spa Day" with the Girls

So you really don't have the time or the money (or maybe even the inclination) to go to a destination spa. As an alternative, create a "Spa Day" with your friends. Agree to meet at someone's house, to do each other's nails, and perhaps hire a masseuse to come and give massages. Sunbathe in the garden and let yourselves completely relax. Give each other facials, or book a beautician to come and give treatments. Play soothing music. Treat yourself to some light, fresh, organic food. Share your dreams and goals, and support each other in achieving them. Even one day like this can have an immensely rejuvenating effect and can be an enormous source of inspiration and strength in your personal growth process.

To renew yourself means reprioritizing your life, being willing to change, having courage, and having a passionate commitment to yourself. It also means stepping out of your comfort zone, taking risks, accepting the support of others, and being willing to totally surrender and just relax. When I take time out for self-inquiry—whether I am going to a spa, having a spa day with friends, undertaking a vision quest, or creating a quiet day for myself—there are some questions I often ask myself. These questions give me a sense of where I am, an overview of my life at this time, and also help me determine where I am going. I wanted to share a few of these questions with you. Perhaps you will also find them helpful on your personal journey to reinvent yourself.

Self-Exploration Questions

- What is my essence?
- What is the current theme of my life?
- What gives me the greatest joy?
- When do I feel the most content?
- Where is my power?
- What do I want out of life?
- Given my current thoughts and actions, what is my probable destiny? Am I happy about this probable future?
- Who do I love and who loves me?
- Where does my spiritual inspiration come from?
- What am I grateful for?

If you really want to reinvent yourself, develop a feeling of gratitude for your life. Whatever you focus on in life expands. If you focus on how miserable you are, you will experience more misery and suffering. If you focus on what is beautiful and splendid in your life, that will expand. Decide who you want to be and live as if that were already a reality. Behave as if your life is already transformed. At the same time, focus on being grateful for your life exactly the way it is. Even if you are not sure what you are thankful for, radiate gratitude for each event in your life. Take time to relax, nurture yourself, and listen to your inner wisdom. Go to a spa. Take a day of solitude and reflection.

Use the energy in your home to create an environment that supports and reflects who you desire to be (see my books *Sacred Space* and *Feng Shui for the Soul*). Begin with simple questions such as: Does this space reflect who I desire to be? Do I need this particular object or is it clutter?

What message about me does it convey? Get rid of items that make you feel bad or have unpleasant associations. Rearrange your home until it becomes an affirmation of the "new you."

The power to change your life comes from taking time to slow down and listen to the urgings of your soul. It comes from living your truth, without question and without hesitation. It comes from creating an environment that supports and nurtures your new beginning. Reinventing yourself is the process of aligning your outer life with the needs of your soul. When you do this, you glow, because your life comes straight from your heart.

15
UNCOILING THE
SERPENT

So much has happened since I started to write this book. When I began, a snake appeared in a dream with a message that if I didn't change my life I might die. Not long after this, it was suggested that I had breast cancer. The synchronicity I've experienced in writing this book has been amazing. The day I received the cancer diagnosis I had been writing about the importance for a woman to heal unresolved sexual traumas, because otherwise it could affect her breasts and sexual organs. The diagnosis prompted me to spend time evaluating my life, searching for answers for those hard questions such as "Who am I?" "Why am I?" and

"What do I stand for?" I also began to address some of the abuse from my childhood. After much soul-searching, I had the second medical test, and was told that I didn't have cancer after all. Also, during the writing of this book, my father died; I healed a lifelong rift with my mother; my daughter left college and started her adult life; I turned fifty; we moved to the country; and the terrorist attacks of September 11 occurred. So many life-changing events happened in such a short period of time.

I am not the same woman now that I was when I started this book. Before I began I didn't really and truly love and cherish myself or see my true value. I now know that I am lovable and glorious. It has been said that you teach what you need to learn, and I needed to learn how to become a Glorious Woman who revered herself. Writing this book has been an odyssey into my realization of my worth as a woman. It initiated an inner journey during which I began to love and appreciate myself. After a lifetime of not really liking myself, this is a miracle to me.

As I was nearing the completion of this book, something wondrous happened. One day I heard a commotion among the workers who were helping my husband with the building work on our new home. I ran outside. Approaching the front door was a huge, thick yellow-and-black snake, perhaps six feet in length. The men were shouting about the snake. One had a threatening hoe held high. The snake was so stunningly beautiful and vital; her skin seemed to glisten in the morning sun. As I looked at her, I felt compassion and love permeate me. A calm filled the air. The workers became quiet and stepped to either side as I quietly walked toward the snake.

I gently reached down and picked her up. She was so heavy in my hands but didn't seem frightened or alarmed. She slowly undulated back and forth as I gently whispered to her, "Thank you for blessing our home. I'm glad to meet you." Carefully carrying her away from the workers, I placed her at the base of Gaia, the Goddess tree, which is one of the 300-year-old oak trees on our property. I watched as she leisurely moved into the grass.

Suddenly I remembered the image of the *yellow-and-black snake* that had appeared in my dream many months before. I knew that snake was dying . . . just as I knew that I was also withering at that time. Now, as I watched the astonishingly resplendent snake slither into the tall grass, I realized that this snake was a potent omen of life, healing, and new beginnings. During the writing of this book, I shed old negative beliefs, like a snake sheds its skin, and in the process I was healed and transformed.

Although I still have days when I'm depressed and I forget that I am deserving of love, and days when I'm critical of myself and others, I don't judge myself so much for these times. I'm more gentle with myself, knowing that every experience is a precious part of the great and grand adventure of being human.

I believe in the miraculous power of intention, and my heartfelt intention is that the energy of this book will allow you to uncoil and come full circle into the glory and pleasure of being a woman. May it carry you on an inner journey during which your ability to cherish and love yourself will deepen and grow. This book is more than paper, ink and binding . . . it is an energy, which carries a spirit of love from me to you. May blessings and love fill you always and forever.

BIBLIOGRAPHY

Al-Rawi, Rosina-Fawzia. *Grandmother's Secrets: The Ancient Rituals and Healing Power of Belly Dancing.* New York: Interlink Books, 1999.

Anand, Margo. *The Art of Sexual Magic: Cultivating Sexual Energy to Transform your Life.* New York: Tarcher/Putnam, 1995.

— *The Art of Everyday Ecstasy: The Seven Tantric Keys for Bringing Passion, Spirit, and Joy into Every Part of Your Life.* New York: Broadway Books, 1998.

Andes, Karen. *A Woman's Book of Power.* New York: Perigee, 1998.

Ardinger, Barbara, PhD. *A Woman's Book of Rituals and Celebrations.* Novato, California: New World Library, 1995.

— *Goddess Meditations.* St Paul: Llewellyn Publications, 1999.

Barrow, John D. *The Artful Universe: The Cosmic Source of Human Creativity.* New York: Little, Brown, 1995.

Bass, Ellen and Laura Davis. *The Courage to Heal: A Guide for Women Survivors of Childhood Sexual Abuse.* New York: Harper & Row, 1988.

— *The Courage to Heal Workbook: A Guide for Women Survivors of Childhood Sexual Abuse.* New York: Harper & Row, 1990.

Beck, Renne and Sydney Barbara Metrick. *The Art of Ritual: A Guide to Creating and Performing Your Own Ceremonies for Growth and Change.* Berkeley, California: Celestial Arts, 1990.

Blair, Nancy. *Amulets of the Goddess: Oracle of Ancient Wisdom.* Oakland: Wingbow Press, 1993.

Bolen, Jean Shinoda MD. *Goddess in Everywoman: A New Psychology of Women.* New York: Harper & Row, 1984.

— *The Millionth Circle: How to Change Ourselves and the World.* Berkeley: Conari Press, 1999.

Budapest, Zusanna. *The Holy Book of Women's Mysteries.* Oakland: Wingbow Press, 1989.

Buonaventura, Wendy. *Serpent of the Nile: Women and Dance in the Arab World.* New York: Interlink Books, 1989.

— *The Goddess in the Office.* San Francisco: HarperSanFrancisco, 1993.

Campbell, Joseph. *The Power of Myth.* New York: Doubleday, 1988.

Camphausen, Rufus C. *The Yoni: Sacred Symbol of Female Creative Power.* Rochester: Inner Traditions, 1996.

Claremont de Castillejo, Irene. *Knowing Woman: A Feminine Psychology.* New York: Harper & Row, 1973.

Curott, Phyllis. *Book of Shadows.* New York: Broadway Books, 1998.

Davis, Elizabeth and Carol Leonard, *The Women's Wheel of Life: Thirteen Archetypes of Woman at Her Fullest Power.* New York: Penguin Books, 1996.

Doulas, Nik and Penny Slinger. *Sexual Secrets: The Alchemy of Ecstasy.* New York: Destiny Books, 1979.

Downing, Christine. *Journey through Menopause: A Personal Rite of Passage.* New York: Cross Road Publishing, 1987.

— *The Goddess: Mythological Images of the Feminine.* New York: Continuum Publishing, 1999.

— *The Long Journey Home: Revisioning the Myth of Demeter and Persephone for Our Time.* Boston: Shambhala, 1994.

Eisler, Riane. *The Chalice and the Blade: Our History, Our Future.* New York: Harper & Row, 1987.

— *Sacred Pleasure.* San Francisco: HarperSanFrancisco, 1995.

Estés, Clarissa Pinkola, PhD. *Women Who Run with the Wolves: Myths and Stories of the Wild Woman Archetype.* New York: Ballantine, 1992.

Fincher, Susanne F. *Creating Mandalas for Insight, Healing and Self-expression.* Boston: Shambhala, 1991.

Franks, Lynne. *The Seed Handbook: The Feminine Way to Create Business.* New York: Tarcher/Putnam, 2000.

Frazer, Sir James. *The New Golden Bough.* Winnepeg: Mentor Books, 1959.

Frymer-Kensky, Tikva. *In the Wake of the Goddesses: Women, Culture and the Bibical Transformation of Pagan Myth.* New York: Ballantine Books, 1992.

George, Demetra. *Mysteries of the Dark Moon: The Healing Power of the Dark Goddess.*

Gimbutas, Marija. *The Civilization of the Goddess: The World of Old Europe.* San Francisco: HarperSanFrancisco, 1991.

— *The Language of the Goddess.* New York: Harper & Row, 1989.

Graves, Robert. *The White Goddess,* 3rd edition. London: Faber and Faber, 1952.

Griffin, Susan. *Woman and Nature: The Roaring Inside Her.* New York: Harper Colophon, 1978.

Harding, Ester M. *The Way of All Women.* New York: Harper & Row, 1970.

— *Women's Mysteries, Ancient and Modern.* New York: Harper & Row, 1971.

Johnson, Robert A. *She: Understanding Feminine Psychology.* New York: Harper & Row, 1977.

— *He: Understanding Masculine Psychology.* New York: Ballantine Books, 1977.

Kenton, Leslie. *Passage to Power: Natural Menopause Revolution.* London: Random House, 1995.

Klein, Tzipora. *Celebrating Life: Rites of Passage for All Ages.* Oak Park, Illinois: Delphi Press, 1992.

Lorius, Cassandra. *Tantric Sex: Making Love Last.* London: Thorsons, 1999.

Mariechild, Diane. *Mother Wit: A Feminist Guide to Psychic Development.* Trumansburg, New York: The Crossing Press, 1981.

Molyneaux, Brian Leigh. *The Sacred Earth.* London: Duncan Baird Publishers, 1995.

Murdock, Maureen. *The Heroine's Journey.* Boston: Shambhala, 1990.

Muten, Burleigh (ed.). *Return of the Great Goddess.* Boston: Shambhala, 1994.

Noble, Vicki. *Motherpeace: A Way to the Goddess Through Myth, Art and Tarot.* New York: Harper & Row, 1983.

— *Uncoiling the Snake: Ancient Patterns in Contemporary Women's Lives.* San Francisco: HarperSanFrancisco, 1993.

Northrup, Christiane, MD. *Women's Bodies, Women's Wisdom: Creating Physical and Emotional Health and Healing.* New York: Bantam Books, 1994.

Ravenwolf, Silver. *To Light a Sacred Flame: Practical Witchcraft for the Millennium.* St Paul: Llewellyn Publications, 1999.

Ryan, M. J. (ed.). *The Fabric of the Future: Women Visionaries Illuminate the Path to Tomorrow.* Berkeley: Conari Press, 1998.

Shlain, Leonard. *The Alphabet Versus the Goddess.* New York: Viking Penguin, 1998.

Starhawk. *The Spiral Dance: A Rebirth of the Ancient Religions of the Great Goddess.* New York: Harper & Row, 1989.

— *Truth or Dare: Encounters with Power, Authority and Mystery.* San Francisco: HarperSanFrancisco, 1987

Stein, Diane. *Casting the Circle: A Woman's Book of Ritual.* Freedom, California: The Crossing Press, 1990.

Stone, Merlin. *When God Was a Woman.* New York: Harcourt Brace Jovanovich, 1976.

Walker, Barbara. *The Woman's Encyclopedia of Myths and Secrets.* San Francisco: Harper & Row, 1989

— *The Woman's Dictionary of Symbols and Sacred Objects.* San Francisco: Harper & Row, 1988.

Watson, Lyall. *The Secret Life of Inanimate Objects.* Rochester, Vermont: Destiny Books, 1990.

Wolf, Naomi. *The Beauty Myth: How Images of Beauty are Used Against Women.* New York: William Morrow, 1991.

Woolger, Jennifer and Roger. *The Goddess Within: A Guide to the Eternal Myths that Shape Women's Lives.* New York: Fawcett Columbine, 1989.

Zweig, Connie (ed.). *To Be a Woman: The Birth of the Conscious Feminine.* New York: Tarcher/Putnam, 1990.

RESOURCES

I give seminars and lectures throughout the world. To receive information about my courses or learn how to enroll in my Women's Mystery School, visit my website at www.DeniseLinn.com or write to me at PO Box 759, Paso Robles, California 93447-0759.

My guided meditation tapes and CDs (including *Secrets & Mysteries: Meditations for Women*), and my feng shui video, are available worldwide from:

QED Recording Services
Lancaster Road, New Barnet, Herts EN4 8AS, United Kingdom
phone: 020-8441-7722
fax: 020-8441-0777
e-mail: enquiry@qed-productions.com
website: www.qed-productions.com

Chapter 3

Flower Essences and Essential Oils

Some of the best flower and environmental essences are available from:

Alaskan Flower Essence Project
PO Box 1369, Homer, Alaska 99603-1369
phone: 1-907-235-2188 (toll-free number: 1-800-545-930)
fax: 1-907-235-2777
e-mail: alaskanessences.com
website: www.alaskanessences.com

A small company that provides excellent essential oils is:

Lifetree Aromatix
3949 Longbridge Ave, Sherman Oaks, California 91423
An information pack and order form are available for $2.50.

Chapter 7

Recommended Website for Health and Well-being

Christiane Northrup, M.D., is a board-certified OB/GYN whose books, *Women's Bodies, Women's Wisdom* and *The Wisdom of Menopause* have both been *New York Times* bestsellers.

website: www.drnorthrup.com

Chapter 9

Sexual Healing

Excellent books by Ellen Bass and Laura Davis:
The Courage to Heal: A Guide for Women Survivors of Childhood Sexual Abuse. New York: Harper & Row, 1988.
The Courage to Heal Workbook: A Guide for Women Survivors of Childhood Sexual Abuse. New York: Harper & Row 1990.

Childhelp USA offers crisis support and referrals for women who have suffered sexual abuse as children. They are an amazing organization. I called to see how effective they were. In less than ten seconds, the counselor found the names of seventy-eight organizations in the Seattle area that could be of help to a woman who was trying to heal sexual abuse issues. They are also able to give referrals in countries and cities throughout the world.

toll-free number: 1-800-442-4453 (to access this from overseas, place your call via the international operator)
for the hearing-impaired: 1-800-222-4453
website: www.ChildhelpUSA.org

Erotic Books, Toys and Videos for Women

Sex therapist and educator Joani Blank started Down There Press in 1975 as a way to provide books on sexuality that were practical and holistic (they also publish Herotica, a series of erotic books written by women). In 1977, dismayed by a lack of resources for women who sought sex information and good-quality sex toys, she opened a shop, Good Vibrations, in San Francisco. She wanted it to be friendly, well-lit and comfortable rather than the conventional "adult" store. Both men and women were highly appreciative of her approach. In 1985 she started the Good Vibrations mail-order catalogue, selling books, toys, and videos. Eventually Joani decided to restructure her business, and it became a worker–owner cooperative. This is *the* resource center for erotica for women. Additionally they sponsor numerous workshops and lectures on the subject. For information about books, videos, DVDs, and excellent quality sex toys, contact:

Good Vibes Catalog
938 Howard Street, Suite 101, San Francisco, California 94103
phone: 1-415-974-8985 (toll-free order line: 1-800-289-8423)
fax: 1-415-974-8989 • website: www.goodvibes.com

Another woman who is pivotal figure in the field of erotica in the US is Lonnie Barbach, who has edited several anthologies of literary erotica. She is on the clinical faculty of the University of California medical school and has a private practice in San Francisco. Some of her anthologies are *Pleasures*, *Erotic Interludes*, *The Erotic Edge* and *Seductions*. Most of the writers are women. The writing quality varies, but for the most part her anthologies are enjoyable and seem to have something for everyone. The stories are more sensuous than pornographic and contain the full spectrum of sexual experience, written for the most part for a female audience.

For erotic books, join the Venus Book club: www.joinvenus.com

Chapter 11

Messages in Water

To view photographs of water altered by various influences, go to this interesting website: www.wellnessgoods.com/art_wat_messages.html

Chapter 14

Vision quests

This wonderful organization leads group quests and has vision quest facilitators all over the world:

Lost Borders, Box 796, Big Pine, California 93513
phone Angelo: 1-530-305-4414 • e-mail: staff@schooloflostborders.com

Retreat Centers and Spas

Esalen is one of the oldest and most respected retreat centers in the United States. It is perched over the Pacific Ocean, has natural hot springs and outdoor hot tubs, and is famous for its massages. The food is organically grown and the workshops are remarkable.

Esalen Institute Retreat Center
Highway 1, Big Sur, California 93920
reservations: 1-831-667-3005 • information: 1-831-667-3000
website: www.esalen.org

Green Valley Spa: Fabulous red rock setting in southern Utah. Fresh air, wonderful rooms, exhilarating hikes, noteworthy classes.

Green Valley Spa and Tennis Resort
1871 West Canyon View Drive, St George, Utah 84770
phone: 1-435-628-8060 (toll-free number: 1-800-237-1068)
fax: 1-435-673-4084
website: www.greenvalleyspa.com

Rancho La Puerta Spa: Gracious Mexican hospitality, great exercise classes, healing food, sacred mountain, a spiritual place for dreams and visions.

Rancho La Puerta Spa
PO Box 463057, Escondido, California 92046-3077
phone: 1-760-744-4222 (toll-free number: 1-800-443-7565)
fax 1-760-744-5007
website: www.rancholapuerta.com

Golden Door Spa: Serene, gracious, elegant, spiritual, in some respects this California spa is a modern-day female mystery school. It's very expensive, but for a once-in-a-lifetime experience, this spa will make you feel like a queen forever.

Golden Door Spa
PO Box 463077, Escondido, California 92046-3077
phone: 1-760-744-5777 (toll-free number: 1-800-424-0777)
fax: 1-760-471-2393
website: www.goldendoor.com

Miraval—Life in Balance: The focus of this gem in the Arizona desert is spiritual awareness and mindfulness. It is a luxury resort, but at the same time, the aim of this spa is to bring your life into balance spiritually and emotionally. Recommended!

Miraval Spa
5000 East Via Estancia Miraval, Catalina, Arizona 85739-8601
phone: 1-520-825-4000 (toll-free number: 1-800-232-3969)
fax: 1-520-818-5870
website: www.miravalresort.com

Canyon Ranch Spa: Excellent medical facilities with numerous exercise programs and treatments. The advantage of this huge facility is that you have the opportunity to try many different kinds of approaches to your health. It can be a bit overwhelming because it is so big, so it might be best to go with a friend.

Canyon Ranch Health Resort
8600 East Rockcliff Road, Tucson, Arizona 85750

phone: 1-520-749-9000 (toll-free number: 1-800-742-9000)
fax 1-520-749-1646
www.canyonranch.com

Brenner's Park Hotel and Spa: Nestled in the Black Forest. Leisure, luxury, and pampering. Thermal baths and springs. Walks in the woods. Old-world charm. Check out the Friedrichsbad in Baden-Baden, which were the original Roman-Celtic baths. The current baths there have been in use for over a century for therapeutic purposes.

Brenner's Park Hotel and Spa
Schillerstrasse 4-6, D-76530 Baden-Baden, Germany
phone: 49-72-21-9000
fax: 49-72-21-3-8772
website: www.brenners-park.de
e-mail: info@brenners-park.de

Spa Chakra: Rejuvenate your spirit as well as your body at these luxurious Australian day spas. Combining leading-edge technology with therapies from ancient origins, these spas focus on the chakras to maximize inner and outer beauty.

Spa Chakra Sydney
The Wharf, 6 Cowper Wharf Road, Woolloomooloo 2011, Australia
phone: 61-2-9368-0888
fax: 61-2-9380-2950
e-mail: spachakra@chakra.net

Spa Chakra Melbourne
Hilton-on-the-Park, 192 Wellington Parade, East Melbourne 3002, Australia
phone: 61-3-9412-3190
fax: 61-3-9412-3191
e-mail: spachakra.melbourne@chakra.net

Hayman Island Spa in Australia comes very highly recommended. They provide a comprehensive set of holistic treatments, fitness activities, and practitioners such as naturopaths, all in a five-star resort. Their website is very comprehensive.

Hayman Island Spa
Hayman, Great Barrier Reef, Queensland 4801, Australia
phone: 61-7-4940-1234 (toll-free number in Australia: 1-800-075-175)
fax: 61-7-4940-1567
e-mail: reserve@hayman.com.au
website: www.hayman.com.au

INDEX